THE COMPLETE IDIOT'S GUIDE TO

Being a Sex Goddess

by Stacy Clark, M.A., and Eve Adamson

ALPHA

A member of Penguin Group (USA) Inc.

ALPHA BOOKS

Published by the Penguin Group

Penguin Group (USA) Inc., 375 Hudson Street, New York, New York 10014, U.S.A.

Penguin Group (Canada), 10 Alcorn Avenue, Toronto, Ontario, Canada M4V 3B2 (a division of Pearson Penguin Canada Inc.)

Penguin Books Ltd, 80 Strand, London WC2R 0RL, England

Penguin Ireland, 25 St Stephen's Green, Dublin 2, Ireland (a division of Penguin Books Ltd)

Penguin Group (Australia), 250 Camberwell Road, Camberwell, Victoria 3124, Australia (a division of Pearson Australia Group Pty Ltd)

Penguin Books India Pvt Ltd, 11 Community Centre, Panchsheel Park, New Delhi—110 017, India

Penguin Group (NZ), Cnr Airborne and Rosedale Roads, Albany, Auckland, New Zealand (a division of Pearson New Zealand Ltd)

Penguin Books (South Africa) (Pty) Ltd, 24 Sturdee Avenue, Rosebank, Johannesburg 2196, South Africa

Penguin Books Ltd, Registered Offices: 80 Strand, London WC2R 0RL, England

International Standard Book Number: 1-59257-282-0
Library of Congress Catalog Card Number: 2004110012

06 05 04   8 7 6 5 4 3 2 1

Interpretation of the printing code: The rightmost number of the first series of numbers is the year of the book's printing; the rightmost number of the second series of numbers is the number of the book's printing. For example, a printing code of 04-1 shows that the first printing occurred in 2004.

Printed in the United States of America

Note: This publication contains the opinions and ideas of its authors. It is intended to provide helpful and informative material on the subject matter covered. It is sold with the understanding that the authors book producer, and publisher are not engaged in rendering professional services in the book. If the reader requires personal assistance or advice, a competent professional should be consulted.

The authors, book producer, and publisher specifically disclaim any responsibility for any liability, loss, or risk, personal or otherwise, which is incurred as a consequence, directly or indirectly, of the use and application of any of the contents of this book.

Most Alpha books are available at special quantity discounts for bulk purchases for sales promotions, premiums, fund-raising, or educational use. Special books, or book excerpts, can also be created to fit specific needs.

For details, write: Special Markets, Alpha Books, 375 Hudson Street, New York, NY 10014.

Publisher: *Marie Butler-Knight*
Product Manager: *Phil Kitchel*
Senior Managing Editor: *Jennifer Chisholm*
Senior Acquisitions Editor: *Randy Ladenheim-Gil*
Book Producer: *Lee Ann Chearney/Amaranth Illuminare*
Development Editor: *Lynn Northrup*
Senior Production Editor: *Billy Fields*

Copy Editor: *Anja Mutic*
Illustrator: *Hrana Janto*
Cartoonist: *Shannon Wheeler*
Cover/Book Designer: *Trina Wurst*
Indexer: *Tonya Heard*
Layout: *Ayanna Lacey*
Proofreading: *Mary Hunt*

Contents at a Glance

Part 1:   Who's Sexy? Yes, *YOU!*   1

   1 Me, a Sex Goddess?   3
      Do you really want to be a sex goddess? You already are!

   2 Invoking Goddess Power   11
      Take your place in the pantheon of sex goddesses across cultures and throughout human history.

   3 Maiden, Mother, Wise Woman   25
      Today's women can transform the ancient paradigm of the triple goddess, using it to choose her own unique experience of the path from maiden to mother to wise woman.

Part 2:   The Sacred Feminine: Honor the Body Goddess   37

   4 The Sacred Cycle of Moon and Menses   39
      Connect the moon phases and sacred sex goddess traditions to the menstrual cycle and the power of the divine feminine.

   5 Embodying Your Sacred Sexuality   49
      Look at your body, mind, and spirit and learn to recognize, nurture, and honor the sex goddess you are!

   6 Your Vagina: The Yoni Blossom   61
      Explore the yoni, the Hindu word for vagina, the source of all. Celebrate the ancient, enduring, and unique creative power of a woman to bring life forth from her own body.

   7 Your Beautiful Breasts   73
      Large, medium, or small, of all shapes, sizes, degrees of firmness, and height, revel in the sex goddess nurturing beauty and power of your breasts.

Part 3:   Prepare Yourself for Love   89

   8 Do You *Feel* Sexy Today?   91
      Explore what makes you feel sexy … and how to feel like a sex goddess every day!

   9 Rituals to Do Before the Loving   103
      Prepare the body, mind, and spirit for sacred sexual union.

   10 Foreplay: A Preview of Ecstasy   117
      Let passion unfold as you learn to connect to your partner while keeping open to that sacred spiritual presence and love.

11 Help Your Man Understand What a Sex Goddess Wants   131
Communicating your innermost desires is essential for the fully realized sex goddess (and sex god)!

Part 4:   Sacred Sex: Making Love Goddess-Style   143

12 Secrets of the Sex Goddesses   145
Discover the secrets of the Greek goddesses, yoginis, and sex goddesses of Tantra, the Kama Sutra, and the Far East.

13 Sacred Sex You'll Both Love   159
Learn about the sacred Five Essentials, many sexual positions for joyful unions, and reaching sex goddess orgasm.

14 The Glow: Coming Together   169
Rituals to honor your yoni and his lingam, while channeling sacred sexual energy for maximum bliss.

Part 5:   After the Loving   189

15 Extending Pleasure   191
What to do if (when ...) (how ...) (where ...) you want more!

16 Embraces and Soft Kisses   207
Understand what happens in the moment, and hours, after physical/spiritual release.

17 Afterglow: Enjoying Your Goddess Energy   221
As the energy of orgasm blossoms in you, hold its glow and embody its wonderful sex goddess power with confidence and joy.

Part 6:   Feeling Sexy Every Day   235

18 Mother Love   237
Discover how sacred sexuality deepens and grows between sex goddesses and their partners through motherhood. Reclaiming your Venus power!

19 On, and Off, the Pedestal   257
Step up, step down, indulge your sex goddess status and enjoy the view—from wherever you chose to stand!

20 A Touch of Sappho and Aphrodite   271
    Explore the sorority of the feminine, and its place in female
    relationships, woman to woman.

21 A Sex Goddess Is a *Love* Goddess   285
    If you embrace and embody the sex goddess, you will possess
    the power to create and inspire love, too!

Appendixes

    A Glossary   295

    B Resources   299

    C Upping Your Sex Goddess IQ   303

       Index   321

Contents

Part 1: Who's Sexy? Yes, YOU!   **1**

1 Me, a Sex Goddess?   **3**

Sex Goddess: You? 4

Hey Sexy, Are You Ready for This? 5

Sex Goddesses Then and Now, Here, There, and
    Everywhere 6

Sex = Creation 8

It Takes Two to Tango..9

2 Invoking Goddess Power   **11**

Hanging With the Goddesses 12

Sex Goddesses from Around the World 13

Sex Goddesses of Africa...14

Central and South American Goddess Power 14

The Sex, Creation, and the North American Goddess ...15

The Power and Passion of the Egyptian Goddess 16

The Sex Goddesses of the Far East 16

Sex Is All Greek (or Roman) to These Goddesses 17

Indian Passion 18

The European Sex Goddesses, from North to South.......20

What Do Asteroids Have to Do with Sex?..................20

Your Own Personal Sex Goddess 21

3 Maiden, Mother, Wise Woman   **25**

Hey Lady, Why Don't You Act Your Age? 26

The Maiden: Embracing, or Re-Embracing, Your Inner
    Virgin 27

The Mother: Transcending the Self...........................29

The Wise Woman: Universal Exploration...................31

The Triple Goddess, Yesterday and Today..................32

Where—and Who—Are You? 33

Part 2: The Sacred Feminine: Honor the Body Goddess   **37**

4 The Sacred Cycle of Moon and Menses   **39**

Your Body and the Lunar Cycle 40

Moon Goddess, Sex Goddess 42

Menstruation in the Real World 44
Honoring Your Cycle 47

5 Embodying Your Sacred Sexuality   49

The Puzzle of Your Body 50
Golden Breath Meditation 52
Your Sensual Chakras 53
  First Chakra: Your Primal Urges *54*
  Second Chakra: Your Inner Fire *55*
  Third Chakra: Meeting the World, Chest Forward *56*
  Fourth Chakra: All You Need Is Love *56*
  Fifth Chakra: Communication Station *57*
  Sixth Chakra: Intuition Central *57*
  Seventh Chakra: Universal Unity *58*
Can You Be *Too* Sexy? 58

6 Your Vagina: The Yoni Blossom   61

Good Morning, How's Your Vagina Today? 62
Your Personal Source of Creative Energy 63
Yoni Types 65
Flying Solo 66
  Ancient Masturbation Wisdom *66*
  Learning Your Body *68*
  Third-Time's-the-Charm Exercise *69*
Yoga for Yoni Health 70

7 Your Beautiful Breasts   73

The Meaning of the Breast 74
  You and Your Breasts: A History *75*
  Breast Man? *76*
Breast Size and the Female Ego 77
  Measuring Your Breast Prejudices *78*
  Love-Your-Breasts Exercise *79*
Three Cheers for Breast Appreciation 80
  The Adolescent Breast *80*
  The Grown-Up Breast *81*
  The Pregnancy Breast *82*
  The Breast-Feeding Breast *82*
  The Aging Breast *83*

Breast Health 84
The Sex Goddess Breast Exploration 84
The Breast: Universal Nurturer 86

Part 3: Prepare Yourself for Love   89

8 Do You *Feel* Sexy Today?   91
Calibrating Your Desire Meter 92
Initiating Sex 96
Express Yourself 98
Sex-Drive Phys-Ed 100

9 Rituals to Do Before the Loving   103
Getting Ready for Love 104
Preparing the Body 104
Breathwork Training for Better Sex 106
Bhramari: Humming Breath 107
Eyegaze Breathing 108
Get-Ready Rituals 108
Relation Meditation 109
Heartlight Meditation 110
Sensuality Meditation 111
Just Say So: The Power of Affirmations 113
Prepare Your Space 114
Eat to Love, Love to Eat 115

10 Foreplay: A Preview of Ecstasy   117
Lip Locks 118
Yoni Kisses, Lingam Licks 120
Lingam Love 120
Yoni Worship 121
Reach Out and Touch ... Yourself! 122
Sensual Focus 123
Touching Each Other 126
Shakti and Shiva, Ready for Union 128

11 Help Your Man Understand What a Sex Goddess Wants   131
I Want You to Want Me 132
It's All in the Delivery 134
In the Other Shoes: How He Sees You 136

Body Mapping 137
How to Be Treated Like a Sex Goddess 140

Part 4: Sacred Sex: Making Love Goddess-Style   143

12 Secrets of the Sex Goddesses   145

Greek to Me...146
Sexy Yoga..146
  Tree Pose *147*
  Yoga Shiva Pose (Natarajanasana) *148*
  Butterfly Pose..*149*
Tantra Secrets 150
Kama Sutra Highlights......................................151
  Yawning Union *152*
  Full Pressed Union *152*
  Packed Union...*152*
  Clasping Union *152*
  Union Like a Pair of Tongs *153*
  Lotuslike Union *153*
  Supported Union *154*
  Suspended Union *154*
Taoist Unions...154
Sex Secrets from Plain Girl 155

13 Sacred Sex You'll Both Love   159

Sacred Sex vs. "Regular Sex".............................159
The Rite of the Five Essentials 161
Positions for Concentrating Sexual Energy 162
  Tiger's Tread *163*
  Splitting the Bamboo *163*
  Swooping Shakti *163*
  Yab-Yum *164*
  Hiding in the Crevice *165*
The Work of the Man 165
Orgasms 101 166

14 The Glow: Coming Together   169

Beyond "Insert Penis Here" 170
  The Sacred Flowering Goddess *170*
  Shiva's Wand of Light *171*

The Flower and the Jewel................................173
Mouth to Yoni 173
Mouth to Lingam................................174
Channeling the Power................................175
Chakra Coordination Exercise 175
Sacred Chakra Breathing Exercise 177
The Inner Goddess Channel 178
Sacred Breathing 179
Know Thyself 180
Sex and Astrology 181
Body to Body, Soul to Soul 182
Secrets to Blissful Union 184
Climaxing Together 185
The Karmic Dance 186

Part 5:   After the Loving   189

15   Extending Pleasure   191

Prolonged Pleasure 191
Heightening the Sensual................................193
Finding Your Rhythm 194
Blossom With Orgasm Energy 195
Screwing 197
Waves of Bliss 197
The Night of One Thousand Hands 197
The Butterfly Pump................................198
The G-Spot 199
Lips That Hold Secrets 200
Withholding Ejaculation 201
Suspended in Rapture 202
Goddess Wildness 203

16   Embraces and Soft Kisses   207

The Aftermath 207
Winding-Down Rituals 209
Double Shavasana 209
The Ritual of the Nine Kisses 210
Hydrotherapy Ritual 211
Rite of Refueling 211
Pillow Talk................................211

Ritual of Silence 212
Ritual of Gratitude 213
Back to the Salt Mines 214
Keeping Your Relationship Sacred, 24/7 214
Agreements for Sacred Couples 216
We Agree to Worship Each Other 216
We Agree to Be Honest 216
We Agree to Accept Each Other for Who We Are 217
We Agree to Do the Best We Can 217
We Agree to Physical Contact Every Day 218
Remember Who You Are 218

17 Afterglow: Enjoying Your Goddess Energy   221

The Energy of Orgasm: Fire and Rain 222
Woman of Many Pools 224
The Energy of the Moment 226
The Energy of Elevation 227
Contagious Ecstasy 227
The Energy of Goddess Empowerment 228
Elixir of Life 228
A Natural Woman 229
Dancing Together, Dancing Apart 231

Part 6:   Feeling Sexy Every Day   235

18 Mother Love   237

Part Sex Goddess, Part Mother Goddess 238
The Erotic Side of Pregnancy 238
The Erotic Side of Post-Partum 239
Deep Intuitive Wisdom 240
Your Partner 242
The Loving Circle 243
Romance, Partnership, and Friendship 244
Tantric Dating 245
The Sacred Bedchamber 247
Destination: The Love Shack 248
Sexy Mama: Your Changing Body 249
Revirginizing 249
Self-Pleasuring 251
All Kegels, All the Time 252

Giving When You Are Depleted: Help Me,
  I'm Drowning! 252
  Revitalizing With Yoga 253
  Source of All: Womb Breathing 254
Loss of Desire 254
A Gallery of Role Models 255

19 On, and Off, the Pedestal   257

Celebration of the Pedestal..258
The View from the Diva Dais......................................259
  Balancing on the Pedestal..260
  Pygmalion's Pedestal: An Ancient Myth.................261
Flirtatious Fun 261
  Pick Me Up 262
  Delightful Dining 262
  Tease Me, Tempt Me 263
  Anticipation ... the Agony and the Ecstasy 263
Public (In)Discretion...264
  Private Indulgences in Public Places 264
  When No Means Know 265
This Vacation Is for Adults Only!..............................266
  One If by Land, Two If by Sea 266
  The Mile-High Club 267
Home Is Where the Sex Goddess Lives......................268
It's *Your* Pedestal 269

20 A Touch of Sappho and Aphrodite   271

In the Media...272
Welcome to the Isle of Lesbos 275
The Cult of Diana 278
Girl Power, Goddess Style 280
Ode to Aphrodite...281

21 A Sex Goddess Is a *Love* Goddess   285

Sex Goddess Energy to Transform Reality.................286
  Love Energy to Fortify Family and Friends.............287
  Life Lessons from the Sex Goddesses 288
  Unleashing Your Creativity 291
Look Within to Change the World 292

Appendixes

A Glossary   295

B Resources   299

C Upping Your Sex Goddess IQ   303

   Index   321

Foreword

For a woman to become a sex goddess, one of her first and most important tasks is to become comfortable with her body and her sexuality. *The Complete Idiot's Guide to Being a Sex Goddess* shows women how to enliven their sexual experience no matter their age, body type, looks, or experience level, and gives valuable advice on how to create more intimacy and pleasure for both women and their partners.

The authors show women important tools, such as how to awaken sensory awareness to increase sensitivity and amplify pleasure, how to add spice to your sensual relationship, and how to practice self-love and self-acceptance. They give encouragement and exercises to help release unwanted inhibitions that make a women's world smaller, and encourage women to acknowledge and make good boundaries to create safety. The book is part information and part instruction, containing both ancient and new techniques for sexual and spiritual fulfillment offered up with a lot of insight and a pinch of good humor.

We all need role models to see what is possible, and goddesses are about the best role models you can get! From maiden, to mother, to wise woman, the sacred pantheons represent women of every age and style. Women can take cues from the goddess culture of both the past and present, as it is a wonderful resource for the would-be sex goddess of today. These archetypes are blueprints for how a woman can be a goddess in a modern world. This perspective can be helpful either to women who believe in the power of the goddesses as spiritual beings, or for women who just need good examples of empowered women.

This book also offers keys to understanding the dynamics between male and female and the sacred dance between the two, and helps to demystify the way men and women act and react to sex, intimacy, and relationship. It gives important advice as to how to negotiate the sometimes difficult passage of communication and interaction within relationship, giving tips for interpersonal skills that can not only make your relationship smoother, but sexier, too!

Approaching sexuality as a sacred act is a very important part of being a sex goddess. Recognizing sex as a natural and sacred act of communion and union helps us to be fully present in the act, and receive the greatest benefits from it. Pleasure is sacred, and has the potential to connect us to the luminosity of our spiritual self when practiced with awareness and intention. *The Complete Idiot's Guide to Being a Sex Goddess* shares techniques from different tantric traditions that illustrate how to practice the art of sacred sexuality.

Cultivating sexual energy and moving it through the body with awareness and intention can be an amazing tool for personal transformation. Through the practice of tantra we can not only have great sex, but we can also help to heal our minds, bodies, and emotions. This sacred art is available to anyone who has the willingness and the desire to apply consciousness to the act of making love. May it serve you well.

Sylvia Brallier

Director of The Tantric Shamanism Institute, Las Vegas, Nevada; www. tantricshamanism.com

Introduction

Everybody, woman or man, has an idea of what "sex goddess" means. Whether you envision a Greek goddess in a flowing toga or a Hindu goddess with four arms floating on a lotus blossom, a Far Eastern geisha or one of today's glamorous couture runway models, well … get ready for a new vision: *you!* Yes, *you*, the young woman ready to set off on her life path; *you*, the bride (whether it is your first, fourth, or eighth marriage!); *you*, the single woman enjoying independence; *you*, the new mom (whether birth or adoptive) at age 20, 30, 40 …; *you*, the confident career woman at any age; *you*, the ageless beauty who only becomes more and more *herself*.

As you read this book, we want you, and your partner, to revel in the exploration of the sacred feminine through spiritual sexuality. May the stories and wisdom of the sex goddesses and their men (mortal and/or immortal) delight, instruct, and inspire you to claim your own sexual power!

How to Use This Book

This book is divided into a six-part exploration of how to nurture and *be* a sex goddess. Join the pantheon!

Part 1, "Who's Sexy? Yes, *YOU!*" introduces you to the many sex goddess stories, myths, and legends and where you fit among them as you choose, adapt, and create sex goddess traditions that identify and embody *your* unique personal sex goddess style. Learn why divine female sexual energy is timeless and how today's woman can move beyond the paradigm of the triple goddess to fast-forward, delay, pause, replay, or reinvent the roles of maiden, mother, and wise woman throughout her life.

Part 2, "The Sacred Feminine: Honor the Body Goddess," looks at the connection between the sex goddess, moon phases, sacred sexuality, and menstruation. Explore your sex goddess nature through a discovery of the chakras, connecting to their divine sexual energy, and understanding how your yoni (that's your vagina) and breasts hold the nurturing source of all that is.

Part 3, "Prepare Yourself for Love," takes a look at what women (and men) think "feeling sexy" means as you search for your inner sex goddess and learn how to nurture and sustain her. The relationship of Shakti and Shiva becomes the gateway to a discovery of Tantric and sacred sexual techniques for sex goddess foreplay, including self-pleasuring (in the company of a partner and alone!). Explore the many ways a sex goddess can prepare her body, mind, and spirit for sexual union, including meditations, baths, clothing, aromatherapy, and environment to produce sacred unions of lasting bliss. Also learn how to communicate your deepest sex goddess desires to the sex god who shares your life, and your bed.

Part 4, "Sacred Sex: Making Love Goddess-Style," draws upon sex goddess traditions to give sexual positions and advice on enhancing the lovemaking experience (for both partners!). Through ancient spiritual sexual knowledge, partners learn how to make divine love. "Coming together" means more than climaxing in harmony (which doesn't necessarily mean at the same time); it means encouraging and realizing the powerful energetic sexual communion two partners can achieve when they make an intimate bond through spiritual sexuality.

Part 5, "After the Loving," shows sex goddesses (and gods) how to prolong their bliss and extend the loving passion through mind, body, and spirit connection. Lovers learn that the energetic sexual bond lasts long after the sex act reaches fruition and the beauty of that sexual energy flows between you and into every area of your lives together!

Part 6, "Feeling Sexy Every Day," takes the sex goddess into the realm of her larger world and explores the many ways to claim the mantle of divinity in the context of the mundane. You'll explore mother love, how to climb onto (and off) the sex goddess pedestal, how you can embrace and strengthen your sex goddess nature by celebrating the sorority of women (empowering yourself with the beauty of female relationships, sexual and nonsexual), and how to move with grace and power to create and inspire in your family, community, workplace, and world.

Following these parts you'll find three useful appendixes: a glossary of terms every sex goddess will find handy, a resources listing of books and websites for further exploration of sex goddess-style spiritual sexuality, and a fun quiz to boost your sex goddess IQ.

Extras

Throughout each chapter of this book, we've added four types of extra information in boxes, to help you learn even more about being a sex goddess.

Source of All

You'll discover the meanings of terms related to sex goddesses, the sacred feminine, and spiritual sexuality that you might not already know.

Initiatress of Love

These boxes contain practical tips and related information to help bring forth your sex goddess nature and inspire intimate, spiritual sexual union with the sex god in your life!

Oracle Wisdom

Like Audrey Hepburn in the classic film *Roman Holiday*, are you brave enough to face the oracle? These boxes give you sex goddess wisdom and inspiring quotations to build your confidence as you join the ranks of divinely inspired, temple priestesses of spiritual sexuality.

Beyond Taboos

There's no limit when exploring your spiritual sexuality. Use these gentle cautions to help direct you on a positive path that safely takes you "beyond taboos."

Acknowledgments

From Stacy:

First, thank you so much to two spiritual sex goddesses: Lee Ann Chearney, who gave me the opportunity to participate in this project; and Eve Adamson, whose gift with words and research resulted in the beautiful book you hold in your hands. Thanks go to my first spiritual teachers: my mother, Linda; my father, Tom; and my maternal grandparents, Claire and R. Z. I am also very grateful to sex gods with whom I've shared communion over my lifetime, especially the most recent, Chris W. Thanks to Kevin P. and Ed K., Robyn, Beryl, Topaz, and Noel, who particularly support me in writing. Finally, thanks to the Sunday Night Priests, a group of friends whose spiritual support has contributed much to my life in the past two years.

From Eve:

So many sex goddesses have influenced and inspired the writing of this book. I would like to thank creation goddess Lee Ann Chearney, who brought us this project; and my co-author, sex goddess extraordinaire Stacy, whose wisdom, experience, and compassion so inform this book. Thanks also to my many sex goddess friends who inspired the writing and enjoyed sending ideas my way, particularly Irene, Rachel, and Ashley. Also thanks to the men who offered advice when I needed some concrete male perspective (that's you, Rico), and thanks especially to Ben, for happiness, for beauty, and for love.

A Special Thanks to the Many Sex Goddesses Who Contributed Their Knowledge, Power, and Unique Style

The publication of this book benefits from the collaboration of many talented sex goddesses who lent their special focus and talent to this book. At Alpha Books, we thank: publisher Marie Butler-Knight, senior acquisitions editor Randy Ladenheim-Gil, development editor Lynn Northrup, and senior managing editor Jen Chisholm. At Amaranth, we thank: creative director Lee Ann Chearney; writers Katherine A. Gleason, Carolyn Flynn, and Deborah S. Romaine; and editorial consultants Laura G. Fahsbender (New York) and Margo Schmidt (Paris). Thanks also to illustrator Hrana Janto for her inspiring drawings.

Illustrations by Hrana Janto

Hrana Janto is an illustrator well known for her paintings of goddesses and mythology. A graduate of the High School of Art and Design in New York City, Hrana received her BFA from The Cooper Union and has also studied at the School of Sacred Arts. Her commissioned works include historical paintings for the PBS series *Bill Moyers' Joseph Campbell and The Power of Myth*, as well as *The Goddess Oracle Deck*. She also contributed illustrations to the best-selling *The Complete Idiot's Guide to the Kama Sutra, Second Edition*, and *Empowering Your Life with Massage*. Hrana lives, paints, and dances in New York state. Visit her website, www.hranajanto.com.

Trademarks

All terms mentioned in this book that are known to be or are suspected of being trademarks or service marks have been appropriately capitalized. Alpha Books and Penguin Group (USA) Inc. cannot attest to the accuracy of this information. Use of a term in this book should not be regarded as affecting the validity of any trademark or service.

Part 1

Who's Sexy? Yes, *YOU!*

Do you want to see a real, live sex goddess? Look in the mirror! That's right, just *look in the mirror*. Maybe you find it hard to see yourself as sexy or even attractive, especially when the grind of daily responsibility mires you. But she's there, that sex goddess who is you, and you don't have to "glam" yourself up to bring her out (though certainly you can ... but we get ahead of ourselves). All you have to do is let her emerge.

Across time, the sensuality and wisdom of the goddess has been ours to draw from and tap into. As women we are of this vanguard, the force of creation and the energy of sacred sexuality. Join us as we time-travel from antiquity to the present in these first three chapters, exploring the many representations and dimensions of the sacred feminine.

1

Me, a Sex Goddess?

In This Chapter

- What is a sex goddess?
- Do you really want to be a sex goddess? (Or maybe you already are!)
- Unleashing your sex goddess power
- The sexual energy of creation
- The sex goddess in partnership

Do you aspire to become a sex goddess? Maybe you know you already are a sex goddess. Or maybe you aren't quite sure what a sex goddess actually *is*, but you kind of like the idea, and that's why you picked up this book (perhaps looking around in the bookstore to be sure nobody was watching, or hoping somebody is watching so they can assure you that you certainly don't need such a book).

Sex is a funny thing in our culture today. Add the word "goddess" and all kinds of images, connotations, expectations, and stereotypes arise in the collective cultural consciousness like so much passion-fruit-scented bath oil in a pink claw-footed bathtub: Mae West, Marilyn Monroe, Madonna, Britney Spears … or perhaps you're more the Christina Aguilera type? Or is Pamela Anderson more of a sex goddess, or Jennifer Lopez, or maybe, to you, Beyoncé or Isabella Rossellini? Or does that girl who beat you out for the last spot on the cheerleading squad in high school best fit the bill as your ideal, the sex goddess you can only aspire to become?

Are these women sex goddesses? And does that mean that somebody like you—somebody who isn't famous or particularly gorgeous or really all that talented a singer, actress, or cheerleader, who doesn't even live in Manhattan, Los Angeles, or Paris, or even have a date for Valentine's Day—even have a chance at being a sex goddess?

Yes, we would say that Mae West, Marilyn, Madonna, and even Britney, Christina, Pam, Beyoncé, and your cheerleader friend (even if she wasn't exactly your friend) may well be sex goddesses, but we would also say, with just as much conviction, that *we* are sex goddesses, and that *you* are a sex goddess, too … or, at least, you can be, if you decide to.

Just because the Roman goddess Venus has automatic deity status and lounges around Mt. Olympus in a toga doesn't mean you can't have goddess status, too. Just because that cheerleader went to the prom with the quarterback and you went with a group of your best gal pals doesn't mean you are any less of a sex goddess than she is. Trust us when we tell you that you can be a sex goddess. In fact, you already are one! It's just a question of accessing the power.

Sex Goddess: You?

All it takes to begin cultivating your inner sex goddess is a little attention: not necessarily to your appearance or your sexual technique (although we will talk about those things later in this book), but to the deepest depths of your soul. That's where your inner sex goddess lies (perhaps reclining seductively on a red velvet chaise draped in silk with a "come hither if you dare" expression … but we digress …).

And that's where you need to look to find her: within your own body, within your own mind, within your heart and emotions and your unique sense of self, and just as important, within your spirit, because a sex goddess balances all these parts in herself. The body and the spirit deserve equal care, attention, nurturing, and yes … seduction.

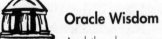

Oracle Wisdom

And the day came when the risk that it took to remain tight in a bud was greater than the risk it took to blossom.

—Anaïs Nin (1903–1977), French novelist

Sex goddesses activate each part of their inner selves, without letting any one part get out of synch and become too dominant or too submissive. It's about balancing the yin and yang, the male and female energies, the essence of life and the recognition of transition into other life stages, the power of creation and the power of destruction, the physical, emotional, and spiritual petals of the complicated flower that is you.

A sex goddess has the ability to be whole within herself, because only then can she truly connect with another human being. To be a sex goddess means to cultivate a deep sense of self and your own connectedness with who you are. And that's what this book is all about.

Hey Sexy, Are You Ready for This?

If you had no interest in being a sex goddess, we imagine you probably wouldn't be reading this book. But we are here to warn you that getting in touch with your inner self and your own sexuality can be a life-changing experience. Are you ready to feel comfortable saying the word "vagina" or its goddess equivalent, "yoni"? Some people have a difficult time saying the words for sex organs out loud. Do you cringe when you say, or hear someone else say, words like "clitoris" or "labia" or even "nipple"? Why should you? There they are, right down there, perfectly viewable with a little twisting and turning (or a hand mirror), and certainly perfectly accessible. Practice saying the words out loud. The more you say "vagina," the easier and more natural it becomes.

Are you willing to look your partner in the eye at the moment of orgasm, sharing the Tantric energy of deep commitment and love? Are you ready to finally *have* an orgasm and fully experience the blossoming of feminine goddess power through your body? Are you ready to like what you see in the mirror, walk down the street with confidence, find yourself slightly titillated by the sound of your own voice? *Are you ready to love your thighs?*

Because that's exactly what happens when you embrace your inner sex goddess. You start to like yourself. You start to recognize that the world is a sensual place and nothing in this world is any more sensual than you, your body, your soul, and your spirit.

Initiatress of Love

Many ancient cultures believed the source of creation for all life and even for the earth itself was a feminine power, "birthing" the universe into existence. The Judeo-Christian version of a male god forming the earth with his divine hands and creating a man in his own image is by no means the first creation story and may even be one of only a handful of creation stories that attribute universal creation to a male figure.

It may be a lengthy journey, and for many of us, it's a journey that lasts a lifetime, but should you decide to seek the sex goddess within yourself, you will start moving down that road. It's an exciting and empowering journey. Are you ready to discover the secrets of the sex goddesses and make their knowledge your own?

Sex Goddesses Then and Now, Here, There, and Everywhere

Part of finding and connecting with your inner self is by looking back throughout history and mythology at other sex goddesses who have found themselves and accepted and embraced who they are as sexual and creative beings, among other things. Such extraordinary women are nothing new. The idea of the sex goddess didn't surface with the advent of movies or popular music or any other contemporary cultural phenomenon. One can argue that the sex goddess has always existed.

A pantheon of both goddesses and gods predates the last 2,000 years of cultural thinking by millennia. Humankind has long understood (though throughout certain periods of history, we seem to experience temporary amnesia) that we are all part of the Divine. Nearly every religion you can name or imagine has this concept embedded somewhere within its philosophies, particularly in its esoteric or "mystery" schools.

But what about the goddesses? And what (you might be thinking, perhaps blushing just a little) about that *sex* part?

Sex parts notwithstanding, goddesses are many, varied, and represent a spectacularly sexy lineup when it comes to world deities starting back in the prehistoric era. Consider Gaea, the Greek goddess who sprang forth from the void and became the earth; or Ishtar, the Babylonian goddess of fertility, love, marriage, childbirth, and the personification of the planet Venus? And of course, we mustn't forget Venus herself, of ancient Rome, the embodiment of sensuality, sexuality, and love. Kali, in ancient India, was a wild, passionate, often violent goddess who was just as likely to ravish a man as cut off his head. (You probably know just how she feels!) On the opposite end of the spectrum, consider Kuan Yin, the Chinese goddess of compassion, who delayed her own enlightenment to selflessly help other sentient beings discover their own inner truths. (You probably know that impulse, too.)

Oracle Wisdom

Sex itself must always, it seems to me, come to us as a sacrament and be so used or it is meaningless. The flesh is suffused by the spirit, and it is forgetting this in the act of love-making that creates cynicism and despair.

—May Sarton (1912–1995), U.S. poet and writer

If we look at more modern times, we can surely discover many of our contemporaries who deserve the title of "sex goddess." Goddesses come in all shapes and sizes, all colors and cultures. They are young and old; they are maidens, mothers, and crones. They are just like us.

No, goddesses aren't meant to be any kind of unattainable ideal, or anything outside of ourselves to be worshipped from afar. These goddesses aren't archaic depictions of female idealism found in ancient stories from lost cultures and time. They are portrayals of ourselves, women with a wide range of experience, sexual beings with bodies, minds, feelings, and spirits.

A sex goddess can be you, cleaning the sink as regally as Vesta, Roman goddess of the hearth. It can be you, nurturing your family as tenderly as Khotun, the Siberian goddess of birth and nourisher of people who lives in a lake of milk and from whose breasts, it is said, the Milky Way originated. You, as passionate and scantily clad as Aphrodite, the Greek goddess of love, beauty, and sexual passion. (Why bother putting on clothes, Aphrodite might have mused, when I'm just going to take them off again?)

One reason for this book is to help women rediscover the Vesta, the Khotun, and the Aphrodite within themselves. We've come a long way since the Victorian days of sexual repression, but many of us still feel a hesitation about embracing our own sexuality, our bodies, and our sensual selves, even as we find ourselves curiously drawn to the *archetypal* images of goddesses whose radiance permeates our thoughts and desires. These archetypes can reveal to each of us our own inner divinity. They can help draw out our yearning to be in closer sensual communion with the natural world, with each other, even with ourselves. They can help you access your own goddess power, bringing it into daily life, whether in the bedroom or out of it, on your own or with a partner. The sex goddesses who came before us can help us, just as we may be able to help those who come after us. Can you *have* too many sensually awakened human beings? We think not.

Source of All

An **archetype** is a model or prototype for an ideal. Influential Swiss psychologist Carl Jung (1875–1965) takes this idea a step further, defining archetype as a symbolic image that exists in the collective unconscious of humans and represents something all people automatically understand. For example, the goddess Aphrodite is an archetype for sexual pleasure.

Sex = Creation

We all know sex is—or should be—more than a matter of inserting tab A into slot B. But what else is it, exactly? One argument we will make in this book (and you're not really going to argue with us about it, are you?) is that sex is a delightfully pleasant source of creative energy.

Sex equals creation, not only because it is potentially a *pro*-creative source (that is, resulting in the creation of brand-new human beings and survival of the species), but because the physical, emotional, and spiritual energy generated by a really good sexual union can become the source for any number of creative pursuits (for you, and for your partner, too!).

At its best, sex itself inspires creativity. Just take a look at the *Kama Sutra* to get an idea of how creative two bodies can get when they put their minds (and genitals) to the task. One (oversimplified) principle of Tantra, an esoteric form of yoga, is that sexual union generates spiritual awakening, "creating" or "birthing" new levels of divine awareness.

> **Source of All**
>
> The **Kama Sutra** is an ancient text from India passed down orally through generations and first organized and edited by Indian sage Vatsyayana in the fourth century B.C.E. Best known for its array of sexual positions, the Kama Sutra also provides guidelines for living, relationships, and morality, as well as techniques for wooing the right partner and for making sex emotionally, spiritually, as well as physically fulfilling. For more information, check out *The Complete Idiot's Guide to the Kama Sutra, Second Edition* (see Appendix B).

Simply put, great sex can engender all sorts of creative energy, which you can then put to use wherever you like: that novel you are writing, that advertising slogan you just can't quite nail down, that problem with your neighbor you haven't been able to solve, that parenting issue, that career as a travel photographer or surrealist painter or part-time jazz saxophonist you haven't quite found the time to pursue.

Get creative, have sex, get more creative, have more sex. Now that's the kind of prescription for enjoying your sex goddess nature we can really get behind (so to speak …).

It Takes Two to Tango

Being a sex goddess has more than a few perks, but one of the greatest is the ability to cultivate deeply fulfilling relationships with other human beings. Sure, we are the first ones to tell you that you don't *need* anybody else to have a really good orgasm, but sexual union with another human being is among the most fulfilling and deeply satisfying experiences humans can have in this life. (Even better than a chocolate soufflé. No, really!)

Ironically, learning to be a sex goddess for yourself and within your own mind, body, and spirit, will do more for your relationship with others than any sort of outward focus on pleasing a partner. Only when you truly embrace your own body, mind, and spirit; only when you learn how to walk through your life sensually awakened and sexually aware; and only when you cultivate your own five senses, honing them for the greatest possible appreciation of the act of lovemaking, will you be a truly active, productive, and potentially fulfilling sexual partner to another human being.

Sexual union is, in large part, a balancing act. The exchange of emotions as well as bodily fluids has the remarkable effect of normalizing both parties involved, so that what seemed excessive in one or deficient in the other somehow equals out. Stress dissolves. Conflicts come clear. Sex can be like that computer program that fixes errors on your hard drive. You aren't sure how it works, but you get a great sense of satisfaction when you get that little message: 37 errors repaired.

When you learn to trust and bond physically and emotionally with another person, things really do start to repair themselves. The simple act of communion with another is what humans were meant to do, and when we do it, we feel good. We feel more whole. We feel more content, calmer, more at ease. We feel more like ourselves, closer to who we are inside. And that makes us better partners for the ones we love.

Oracle Wisdom

Sex and laughter do go very well together, and I wondered—and still do—which is the more important.

—Hermione Gingold (1897–1987), English actor

Sex can do all that? Sure it can, with a holistic approach. Sure it can, if you are a sex goddess and know what you are doing. And that's our purpose here: to help you figure out exactly what you are doing and guide you toward finding the sex goddess we know you are waiting to become. We're here to help you feel empowered to have a really good time with the one you love.

And what's so wrong with the pursuit of sensual desire? We say: absolutely nothing. It's what we are built to do. Why waste another minute *not feeling?* As a sex goddess, you have so much to feel, so much to see and hear and smell and touch and taste. C'mon girlfriends, the world is full of senses to experience, people to love, sex to be had. You've got a sex goddess in you. Let's dive into your mind and heart and soul and bring her goddess power (*your* goddess power!) into the light.

The Least You Need to Know

- A sex goddess is any woman who pursues knowledge and sensuality, balancing all the different elements of the internal self, including male and female energies, the urge for creation and for destruction, at every stage of the life cycle, from maiden to mother to wise woman.

- For thousands of years before recorded history, cultures have honored goddesses of creation, fertility, childbirth, motherhood, passion, and sexuality. Sex goddesses are nothing new!

- Sex is intimately linked with creativity, both because sex can result in the creation of human life and because many creative pursuits can benefit from sexual energy.

- Becoming a complete, confident, and sensually aware woman—a sex goddess— helps make sex with another human a truly fulfilling experience.

Chapter 2

Invoking Goddess Power

In This Chapter

- Hanging out with Athena
- Your personal sex goddess world tour
- The fantastic four: Ceres, Juno, Pallas Athene, and Vesta
- Building your personal sex goddess pantheon

How would you like to hang out with a goddess? Sex goddesses have power, sensuality, and creativity. They have existed for many thousands of years, and their stories still stay with us. They exist today, in the powerful and sensual women all around you, and they can influence each of us with their stories, experience, and qualities, both those we wish to imitate and those we wish to avoid.

Invoking sex goddess power is more than a matter of wishing to be sexier or less inhibited, wanting to find love, either for the night or for a life-time. It's a process of learning and taking the knowledge of other sex goddesses into our hearts, minds, and bodies so that we become part of that pantheon of women, both real and imagined, living and symbolic, who understand what it means to live in a body with senses and urges, passions and fears, and a never-ending flow of love moving in and out of us. Let's get to know some of these sex goddesses. Pretty soon, you're going to feel right at home.

Hanging With the Goddesses

Imagine spending an evening with Baubo, the Greek goddess known for telling sexually charged jokes and lifting up her skirt to flash people who were getting too melancholy. Talk about taboo—Baubo was famous for doing, saying, and displaying the most outrageous things, just for a good laugh. We think she'd be a lot of fun at a party.

Beyond Taboos

The Greek goddess Baubo was known for sexually explicit talk and behavior. In some depictions, she is a body without a head, with breasts and nipples for eyes and a talking vagina for a mouth. Sound offensive? In fact, Baubo represents the humor and levity that is possible for a woman who can truly embrace her sexual parts, not as a replacement for her personality but as an integral part of who she is. Sometimes we have to overemphasize something to balance out a history of repressing it!

Or maybe you would prefer to go horseback riding with Athena, the gray-eyed virgin Greek goddess of war and handicrafts. You could talk about the arts, protecting the innocent, fighting the good fight.

Maybe Aphrodite could share a few trade secrets for advanced sexual techniques. After all, this goddess of pleasure was famous for her many sexual exploits. Or maybe you and Persephone could talk about the pros and cons of a long-distance relationship. (She only gets to spend half the year together with her husband, Hades, king of the underworld; the other half of the year, Persephone comes up to the surface to live with her mother and be sure spring and summer are in full bloom.)

Maybe you love to be out in nature and you would get along great with the Greek goddess of nature, Artemis. Imagine a goddess retreat, a group of women hiking, camping, and talking around a campfire. Think of the stories around *that* campfire, if you invited Baba Yaga, the Russian thunder witch and grandmother of the devil, along with Lilith, the first woman who ran away from Adam because he kept telling her what to do.

Maybe you would also invite Hathor, the Egyptian cow goddess of love and joy, to be sure everyone remained in good spirits. Haumea, the Hawaiian goddess of childbirth, whose children were born from different parts of her body and who could change herself from young to old to young again whenever she wanted, might have some interesting childbirth stories to tell.

Of course, you can't *really* hang out on the weekends with a bunch of goddesses. Or can you? Sure you can! Not only are you hanging out with goddesses every time you get together with girlfriends, but you can invoke the power of mythological goddesses from all over the world to guide you in your quest for happiness, love, wisdom, … and really great sex!

Sex Goddesses from Around the World

Sex has been around for about as long as, well, life itself! This powerful force drives life, the propagation of species, and to a large extent, the bond we feel for one another, so it's no surprise that every culture throughout history and from every corner of the globe has incorporated themes of love and sexuality into their theology and mythology. In many cultures, goddesses personified ideas about love, sex, passion, fertility, birth, motherhood, and the basic urge to partner with another human being. (Mythologically, it seems that many of the gods and goddesses just can't seem to leave us humans alone. We think it's because we're just so sexy!)

Let's take a closer look at some of the sex goddesses from different cultures throughout history. The goddesses listed here are just a small sampling of the thousands of goddesses of sex, love, passion, fertility, creation, destruction, motherhood, spousal fidelity, spousal infidelity, death, and resurrection that grace the mythologies of world cultures.

Initiatress of Love

The more you learn about sex goddesses from here, there, and everywhere, the more you will find the ones who attract you, the ones you can relate to, and the ones you can visualize or call up for inspiration when you need an infusion of passion in your life, a helpful increase in fertility, the courage to speak your mind, the patience to be a good mother, or the willingness and desire to take on and maintain a partnership. Keep a list of your favorite goddesses, and keep adding to it.

Not every sex goddess, in this list or any other, has a happy story (welcome to real life!), and not every couple has a happy ending. The wide range of sex goddesses around the world, however, represents the great variety of life, experience, and passion that humans know so well.

Sex Goddesses of Africa

In African mythology, goddesses often represent creation, fertility, childbirth, and the moon. Here are a few of our favorites:

◆ 'Aisha Qandisha, a free-spirited, beautiful, and sexually active Moroccan spirit with the legs of a goat and pendulous breasts.

◆ Ala, a Nigerian symbol of Earth, death, and fertility; a guardian of children; and a guide to moral behavior.

◆ Crocodile Woman, a Sudanese birth goddess who took the form of a crocodile to protect infants.

> **Oracle Wisdom**
>
> Chi, a Nigerian earth goddess and creator of life, protects the good, punishes the corrupt, and is both male, in the form of a sky god, and female, in the form of an earth goddess. This androgynous goddess can help us get in touch with both the male and female energies within each of us.

◆ Ekineba, a West African masquerade goddess who taught the dancing and drumming used at masquerades.

◆ Inkosazana, a Zulu sky goddess called the "Princess of Heaven." This goddess appeared as the rainbow, the rain, and the mist, and governed the growth and harvest of corn. Sometimes, to a lucky few, Inkosazana appeared as a young woman who delivered an important and secret message.

◆ Juno Coelestis, a North African goddess of sacred temple sexuality who was associated both with fertility and debauchery.

Central and South American Goddess Power

In Central and South America, goddesses were often virgins or mothers and associated with water or the moon.

◆ Erzulie, a Caribbean moon goddess who could bring beauty and fortune or jealousy and discord. In her appearance as a water snake who ate bananas, Erzulie was the goddess of salt water and fresh water.

◆ Ichpuchtli, an Aztec earth goddess of flowers, lust, and pleasure, who represented feminine beauty.

◆ Ix Chel, a Mayan rainbow goddess and wife of the sun. She had both a benevolent form as goddess of weaving, healing, medicine, childbirth, and sex, and a malevolent form as goddess of destruction through water.

♦ Olokum, a Puerto Rican hermaphrodite sea goddess who ruled the ocean, including the mermaids and the tritons (half men, half fish).

♦ Cocamama, a Peruvian sex goddess with many lovers and also the mother of the coca plant, which brings health and happiness.

♦ Mariana, a Brazilian goddess of healing, children, and love, who protected sailors.

Oracle Wisdom _____

Cavillaca was an Incan love goddess. One day, the god Viracocha, disguised as a beggar, placed some magical fruit next to Cavillaca. She ate it, immediately became pregnant, and gave birth to a child. But when she discovered that she had been tricked into pregnancy, she took her child and leapt into the ocean. She and the child became rocks in the sea for the waves to break against. Viracocha was left on the shore to grieve his loss and regret his subterfuge.

The Sex, Creation, and the North American Goddess

North American or Native American goddesses are frequently attributed with having created the world.

♦ Anog Ite, a Dakota "two-faced woman" and daughter of first woman and first man, taught a form of basket-making that conflicted with a woman's traditional role and was thought to lead to lesbianism.

♦ Awitelin Tsita, a Zuni creation goddess with four wombs who engaged in continuous sex with the sky until all her wombs were filled. She then gave birth to the human race.

♦ Ca-the-na, the Mohave "Venus" and goddess of love and sex, whose worship promoted fertility.

♦ Kokopell' Mana, a Hopi goddess of sex and fertility charm who liked to challenge men to a race. As they'd start to run, she would lift her dress as a distraction and then she would catch them, throw them to the ground, and pretend to ravish them.

Oracle Wisdom _____

Bear Maiden, a North American guardian goddess and black bear, wandered the woods in the form of a young woman. When a young hunter killed Bear Maiden's enemy the grizzly, they fell in love and married. Several years later, however, Bear Maiden's husband regained interest in a past love, so Bear Maiden took their child and turned herself and the child back into bear form, disappearing forever back into the forest.

◆ Korawini?i, a North American sex goddess who attracted many men but killed them during sex because she had teeth in her vagina. Finally, clever Coyote was the only man left on Earth. He turned his penis into a stick, which broke off Korawini?i's vaginal teeth, allowing her to finally bear children successfully.

◆ Soatsaki, a Blackfoot feather woman and sex goddess whose lover, Morning Star, brought her to heaven by pulling her on a silken spider's web. Isn't that romantic?

The Power and Passion of the Egyptian Goddess

In Egypt, sex goddesses had great powers, often rivaling or exceeding the powers of the male gods.

◆ Anatha Baetyl, the lion goddess, wife of Jehovah, and the goddess of both love and battle.

Oracle Wisdom

Ken, the Egyptian equivalent of the Roman Venus, is the goddess of love and sex. Worshipped in ancient Egypt and even mentioned in Hebrew scripture, Ken is usually depicted standing on a lion, holding two snakes in one hand (perhaps representative of the phallus) and a flower in the other hand (perhaps representative of the yoni, or vulva—see Chapter 6).

◆ Autyeb, the goddess of happiness and the personification of joy.

◆ Isis, the notoriously powerful goddess of love and sex, was the daughter of Nut, the goddess who created the universe according to the Egyptians, and the wife of the hawk god Osiris. Called Queen of the Earth, The Moon, Goddess of Life, and Queen of the Stars, Isis was originally worshipped on her own, and later in partnership with Osiris.

◆ The Zodiacal virgins, goddesses of love and sexuality, were the personification of the planets in the zodiac sign of Virgo.

The Sex Goddesses of the Far East

Known for inventive and creative sex, the Far East has many sex goddesses, often born of mystical elements.

◆ Akaru-hime, a Japanese goddess of magic and sex, was born when her mother gave birth to a red jewel, which found its way into the hands of a Korean prince who put the jewel in his bed, where it turned into the beautiful Akaru-hime.

When her husband began to treat her badly, Akaru-hime left him to return home to Japan, where she was worshipped and asked to provide safety to those at sea.

♦ Bai Mundan, a Chinese goddess of wealth, beauty, love, and sex, was sometimes called the White Peony, to represent both wealth and beauty. Bai Mundan's job was to distract religious ascetics with her promise of wealth and pleasure.

♦ Iku-tama-yori-bime, a Japanese goddess called the life-spirit or lucky-spirit princess. A handsome prince visited Iku-tama-yori-bime each night but always disappeared in the morning. In love and curious, the goddess tied a thread to her lover's clothes and followed the string the next day, discovering that he was a mountain god.

♦ Inari, a Shinto vixen goddess of commerce, travel, wealth, and love, was invoked in Japan for prosperity, longevity, and successful love relationships.

♦ Jiutinan Xuannu, a Chinese goddess called the Dark Maiden, decided to come down from heaven to live with a mortal for a while, just to see what it was like.

♦ O-ichi-hime, a Japanese goddess of sexual attraction and fertility, both for humans and plant life.

♦ Suseri-bime-no-mikoto, a Japanese underworld goddess of physical prowess and sex.

Oracle Wisdom

Izushi-otome-no-kami, the Japanese goddess of love, attracted the attention of two brothers. The older brother, Autumn, didn't interest her, but the younger one, Spring, with the help of his mother (Mother Nature, of course), donned a costume of wisteria vines to spark the goddess's interest. It worked, and she took him into her home and they made love and became husband and wife. Autumn refused to give the lovers a wedding gift, so Mother Nature punished him by making him wither, hence the withering autumn leaves.

Sex Is All Greek (or Roman) to These Goddesses

Who better personifies the sex goddess than the Roman Venus or the Greek Aphrodite? When most people say "goddess," they probably think "Greek goddess," and indeed, many goddesses from this area of the ancient world embodied love, sex, and passion.

◆ Aphrodite, one of the chief 12 gods of Olympus, was the goddess of beauty, love, and sex. Born of sea foam into which Cronus had tossed the severed genitals of Uranus, Aphrodite was irresistibly beautiful, but she married the ugly fire god, Hephaestus. Aphrodite was famous for having many affairs during her marriage, including one with the god Adonis and the god of war, Ares. The philosopher Plato gave Aphrodite two names: Aphrodite Urania, to represent spiritual love, and Aphrodite Pandemos, to represent sexual love.

◆ Maia, the goddess of spring and warmth, including the heat of passion and sexuality. She was worshipped on May 1, as the earth becomes warm after winter.

◆ Medusa, the snake-haired Gorgon goddess of magic, sex, and ugliness. Her startling appearance didn't keep this powerful goddess from sleeping with Poseidon.

◆ Selene, the goddess of the moon, fell in love with a mortal named Endymion. She cast him into a state of perpetual sleep so she could make love to him every night. They produced 50 daughters.

◆ Venus, the Roman incarnation of Aphrodite, a powerful goddess of sensual love, was considered to be the mother of the Roman people.

◆ Virilis, the Roman goddess of love and sex, was the sexual incarnation of the Roman goddess Fortuna. Women worshipped her in this incarnation so they could remain sexually provocative to their husbands.

Oracle Wisdom _____

Eurydice, the Greek goddess of love, sexuality, and unhappiness, was deeply in love with Orpheus, who loved her just as deeply. While trying to escape the advances of another man, Eurydice accidentally stepped on and was bitten by a poisonous snake. She died and was transported to the underworld. Orpheus went in desperate search of her. The underworld gods told him that he could take Eurydice back only if she walked behind him and he did not look back. Afraid he was being tricked, Orpheus took just one quick glance behind him, and his love vanished forever. Some versions say he consequently hung himself in despair.

Indian Passion

In India, home of the Kama Sutra, physical pleasure is one key to spiritual enlightenment and a sacred (and creative) undertaking.

♦ Ahalya, a Hindu goddess of beauty, love, and sexuality, caught the eye of the god Indra, who conspired to distract Ahalya's husband Gautama so he could seduce her. Indra turned himself into a rooster and crowed at midnight, luring Gautama out of the house to do his morning exercises. Indra then assumed Gautama's form and went inside to make love to Ahalya. When the couple discovered Indra's deception, they punished him by covering the entire surface of his skin with images of yoni, the symbol for the female reproductive organ.

♦ Amrit, a Hindu goddess of immortality, sex, and magic, first appeared at the Churning of the Ocean of Milk, the primordial source of all life according to Indian mythology. Goddess of love potions and water life, Amrit's belly was said to contain the water of everlasting life and anyone who drank it would become immortal. One day, a cow accidentally punctured Amrit's belly with his horn and all the water leaked out. After that incident, death appeared, and the cow was punished by forever having to work behind a plow.

♦ Arundhati, a Hindu goddess of fidelity, was invoked during marriage ceremonies and pictured standing on a lotus leaf as it floats in the water.

♦ Durga, the avenger, was a composite of many different Hindu goddesses and demons representing the cycle of life and death, war, creativity, intelligence, and sexuality. A warrior out for blood, Durga was a symbol of the struggle against evil and of powerful intellectual exploration.

♦ Kali, a Hindu goddess of life and death, was both a creator and a destroyer, devouring humans and protecting them, depending on the situation. Often pictured as black, "the color in which all distinctions dissolve," and naked, she represented the ultimate realization of truth.

♦ The Nayikas, a group of deities who personify illicit love, include Aruna, Balini, Candi, Jayini, Kamesvari, Kaulesi, Medini, Sarveshvari, and Vimala.

Oracle Wisdom

Anasuya, the beautiful goddess of education, knowledge, justice, and love, sat on the bank of the Ganges one day when the three gods, Shiva, Vishnu, and Brahma, appeared and became overwhelmed with passion for her. They tried to take her by force, but she prevailed, commanding them to act like the holy beings they were and consider her as their mother and only their mother. Abashed, the gods obeyed and left Anasuya unharmed.

The European Sex Goddesses, from North to South

The Far East and India may be most famous for their unbridled and powerful sex goddesses, but the European continent has its fair share of sex goddesses, too.

- Frau Welt, the German mistress of the fairies, represented love and sex. To the medieval religious authorities later in Europe, she also represented the devil. It was said that Frau Welt liked to seduce humans.

- Frigga, a Scandinavian goddess of conjugal fertility and love, was a devoted wife, helper, and mother who weaved clouds and spun golden threads that symbolized the rays of the sun.

- Geion, a Scandinavian goddess who was a guardian of young people, virgins, and those who will never marry.

- Grimhild, a Scandinavian goddess of love and sex and a sorcerer who made a magic potion to help the god Sigurd fall in love with her daughter, Gudrun.

- Hnoss, also called "Jewel," a Norse goddess of love, sex, and metal who represented sensuality and infatuation.

- Walden Wip, a German forest goddesses who performed magic and healing and enjoyed seducing men.

> **Oracle Wisdom**
>
> Ingeborg, the northern Teutonic goddess of love, sexuality, and the sun, fell in love with the sun god, Frithiof, but was promised to the elderly King Ring. During this marriage, she had an affair with a mortal, whom she blinded so he would never look upon another woman. When the elderly king died, Ingeborg married her first love, Frithiof.

What Do Asteroids Have to Do with Sex?

In ancient Greece and Rome, gods and goddesses often represented planets and stars. But it wasn't until the nineteenth century, when the first four asteroids were discovered in an asteroid belt teeming with the catapulting heavenly bodies, that astrologers attributed important Greek or Roman goddesses to each of these four asteroids. In *astrology*, each planet reflects certain aspects of human personality and behavior. The four asteroids, just like the planets, also reflect upon who we are and what we do, according to their position when we were born and how they move as we move through our lives.

> **Source of All**
>
> **Astrology** is the study of the influence of heavenly bodies, such as stars and planets, on human behavior and personality.

These four asteroids, governed by goddesses, influence certain aspects of love, sex, and relationships. Here is a summary:

♦ The first asteroid is named after earth mother and goddess of the harvest Ceres, the Roman equivalent of the Greek goddess Demeter. The position of this asteroid influences the individual's ability to nurture and take care of those she loves.

♦ Juno, the Roman goddess of families and the wife of the god Jupiter, protects women, marriage, and children. Unlike her Greek counterpart Hera, Juno handled her marriage in a rational and secure way, with her own agenda and activities. Her asteroid influences the individual's level of long-term commitment in love relationships.

♦ Pallas Athene, or Athena, the virginal Greek goddess of war, goodness, and household affairs, influences the way we use our creativity to solve problems in our lives and in our relationships.

♦ Vesta, the Roman goddess of the hearth, influences the ways in which we commit ourselves, body and soul, to a purpose, and the ways we express our sexuality.

Initiatress of Love

A detailed astrological chart will tell you exactly how Ceres, Juno, Pallas Athene, and Vesta influence your own personality. If you ever have an astrologer do a reading for you, ask for a reading of the four asteroids in your birth chart, or the chart of your solar return for the year.

Taken together, these four asteroids represent the experience of a committed love relationship, family life, and what it takes to love and live with another human being.

Your Own Personal Sex Goddess

When you learn about many different goddesses, you can take their stories and incorporate them into your own life, as inspiration and a source of power. Throughout this book, we will continue to tell goddess stories, and as we do, we hope you will take to heart those who speak to you, adding those goddesses to your own personal list of favorites.

For example, maybe you are in love, and the bond between you and your partner is strong and enduring, one of equality and mutuality. Perhaps you will take on Isis, the Egyptian queen of the earth, as a personal favorite, because of her strong bond of loyalty, love, and unabashed sexuality with her husband, the hawk god of light Osiris. When Osiris was killed and chopped into pieces by his evil brother, a god of darkness named Set, Isis searched the earth for him, enduring many trials and adventures in her quest to retrieve the pieces of her husband. When she finally found him, she put him back together. But there was one piece missing—his penis. So ever the resourceful lover, she made one of gold and attached it to him. Using this new organ, Osiris and Isis conceived their son, Horus, who later exacted his revenge by killing Set. Together, Horus, Osiris, and Isis formed a triad worshipped by the ancient Egyptians. (Now that's a family that sticks together!)

Perhaps at this point in your life you aren't interested in commitment but in exploring the range of options life has to offer. You may relate to Jiutinan Xuannu, the Chinese Dark Maiden, who decided to come down from heaven to live with a mortal for a while, just to see what it was like. She cast herself into a picture, which a man brought home, hung on his wall and worshipped. Whenever he returned home after work, he found food on the table and the house cleaned. One day he decided to hide and see what was going on. He saw a beautiful woman cooking and cleaning and noticed the picture on the wall was blank. He jumped out, hid the picture, and the goddess told him she would live with him as his wife for a while. They lived happily, had a daughter, and finally, after a few years, the goddess asked for the return of the picture, went back into it, and returned to heaven, leaving her husband with only an image to worship once again. Jiutinan Xuannu was ready to move on to something new.

Oracle Wisdom

Sex appeal is fifty percent what you've got and fifty percent what people think you've got.

—Sophia Loren (1934–), Italian actor

Perhaps you are protective and strong in your relationship and have learned that you and your partner can stick together in a world of adversity, somewhat like Suseri-bime-no-mikoto, a forceful and protective Japanese goddess who fell in love and married Opo-kuni-hushi. Her father tried to harm his son-in-law by sending him to sleep in various dangerous places filled with snakes, centipedes, or wasps. Suseri-bime-no-mikoto sent her husband off with a magic scarf to protect him from danger and then negotiated their release from her father's influence and territory. In Japan, depictions of the amorous couple show them in various forms of conjugal embrace. Perhaps they know some techniques we can all learn from.

Keep an eye out for the sex goddesses who sound a little bit like you, but don't neglect the ones whose strengths you admire, those who do the things you wish you could do. Sex goddess inspiration exists everywhere. Just open your eyes, crank up your senses, and soon you'll feel perfectly natural as a member of the pantheon.

The Least You Need to Know

♦ You can relate personally to many sex goddesses from mythologies around the world for inspiration in your personal life, love life, and sex life.

♦ Goddesses throughout history and around the world have stories and themes that can help each of us understand what it means to be a sex goddess.

♦ The first four asteroids, discovered in the nineteenth century, are named after four goddesses. In astrology, they influence our personalities and behavior: Ceres governs our nurturing ability, Juno our long-term commitment, Pallas Athene our creativity in problem-solving, and Vesta our spiritual commitment and sexual expression.

♦ Keep a list of your own personal sex goddess favorites, both those you can relate to and those who inspire you to try something new.

Chapter 3

Maiden, Mother, Wise Woman

In This Chapter

- ◆ The ages and stages of pleasure
- ◆ The female trinity: maiden, mother, wise woman
- ◆ Triple goddesses, ancient and contemporary
- ◆ Finding your place (or places!) in the life cycle

Once upon a time, a baby girl is born. Nurtured through childhood, she eventually reaches puberty and becomes a young woman. Virginal and pure, this young maiden eventually finds a mate, marries, learns the ways of love, and has a child. Now a mother, the woman learns to nurture her own children, and as they grow and become adults themselves, she ages. Eventually, her childbearing years end and she moves beyond motherhood to become a wise woman, well versed in the ways of the world, the world of women, and the cycle of life.

Nice story, isn't it? Well, sure, for some women, both in the past and today, life does resemble this story. Many of us are still schooled in the notion that such a progression is the ideal one, the one to be sought after.

If we don't follow it—say, by not becoming a mother, or becoming one "too early" or "too late," or lapsing back into youthful maidenlike behavior after a divorce or after our children move away, or choosing not to behave like a maiden in search of a man, or remaining sexually interested and active past the childbearing years, or choosing a same-sex partner and re-directing the *entire* scenario—we have somehow missed the feminine boat, done something horribly wrong, failed to fulfill our genetic destiny.

We think not.

All it takes to understand the far-reaching options, implications, and flexible nature of the female life cycle (and sex cycle) is to take a look back at how this cycle has played itself out in other times and other cultures, both in myth and in history. We love the maiden-mother-wise woman paradigm because it is both descriptive and comprehensive. But what is it exactly that characterizes a maiden, a mother, or a wise woman? Maybe the answer isn't what you expect. Maybe it's much more.

Hey Lady, Why Don't You Act Your Age?

Age. It's only a number, right? This is true, in a way. You can be 40 and feel 20 (or 20 and feel 40!), but even more than your age, your *stage* does affect who you are, how you feel, and what you can do (at least reproductively … and in some instances, legally!).

As women, and also as humans, we all go through stages—birth, or our introduction into this world and this body, infancy, childhood, adolescence, adulthood, midlife, the senior years. And eventually, all of us move on to the next stage, into whatever comes after this world and this life.

> **Initiatress of Love**
>
> How old do you feel? Pick an age, and imagine you are that age. How would you behave differently? Consider another age. How does your behavior change again? Try "acting" a different age for a few hours, seeing the world through the eyes of an older or a younger woman. What do you learn? What do you see differently?

These stages mean certain things for women and certain things for the budding, or the experienced, or the downright sagacious sex goddess. And because they are so meaningful and universal, cultures and people long before us honored these stages, named them, and even represented them symbolically.

Trinities, triads, and triangles have long held a significant and symbolic role in many cultures, philosophies, and spiritual practices. The holy trinity of Christianity (the father, son, and holy ghost) is just one of hundreds, perhaps thousands of examples of spiritual trinities. One of the most ancient and honored of those trinities is the female trinity, represented by the maiden, the mother, and the wise woman (some people say "crone," but other people just don't like that so we'll go with the wise woman option).

Each of these three sex goddess stages represents certain archetypes for women. The stages begin with the onset of puberty, when gender traditionally begins (children have often been considered genderless). Let's look at them individually.

The Maiden: Embracing, or Re-Embracing, Your Inner Virgin

The maiden stage begins at puberty and lasts, traditionally, until a woman loses her virginity. Maiden, in many cultures, is akin to the word "virgin" and implies a pure, undefiled nature and innocence. Yet in many ancient cultures, maiden or virgin didn't mean "she who hasn't had sex yet." Instead, a virgin was a woman who belonged to no man. Whether or not she had ever had sex was irrelevant. A virgin was her own woman, and we like to think of the term that way today. Virgin goddesses such as Athena and Artemis were wise, powerful, often warriorlike, and protective. They ruled nature, harvests, and animals. They watched over childbirth, protected babies, and shielded mothers from harm. They belonged to no one other than themselves.

In Western culture, there's a prevailing idea that the maiden or virgin is eventually "defiled" or brought into womanhood by a man. She "loses" her virginity in the same way she might lose her car keys (never to find them again), or perhaps even more apt, in the same way she might lose her reputation, her innocence, or her former life. Virginity gets stolen away, and isn't it a little bit sad? But in ancient cultures, the connotations of maidenhood were a little bit different.

Oracle Wisdom

How can a virgin goddess be a goddess of fertility, sexuality, and childbirth? Many virgin goddesses ruled these areas even though they were "maidens" who, technically, had no experience with childbirth. Yet in the realm of the goddess, the experience of womanhood is an interconnected chain and each part shields, protects, and is connected to every other part.

In many ancient myths, goddesses went after human men, or gods, choosing on their own to move from one stage to the next. Maidens were hardly victims, or subjugated, or "led" anywhere by anyone. Yes, there are also stories about gods pursuing maidens, both goddesses and "mortals," to try to steal away their virginity. These gods were often punished by other, more noble and protective gods, and often by mother goddesses, too. But our point is that this is not, by any means, the only scenario.

To counteract this idea, many women today don't like to consider the idea of virginity at all. So what if you are a virgin or aren't? Does having sex really change you at all? What does it have to do with who you are? And what exactly counts as sex anyway?

Why should penetration by a man define anything about you? Why should it make you suddenly belong to someone else? Isn't your maiden stage your own business, and shouldn't you be able to move on to the next stage whenever you darn well please? Can't you stay a maiden even if you decide to become sexually active? A woman's maiden stage belongs to her and no one else, and in our current culture, for the first time in centuries, women can embrace this notion and practice it. Be a maiden for as long as you like, gals! You can enter into a committed relationship when you are ready. (And even then, we won't say you belong to someone else. Perhaps you belong to each other.)

Initiatress of Love

One can hardly mention virgins without considering the Virgin Mary, mother of Jesus, "known" only by God when she gave birth to the Son of Man. When Christianity began to spread, many ancient statues of other goddesses were slightly altered to be statues of the Virgin Mary, drawing her into a long line of goddesses dating back into prehistory. But was Mary both a virgin and a goddess? In Christianity, and particularly in Catholic mysticism, yes. Mary belonged to no man, only to God, when she became a mother. Like many goddesses before her, she was her own woman as she became a mother, and her spirituality was forever after entwined with her sexuality. She was a vessel for the Holy Spirit.

One reason for this re-appraisal of the technical definition of "maiden" is the fact that most women in our current culture become sexually active, moving on from virginity, long before they have even the slightest inclination to start having children. Where do we fit into this triad when we have experienced sexual pleasure but haven't yet become mothers?

The sex goddess of the twenty-first century has a great opportunity to continue the evolution of the female trinity. To exist in the maiden stage is to exist in youth (not necessarily technical youth, but spiritual youth), in conquest of love or human connection, not yet taking care of others but only of oneself.

Better yet, because maidens don't need to be limited to a virginal state (or to a technically virginal state), we can become mothers and then go back to being maidens again if we darn well please. We can seek love again when a former love has ended or embrace celibacy if we choose to or explore other pursuits beyond the search for mate, family, and domesticity, such as painting, environmentalism, starting your own company, or doing something else we've always wanted.

Maidens can love, physically, emotionally, and spiritually. They are joined to no one and remain open to the possibilities of life. The notion of maidenhood is as fluid as history, as changeable as myth, and as unique as the sex goddess who chooses to embrace this stage.

The Mother: Transcending the Self

The word "mother" carries with it just as much baggage as the word "virgin." Mothers are, of course, women who have had children, right? They may have careers or not, they may be married or not, but they have experienced pregnancy, childbirth, and the sacrifices inherent in raising children. Even in their work, their relationships, and in every aspect of their lives, mothers have learned to give themselves over to other people, causes, and forces. Their lives are no longer their own. They are self-less, taking care of their partners and their children, keeping the house, fulfilling their domestic role … right?

Well …

Sure, sometimes mothers do these things, and sometimes they don't. Just as the maiden stage is fluid, changeable, and diverse, so is this second stage of the female trinity. The mother stage is really the stage of the sex goddess with life experience, sexual experience, and an understanding that, at a certain stage, it feels right that the mainte-nance, care, and nurture of relationships supercede the quest for selfhood. Where the maiden explores the self, the mother explores the bond between herself and others.

Oracle Wisdom

In search of my mother's garden, I found my own.
—Alice Walker (1944–), U.S. writer and poet

To embrace the mother stage of the female trinity is not necessarily to have become pregnant and experienced childbirth. A mother may adopt children or work in a field where she nurtures children (such as teaching). Or she may instead be in a committed long-term relationship with another human being or work in a field where she cares for or works in defense of other people or animals or the earth.

The mother has reached a stage of maturity that nobody can force on her. It happens at a certain point in life and even she can't necessarily bring it on or even define when or why or how it occurred. The mother understands what it means to be beyond the self. She begins to apprehend the unity in all things, the connection between all beings, the divinity in herself and in others. The mother recognizes the concept of *other* in a new way, not as something foreign, or something to pursue, attain, or flee from, but as part of a universal flow of being.

Again, the mother stage doesn't have anything to do with the technical aspects of sex, reproduction, and aging. It is a spiritual state. A woman can enter the mother stage even if she has never had sex, just as a woman can remain in the maiden state even after her first sexual encounter. A mother doesn't need to be in a traditional partnership with a man or even with a child. A mother is in partnership with humanity and recognizes that compassion, empathy, and helping others is more fulfilling than the pursuit of the self.

Or we might phrase that a little differently: The mother recognizes that the nurture of relationship *is* the pursuit of the self. They are one and the same. To be is to recognize the self in others, and the others in the self. It is to embrace the ultimate unity of all things.

Oracle Wisdom

The first problem for all of us, men and women, is not to learn, but to unlearn.
—Gloria Steinem (1934–), U.S. writer and journalist

"Wow," you might be thinking." I thought I was a mother, but I didn't really think of all *that* stuff!" Maybe you wouldn't describe your view of life in quite this way, but if you have learned how to have and nurture relationships with others and if caring for others, whether your own children or any other living things or anything you create, has become a priority in your life, you have entered the stage of the mother.

That doesn't mean you won't ever go back to the maiden stage, today, tomorrow, or in a few years. Maybe you will and maybe you won't. The female trinity isn't a linear thing; it is triangular, and you can jump around all you want! Being a mother doesn't mean you don't ever think about yourself, pursue your own pleasures, and seek personal fulfillment. It is simply a new stage of maturity, one that recognizes, as we have explained, the fulfillment that comes from bonding with others and the discovery of the likeness we all share.

Another advantage to being in the mother stage is that this personal recognition of the importance of relationships catapults the woman to a new level of sexual prowess, understanding, and enjoyment. Sex in pursuit of personal pleasure is all well and good. We are the first to agree with you on that one! But sex in pursuit of the unity inherent in a relationship between two people is an entirely new game with different rules and a much better prize at the end.

This is a whole new level of sex that transcends your basic perfectly enjoyable orgasm. This level of sex encompasses the unification of two spirits, and pleasure becomes an ultimate communion of two into one. If that's not incentive to move on to the mother stage, we don't know what is!

The Wise Woman: Universal Exploration

What does it mean to be a wise woman? Traditionally, this third stage starts at menopause, when the mother leaves the childbearing years behind and moves into the next stage of physical, emotional, and spiritual advancement. Life no longer means caring for others, because the others have grown up and moved on to their own next stages. As children move on, work evolves, and relationships change, the woman beyond motherhood enters an entirely new stage: the stage of wisdom.

The new quest in this life stage is marked by an accumulation of knowledge with a more over-reaching perspective. No longer compelled to serve, the wise woman becomes compelled to *know*. This exciting stage of life has nothing at all to do with menopause, although the onset of the stage often correlates, more or less, with this biological phase.

Initiatress of Love

A woman doesn't typically attain enough wisdom to really understand what it means to enter the realm of the wise woman until later in life.

Unlike the maiden stage, where the pursuit of the self governs the psyche, and unlike the mother stage, where the pursuit of relating to others prevails, the wise woman stage is marked by the pursuit of relationship to the world as a whole, to universal understanding and a unity, not just with the other, but with the *all*. The wise woman stage is a natural by-product of simply living a long time with mindfulness and awareness. The more we experience, the more we understand. The more we know, the more we realize we *don't* know, and the more we love, lose, suffer, grow, and feel, the more we experience the compulsion to bring all these details of life together in a more meaningful way.

Although traditional ideas in Western culture tell us that the post-menopausal woman is no longer interested in sex, and although the body does erect certain barriers toward easy intercourse, our world has also changed in many ways in this regard. Women past their childbearing years experience a new sexual freedom, one they could never have understood as maidens and mothers.

Despite the fact that the possibility of pregnancy can easily be thwarted via birth control, sex at the mother stage is about the bond with the other. For the wise woman, sex becomes even more than this bond. It can potentially transcend relationship to reach a whole new level of enlightenment. For the wise woman, sex can become an entirely new method of relating to the world. This is the level of sex described in the Kama Sutra and in the practice of *Tantra*, sex de-signed for spiritual enlightenment and ecstasy of the entire body, mind, and spirit, rather than just the genitals.

Another aspect of the wise woman stage is the proximity to that ultimate transition—the transition out of this world and the physical body the woman has come to know so much about. (Yes, we mean death.) This proximity to the death transition doesn't exactly lend urgency to the explorations of the wise woman, but it does shade the retrospective on life. The wise woman comes to see the web of life as an intricate series of cause and effect, of chain reactions and inter-relations, not just between people but between all things connected by the ebb and flow of life-force energy.

> **Source of All**
>
> *Tantra* is a Sanskrit word meaning "weave," and it refers to an ancient Indian system of philosophy and psychology that considers the realm that lies beyond oppositions in the universe, to encompass a reality that is ultimately unified rather than opposed. One method for comprehending this unification is through certain sexual practices.

No act is without its effect on the universe as a whole, both on the microcosmic and macrocosmic levels, and not a single human exists without a multitude of influence on the universe as a whole. With this understanding comes wisdom, and the wise woman is all about wisdom.

The Triple Goddess, Yesterday and Today

This female trinity—the maiden, mother, and wise woman—surfaces in cultures all over the world, and wherever it arises, it manifests itself in similar ways. Typically, the maiden incarnation of the triple goddess is young, beautiful, and desired by all. The mother is typically a protector and facilitator of communication and interaction. The wise woman often encompasses many incarnations and is sometimes linked with death. The triple goddess also surfaces in other similar ways: creator, protector, and destroyer; spring, summer, and winter; birth, growth, and death; waxing, fullness, and waning.

In ancient Rome, Lucina, Diana, and Hecate formed a trinity of lunar goddesses. Lucina, bringer of light, was often pictured holding a flower and a baby. She represented birth and was sometimes associated with the Greek goddess Juno, protector of children. Diana (or Artemis in Greece) presided over the moon and the forest. Diana represented a triad herself: heaven, earth, and death as well as birth, growth, and death of the forest, but she is primarily associated with growth. Finally, Hecate was an underworld goddess of darkness and death and was often pictured holding a torch to illuminate knowledge to help with important decisions.

The Three Fates of ancient Greece are another trinity that represented the process of fate throughout existence. Clotho appeared at birth and pulled the thread of a human's destiny from a spindle. Lachesis measured out the length of each thread, determining the length of life, and Atropos cut the thread, determining the moment of death.

In India, this trinity, or trimurti (the Sanskrit word), consists of Lakshmi, Sarasvati, and Devi. Lakshmi, the maiden incarnation, was a beautiful young goddess born out of the primordial sea of churning milk holding a lotus blossom and dazzling all the gods with her beauty. Sarasvati, the mother incarnation and sometimes called the white goddess, is credited with giving the Sanskrit language to the people of India, thus facilitating communication between people. Devi, the wise woman incarnation, is among the most important Hindu goddesses and appears in many different incarnations, sometimes as a young girl, sometimes as the "universal mother," and sometimes as a destroyer; a goddess so various that she possesses great wisdom.

> **Oracle Wisdom**
>
> Quadriviae, Western European goddess of the crossroads, was in and of herself a triple goddess of birth, growth, and death who created and sustained herself.

The Celts had several goddess trinities. One included Banba, Fotla, and Eire, a trinity that symbolized the spirit of Ireland (Ireland was named after Eire). These three sisters all represented earth, nature, and family. Another goddess who was in herself a trinity was the Welsh goddess Gwenhwyfar. She appeared in three forms in Arthurian legend, as three wives of King Arthur associated with birth, growth, and death.

For all you Trekkies out there, one of our favorite contemporary examples of the triple goddess appears on the television show *Star Trek: The Next Generation*. Deanna Troi, the beautiful, desirable, and intuitive counselor, is the maiden. Beverly Crusher, the doctor, is the mother. She is an actual mother and a healer to the crew. Finally, Guinan, the bartender, dispenses wisdom to all who wander into her realm. She is the quintessential wise woman.

Where—and Who—Are You?

As you consider the many triple goddesses out there—the maidens, the mothers, the wise women—think about where you fit in this life cycle. Are you just beginning your journey into yourself? Are you searching for a partner, or just getting to know someone? Are you young (mentally, emotionally, and/or physically)?

Perhaps you have moved into the mother stage, into a committed relationship, into a parenting or caretaker role, into a profession of service to humankind, or simply into a place where you are more comfortable with yourself and better able to reach out to others.

Maybe you have moved beyond the caretaker stage into a new level of understanding about yourself and the world, a place where you can pass your wisdom on to others as you move through your life guided by a greater vision.

Initiatress of Love

Consider the goddesses who are a little like you. Are you like Juno, goddess of the hearth and home? Are you like Aphrodite, gorgeous and desired by all? Are you like Artemis, the huntress who gallops through the forest and wants nothing to do with men as she pursues her own causes? Are you like Kali, the destroyer, or Hecate, the wise woman of the darkness?

Or as we have mentioned earlier in this chapter, perhaps you look back over your life and see how you have moved from maiden to mother back to maiden and then skipped back to wise woman. Consider how you fit into this cycle, both now and in the past.

Finally, consider how the stage of life you are now in becomes reflected in your sexual self. For the maiden, sex is an exciting exploration of self. For the mother, it becomes a powerful and meaningful bond with another. For the wise woman, it can be akin to enlightenment itself. Throughout the rest of this book, we will explore all the ways in which you can fully enjoy and most benefit from the delights each of these stages has to offer.

The Least You Need to Know

- Every stage of life, from infancy through old age, means something different for the sex goddess, but the three key stages of the sex goddess cycle are the maiden, the mother, and the wise woman.

- The maiden stage represents youth and exploration of the self; the mother stage represents maturity and moving beyond the self to understand the deeper relationship of the self to the other; the wise woman stage represents enlightenment and the eventual understanding of the universal unity of all creation, as well as an ability to share that knowledge with others.

- The female trinity surfaces in many different cultures and mythologies throughout history, from the ancient Roman Lucina (birth), Diana (growth), and Hecate (death) to *Star Trek: The Next Generation*'s Deanna Troi (the maiden), Dr. Beverly Crusher (the mother), and bartender Guinan (the wise woman).

♦ Sexually, the maiden stage represents the pursuit of pleasure for the self and an exploration of one's own body. The mother stage represents sex as a deeper connection to another person. The wise woman stage represents sex as a method for pursuing a higher state of spiritual enlightenment.

Part 2

The Sacred Feminine: Honor the Body Goddess

To know your body is to love and respect your body, and to understand, intimately, its ability to give and receive pleasure. How well do you know *your* body? Do you look at it, touch it, see and feel the ways your lover enjoys it? Do you know what pleases you?

Maybe you know your body well, or maybe you're shy and uncertain about exploring its mysteries. The power of the sex goddess arises from knowing and experiencing. These chapters guide you in exploring and appreciating the delights of your body from head to toe—with special attention to those parts that are uniquely and pleasurably feminine.

Chapter 4

The Sacred Cycle of Moon and Menses

In This Chapter

- ◆ Your body and the moon
- ◆ The ebb and flow of the moon goddess
- ◆ Your menstrual cycle in the real world
- ◆ Honoring your body, your cycle, and your sexual energy

"That time of the month." "Period." "A visit from Aunt Flo." We have lots of euphemisms for menstruation in our culture, but most people don't like to talk about it in very much detail. It's not exactly an appealing subject, we think. At best slightly embarrassing, at worst painful and debilitating, menstruation has a bad rap in our world today.

Yet this natural cycle is an integral part of a woman's body during the childbearing years, so why do many women see it as negative? Other events in our lives can be painful and messy—for example, childbirth—but we relate to them with joy. Why not menstruation?

In ancient cultures, menstruation marked a sacred time. It meant evidence of a woman's fertility, so women were often treated with a special reverence during this time. In the practice of Tantra, menstruation signaled a time when a woman existed somewhere between the earthly and the heavenly worlds. Associated with the cycles of the moon, menstruation also linked women to the greater cycle of life, the flow of the tides, and the motions of the planets. Menstruation gave women a sort of lunar divinity.

So what happened between then and now? How did your "period" transform from something sacred to something embarrassing? Can you reclaim that sacred nature for yourself, your own cycle, and the sexy moon goddess within?

Your Body and the Lunar Cycle

Some people believe that long ago, when people lived closer to nature and in harmony with the earth, women had menstrual cycles that coincided with the lunar cycle. With each full moon, women would experience ovulation and with each new moon, menstruation. Now wouldn't that make getting pregnant, not to mention birth control, a whole lot easier?

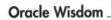

Oracle Wisdom

We've surrounded the most vital and commonplace human function with a vast morass of taboos, convention, hypocrisy, and plain claptrap.
—Ilka Chase (1905–1978), U.S. writer and actor

We know today that menstruation, in addition to many other bodily functions related to our sexual selves, is governed by hormones. The ovaries, those two egg-producing structures within our lower abdomen, produce estrogen and progesterone; the adrenal glands, just above the kidneys, also produce estrogen. In our bodies, these hormones work in cycles. Estrogen levels rise, causing the uterus to accumulate a nourishing lining in case of pregnancy. Then, about 28 days into the cycle, estrogen levels suddenly drop and the uterus sheds its lining. This is menstruation.

But what does the ebb and flow of estrogen have to do with the moon? Does it mean they are necessarily connected just because they both ebb and flow? Not if you are doing a logical proof in philosophy class, but in the natural cycle, sure. Our bodies are made largely of water, and menstruation also involves the flow of fluid through the body. The moon is the nearest heavenly body to the earth, and it exerts a gravitational pull as it circles around us. The more in tune we are to the natural world, the more sensitive we become to the cycles of nature, the more we will feel nature.

Evidence for this natural connection is the many moon goddesses in ancient myth. When humans still lived close to the earth, they recognized the connection between woman and the moon. As we moved in our lifestyles farther away from nature, our bodies also moved out of synch with the cycle of the moon. The idea that women were somehow linked to the moon and men to the sun as part of a system of balance stayed with us in theory, but the practice of it has faded. As we worked to conquer the earth, bending its resources to our needs, we lost respect for the natural cycles and the ebbs and flows of the planet. And as with so many things, when we stop paying attention to something, or stop respecting its natural movement, we lose touch with it, and cease to be a part of it.

Today we live in houses well insulated from the elements and conveniently temperature controlled. We wear clothes that we buy in stores or on the Internet (mailed to our doors) to protect us from the feel of the air or the rays of the sun, and shoes to protect us from the earth underfoot. We eat food grown, picked, slaughtered, processed, and packaged somewhere far away, apart from those few tomatoes and herbs from the backyard garden that grow in soil bought in plastic bags and depleted of its rich mineral content. We talk to each other through electronic, cyber, and virtual filters, and we get from place to place inside gas-powered, well-sealed, moving metal vehicles.

Some of us go for walks outdoors, or hikes, or even camping. Some of us try to buy more natural foods and clothes and do things that won't harm the earth *too* much. But still, life in the twenty-first century is a whole lot different from living in a tent or in a tree, growing and killing your own food, making your own clothes, and defending yourself against constant environmental adversity.

Life is certainly safer, if not less stressful, but it's no wonder our bodies are out of touch with the moon. How often do we swim naked in the sea beneath the stars in the light of the moon herself? How often do we wander in a moonlit forest or lie in a field and gaze at the moon? How often do we organize sacred ceremonies around reverence for the moon or honor the goddesses, like Selene and Mene, who represent the moon? (Mene is the Greek goddess of the menstrual cycle. She rules over the months of the year.)

Sure, some of us might do some of these things once in a while. And sure, we might notice a particularly large, bright, or strangely colored moon as we drive down the highway or walk up the road. We may even stop to look at it for a moment or two. In some ways, the moon seems to influence us whether we like it or not. Emergency room nurses report surges of women going into labor during the full moon, and some police officers swear that crime surges with the full moon, as if that bright round orb in the sky really is making everybody feel just a little bit restless and crazy.

What if we were to harness this power by paying attention, purposefully and with our full awareness, to the cycles of the moon and the way they affect us? You can get back to your lunar center and recognize the effect of the lunar cycle on your body, and you don't even have to run naked through the moonlight to do it! Not that we would stop you if you really *wanted* to run naked through the moonlight, but we certainly aren't going to *make* you do it. Instead, the process of getting "back to the moon" can be a gradual (and healthful) sequence of small adjustments.

> **Initiatress of Love**
>
> Keep a lunar journal to track the moon cycles, your menstrual cycles, and the relationship between the two. Sometimes simple awareness is all it takes to synchronize the two. Also write about how you feel and what you think about as you observe the moon in its cycle and your body in its own cycle.

First, begin to keep track of the lunar cycle. Many calendars already list the cycles of the moon. On full moons and new moons, make a point to go out in the evening and take a look at the moon. How is it different than last month's full or new moon? Or take a look at the moon each evening at the same time. Make it a habit, and you'll soon notice the subtle but visible daily changes in our earthly view of the moon.

Move your regular exercise routine outdoors in the evenings, if weather and safety permit. If you can't see the moon from where you live, take a drive in the evening out to a place where you can spot the moon. A monthly full-moon and/or new-moon evening drive can become a goddess tradition in your life, and even in your family.

Most important, simply bring your awareness to the moon, and not just when you see it. Think of it often, up there in the sky above, circling around us in its nurturing orbit and, just like a good mother, far enough not to interfere too much and close enough for us to still feel her presence.

> **Source of All**
>
> Yin/yang is a Taoist concept of balance in the universe. All things are associated with either yin—female, dark, moist, lunar energy—or yang—male, light, dry, sun energy. The yin/yang symbol represents the balance of these energies in the universe.

Moon Goddess, Sex Goddess

Because the menstrual cycle has long been linked with the lunar cycle, the thousands of moon goddesses in mythologies all over the world often represent fertility, both of the earth and of the female body. Obviously, fertility is linked to sex, the planting of seed in the fertile ground resulting in the spontaneous creation and growth of a new life.

But the moon and moon goddesses are more integrally linked to the cycles of the earth and the body. They also serve as the yin to the sun's yang. The idea of *yin* and *yang* is an ancient one, with roots in

Chinese Taoism. According to this idea, everything has a yin and yang quality, and these opposites combine and integrate to form a balance. In life, in nature, and even in sex, a good balance of yin and yang makes for a more fulfilling and complete whole.

Traditionally, yin is associated with the female essence, the moon, darkness, and moisture, while yang is associated with the male essence, the sun, light, and dryness. In the Kama Sutra, yin essence refers to the flow of moisture triggered by sexual excitement and release in a woman, and this fluid was thought to possess mystical and beneficial energies. Yang essence refers to the fluid ejaculated by the man. But that doesn't mean a yin/yang connection can't happen between two women or two men. Just as many gods and goddesses are androgynous and contain both male and female energies, so each of us in the real world has our male and female sides, energies, and inclinations.

We only label these as "male" and "female" due to tradition, but you might feel more comfortable calling these energies "yin" and "yang." You and a female partner may balance each other well, with your flowing and changing yin and yang energies. In the same way, a man and a woman can balance each other well, even if it is the woman who tends to have more yang energy and the man who tends to have more yin energy. It is not about who has what or who does what. The point is in the balance.

The yin/yang symbol, a circle in which white and black spiral around each other, with a black dot in the center of the white and a white dot in the center of the black, represents this integrated balance of opposing forces.

The essential balance of male and female fluids creates the sacred whole of the yin/yang balance in the Kama Sutra.

> ### Oracle Wisdom
>
> Sometimes the pairing of opposites is less than harmonious. The Masai moon goddess of Eastern Africa, who governed disorder as well as the moon, married the sun, but the two got into a terrible fight and were both covered in scars. The sun felt humiliated by the marks of the battle, so he shone so brightly that nobody could see his scars. But the moon wanted everyone to see the marks of her combat with the sun. She chose a dimmer light, making the scars on her face fully evident. Do you have some of the Masai moon goddess in you, proud to show the marks of your life experience rather than feeling compelled to hide them behind a mask of light and happiness?

Although the idea of yin/yang comes from the East, many ancient cultures from all over the globe contain this or a similar philosophy. Moon goddesses from many mythologies are often paired with sun gods in a similar sort of balanced integration.

An African moon goddess from Ghana named Obosom was androgynous, combining opposites within a single deity. Obosom was the visible physical manifestation of the moon's vital force. Can you feel the power of Obosom within you as you look at the moon, stirring both your male and female energies and making you feel whole and complete within yourself?

> ### Source of All
>
> The **Book of the Dead** is an ancient Egyptian book of spells, prayers, and hymns written in about 300 B.C.E. and designed to secure safe passage for the dead from this world into the next.

The woman-light of the shadows, an Egyptian moon goddess, was called "The Light That Shineth in the Darkness, the Woman-light." Rather than lingering near the sun to reflect his light, the mythology from the ancient Egyptian *Book of the Dead* represented this lunar goddess as the protector of the moon god Thot. Do you feel that your partner also has lunar qualities, a feminine aspect, a quiet inner darkness, and do you sometimes feel compelled to serve as protector?

Menstruation in the Real World

"Moon goddesses or no moon goddesses," you may be thinking, "weren't we talking about menstruation? Because whether the goddesses had to experience it or not, menstruation in the real world is, well, mostly just not fun!" We hear you! Whether you aren't sexually active with a partner or sexually involved and either trying to become pregnant or with no such desire, you may just wish the whole messy monthly business would hurry up and be over with.

However, whenever we bring negative energy to something, it increases our overall negative energy. The fact is that the cycles within your own body as well as the cycles of the moon will have a profound and rhythmic effect on your sexual identity. Why not use this rhythmic power to your advantage instead of complaining about what you could as easily revere and treasure? Just think about how much easier life is now that we have things like tampons and panty liners! Women used to have to wad up a rag and stick it in their britches to catch the menstrual flow. (Hence the term "on the rag." Nice, huh?) These days, we can slip in a little tampon and be done with it.

Initiatress of Love

You can still have sex during menstruation, if you feel like it, and knowing exactly where you are in your cycle can help you get the most out of sex, wherever you are in the month. Your cycle will impact how you feel about sex, how much you feel like engaging in sex, and how much you enjoy it. It might also impact how your partner feels about sex, so be open about where you are in your cycle to your sexual partner. You may also have heard that orgasm can help relieve menstrual cramps ... but if you just feel too crampy and bloated to even entertain the idea of an intimate encounter, you probably won't feel inspired to try it. At other times in your cycle, nothing sounds more pleasurable than sex with your intimate partner. (That's a week of opportunities!)

To take advantage of your cycle, get back in touch with the rhythms of your own body and make the most of each stage, whether you are feeling exuberant and experimental or sensitive and in need of a little gentle romance. Let's take a look at what exactly is going on down there.

As we've already mentioned, hormones in your body don't remain at a steady state. They ebb and flow, increase and decrease, according to the complex and precisely regulated needs of your body. When it comes to menstruation, estrogen is one of the key hormones that can impact how you feel, both physically and emotionally. Estrogen level peaks during ovulation, about two weeks before menstruation begins. This is your most fertile time because your body is releasing an egg that could, potentially, be fertilized, so your body kicks into high gear and makes you feel like you really gotta get you some love!

You will probably feel pretty darned sexy during this time, and your desire level may be high, although this isn't always true because many other things in life also impact desire. Apart from feeling sexy, you will probably feel more confident, attractive, and energetic during this time. You may feel invulnerable to criticism, on top of the world, capable of accomplishing just about anything. Your body sheds excess water weight so your stomach is flatter, and your skin is even likely to be clearer.

Unfortunately, this enjoyable stage doesn't last all month. It only lasts for a few days, maybe a week, tops. As estrogen levels drop, some women begin to experience a more emotional time. Some may feel more insecure, more easily irritated, and less social. It starts gradually, as energy level decreases. You might begin to feel more scattered, more forgetful, more "spacey."

But what's wrong with that? Who says you have to be the life of the party and quick on the uptake every single day? When we deny the effects of hormones on our bodies, this "low" period, during which some women may need a little more downtime, can feel like "something wrong." "What's wrong with you?" people might ask. "Two weeks ago you were feeling so good about yourself!"

Some women report what feels like a personality change during this pre-menstrual time, but rather than thinking you are somehow not yourself, why not see it the way a moon goddess would—as a time when you are every bit your self. And that self is cyclical and ever-changing, with every right to want to be alone for a while, have a little less to do, sleep a little more, eat a little less, and reflect on life. Why not spend more time turning inward and relish the meditative mood?

Beyond Taboos

The pre-menstrual time can be a low period for some women, and respecting this time and adjusting to it can help re-integrate this natural part of the cycle into regular life. However, some women really do experience a severe form of "pre-menstrual syndrome," or PMS, when they lose control of their behavior and/or become truly depressed. If you feel like your PMS is something you can't control and it is impacting your life in a negative way, please see your doctor or a counselor. This condition is not your fault—sometimes hormones fluctuate a lot—and it is fully treatable, so don't hesitate to seek help.

As you get in closer touch with the way your cycle affects your body, your emotions, and your mind, you may find that you begin to enjoy the ebb and flow of your own body. Remember the moon and the way it, too, moves and changes, showing us more or less of the sun's light, depending on the cycle. Sometimes the moon shows off her full illuminated glory, and sometimes she retires into darkness. Let the moon empower you to do the same, according to the rhythms within you.

And as for your sex goddess side? When it comes to menstruation, we think sex goddesses are all the sexier. Not everyone thinks that way, and you and/or your partner may prefer not to engage in sex during this time. Or you may decide to go for it, and why not? The yoni, or vulva, is full and well lubricated during this time (although as your menstrual flow tapers, you may experience some dryness). Sex feels a little different during this time of the month, but no less enjoyable. And yes, orgasm really can relieve menstrual cramping! You can also use this time to enjoy your partner in other ways, sexually or not.

The point is that a sex goddess does what feels natural and comfortable, and the first step in this process is to feel natural and comfortable about the cycles in your own body. Only then can you feel natural and comfortable about whom you choose to share your body with, and when and how you do it.

(For starters, may we suggest kissing in the light of the moon?)

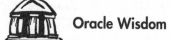

Oracle Wisdom

The moon develops the imagination, as chemicals develop photographic images.
—Sheila Ballantyne (1936–) U.S. writer

Honoring Your Cycle

Life is a cycle. The earth, the moon, and the planets move in circles, slowly turning, their surfaces changing with the presence or absence of light and heat. The earth is covered with life: animals, plants, people; each is born, lives, and dies. These beings breathe, grow, change, eat, sleep, and copulate, each in their own way. Within the body of each being, fluids move, organs pulse, life flows.

The menstrual cycle is just one of many cycles within and around a woman, and part of being a sex goddess is learning to recognize, participate in, live in awareness of, and fully honor this cyclic existence.

Know your body with all its parts, and the way it changes, and you will know yourself more deeply. This inner knowing and willingness to move to your own inner song will put you in better touch with who you are on all levels, making you more responsive to touch; to the back-and-forth flow of emotion between two people; and to the cycles of anticipation, pleasure, and release inherent in the cycle of lovemaking. See how awareness of our world is so intimately linked with awareness of our own bodies? This is what sex goddesses know, and the lesson lasts a lifetime. Fortunately, this is one lesson we can all enjoy for as long as it takes to learn.

The Least You Need to Know

♦ Long ago, women menstruated in coordination with the lunar cycle, but today we have become largely alienated from the cycles of nature and no longer enjoy this synchronicity with the moon.

♦ Moon goddesses appear in many different mythologies worldwide. They often rule over fertility, both of the earth and of the body, and are paired with the sun or other balancing counterparts, sometimes within themselves.

♦ In traditional Asian philosophy, the moon represents yin, the dark, female energy, which is balanced by yang, the light, male energy represented by the sun.

♦ Rather than fight or suffer from your menstrual cycle, learn to recognize how it affects your body physically, emotionally, and mentally, so you can live in harmony with the needs of your changing cycle.

♦ The more you honor the cycles of your body with full awareness, the more you will enjoy sexual pairing according to the arc of your cycle.

Chapter 5

Embodying Your Sacred Sexuality

In This Chapter

- ◆ Your body: more than the sum of its parts?
- ◆ Chakra talk
- ◆ Your inner river of sexual energy
- ◆ Why you are sexy right here, right now

Whether you love it or criticize it, flaunt it or hide it, think some parts are great and others need an overhaul, or really don't think about it all that much, there it is, wrapped around your brain, container for your spirit, your own personal vehicle, standing there staring back at you from the full-length mirror: your body.

Women have a complicated relationship with their bodies. Some of us obsess about them, some of us totally neglect them, and some of us take care of them like they are our most precious possessions. Whatever your attitude, like it or not, this is the body you have right here, right now. As a sex goddess, your body is one of your greatest tools for apprehending pleasure, connection to others, and enlightenment.

Why ignore your body, or dislike it, when it can bring you such bliss? Maybe you could honor it a little bit more, take care of it a little better, and learn to really, really love it, no matter what its shape, size, age, fat-to-muscle ratio, or its abilities or flexibilities. It's all yours, so why not make the most of it?

The Puzzle of Your Body

You've probably done some kind of puzzle in your life, and if you have, you know that you start with a box full of pieces. Each piece is interesting and perhaps colorful in its own way. Each has a certain shape and fits together with some of the other pieces. When you put together small chunks of the puzzle, you might begin to see part of a bigger picture, an idea or a section. Yet when you put that last piece in and the puzzle is finally whole, something almost magical happens: The puzzle becomes a picture.

Suddenly, when all the pieces are together, the picture jumps out and becomes separate from all those pieces, somehow becoming more than the sum of its components. The way a picture emerges when the puzzle comes together seems to have little to do with that box of pieces you started with. Yes, that's all there is, really—a bunch of pieces fitting together. But just look at that picture!

Your body is a little like that. Yes, you've got hair, elbows, thumbs, a heart, a rib cage, a brain. Those little wrinkles in the corners of your eyes that show whenever you smile. Those little dimples on the backs of your upper thighs. But any one of those parts taken by itself has very little to do with the picture that is the whole you, the you people see every day, the you who is so much more than a sum of body parts.

> **Oracle Wisdom**
>
> The body has its own way of knowing, a knowing that has little to do with logic, and much to do with truth, little to do with control, and much to do with acceptance, little to do with division and analysis, and much to do with union.
>
> —Marilyn Sewell (1941–), U.S. minister and writer

When you look in the mirror, chances are you focus on some of those parts rather than on seeing the whole you. You might obsess about those forehead wrinkles or gray hairs or that little jiggle that didn't used to animate your rear view quite so much. Maybe you focus on your gorgeous eyes or shiny hair or the muscle definition in your shoulders. But the whole you is something much, much more than slim ankles or double chins or breasts in any stage of perkiness, or lack thereof.

It can be hard to see this, especially when you are in the habit of scrutinizing your body. How can you possibly be objective about something that is so much a part of your self-esteem? This new body-focus takes awareness, as well as a willingness to let go, even if just for a little while, of that focus on the parts in favor of the whole.

Feeling negative about your body can put a real damper on your enjoyment of physical pleasure, and seeing your body as a string of parts that need improvement can make you self-conscious about what your partner sees during sex. You can even begin to objectify yourself: "Why do I think I should get to have physical pleasure when I can't even lose 10 pounds?" "How can my partner stand to look at my stomach?" "Nobody with thighs this jiggly/arms this bony/hair this gray could really be sexy!"

This destructive pattern disregards most of what makes you the unique, beautiful, sexy, physical/emotional/intellectual/spiritual being you really are. If this sounds like you, the first order of sex goddess business on your sex goddess to-do list is just this: "Tweak body image."

Initiatress of Love

Write your own body image to-do list to post in a visible place, reminding yourself to replace destructive body image thoughts with a positive, affirming attitude. Your to-do list might look something like this:

- ◆ Think of my best feature.
- ◆ Wear something sensual.
- ◆ Hug somebody.
- ◆ Apply lotion to every inch of my skin.
- ◆ Look in the mirror and tell myself: "I look *good!*"

Yes, easier said than done, we understand that. But have you ever noticed how some women ooze sexuality despite obvious physical "flaws"? We know a girl who is significantly overweight by conventional standards but whose stylish clothes, sexy hair, swingy walk, and easy self-confidence turn heads every time she enters a room. Most of us also know people with so-called "perfect bodies" who don't seem even a little sexy because of the way they act. Sexiness isn't in the body, gals. It's in the mind and the heart.

Initiatress of Love

Yoga is a great way to get in closer touch with your body. Whether you are new to exercise or already in good shape, yoga can challenge every fitness level with increased flexibility, balance, strength, and inner tranquility. For more information on yoga, see *The Complete Idiot's Guide to Yoga, Third Edition,* by Joan Budilovsky and Eve Adamson (see Appendix B).

Another friend of ours knows this but still asks: "But what can I do to feel like that? I've been told by a past boyfriend that he broke up with me because of my weight, and now I can't feel attractive anymore." We are social animals, and what other people think about us and say to us—especially those we love—can make a pretty big impact that can be difficult to overcome. But with mindfulness and a dedicated effort to exhume that sex goddess you have within, you can do it. The people who have told us hurtful things weren't good matches for us and have nothing to do with who we are inside. You may have to keep reminding yourself of this every single day. It's worth the work to finally free yourself from the bondage of negativity. The more you remind yourself of how sexy you really are, the more easily you will recognize it to be true.

Golden Breath Meditation

One way to accomplish this gradual body-image tweaking is through daily meditation. Spending a short time each day in quiet meditation and reflection can make a big difference in how aware you are of your own body and your own mind. Although there are many different types of meditation (for more on meditation, check out *The Complete Idiot's Guide to Meditation, Second Edition*, by Joan Budilovsky and Eve Adamson; see Appendix B), this is one we like to use to help solidify a positive sense of body image:

1. Find a quiet spot where you won't be disturbed for 5 or 10 minutes.

2. Sit comfortably, and pay attention to the feel of your breath flowing in and out of your body.

3. Close your eyes and bring your attention more closely to your breath.

4. Imagine your breath is made of energetic golden light. Keep your eyes closed, and visualize this light moving in and out of you as you breathe.

5. Now, imagine that the golden light begins to suffuse your entire body with every inhalation, radiating out of you, illuminating you.

6. Next, picture a beautiful golden goddess standing in front of you. This goddess is Gauri, the Golden Lady, a Hindu goddess of shining light. She holds out her hands to you. Imagine taking her hands.

7. Gauri's golden light begins to flow into you, mingling with the golden light filling you with each breath. Imagine the golden light swirling and dancing within your body, filling it up.

8. Imagine your whole body filling with golden light so that all your features, your shape, your height, your size, your imperfections, and even your perfections disappear and you become a glowing figure of light. You are joined with the Golden Lady in this moment, two perfect golden goddesses whose power is mutual, flowing back and forth.

9. Keep breathing and visualizing yourself in this golden glow. Imagine that this light has set your spirit free to infuse every cell of your body so that your physical self has become completely integrated with your spiritual self.

10. Imagine Gauri releasing your hands and fading back into the ether. And yet, the golden light remains within you, your spirit a golden flicker within your glowing body, dancing, laughing, leaping. You, distilled to your joyful essence. There you are! A golden goddess yourself.

11. Stay here for a few minutes, glowing, letting your spirit dance. When you are ready, slowly open your eyes.

12. Throughout the day, recall this meditation and the feeling of golden light radiating and dancing within. Remember Gauri, and thank her for the infusion of golden goddess light.

13. Do it all again tomorrow.

Your Sensual Chakras

In the East, traditional healers viewed the body differently from those who practiced healing in the West. The Eastern philosophy of healing is based on the idea that meridians of energy flow through the body, up and down, animating the body and giving it life. We breathe energy in and out, and it travels through us via a series of swirling energy centers called *chakras*.

Chakras are a little like train stations for energy, and each chakra has a different function and color. You can't see them, and you won't find them in anatomy textbooks, but they are an integral part of ancient healing practices as well as esoteric sexual enlightenment practices.

At the base of the spine, according to the Tantra and a practice of yoga called *kundalini yoga*, is a coiled "serpent," or source of potential energy. This kundalini energy can be awakened through certain practices, including those involving sex. Sometimes likened to a woman or a snake within the body, kundalini energy, when awakened, travels up through the chakras to the crown of the head. This very physical experience is intense and enlightening, and it is the goal of kundalini yoga, which seeks to awaken the kundalini under controlled conditions for the purpose of spiritual, ecstatic understanding.

> **Source of All**
>
> Chakras are spinning energy centers in the body, and each chakra is the source of certain specific energies. Although the body contains many chakras, the seven primary chakras are located along the center of the body, from the base of the spine to the crown of the head. **Kundalini yoga** is a type of yoga that awakens and channels kundalini, an intense psycho-sexual energy that travels through the center of the body to the crown of the head and can bring enlightenment.

Each of the seven chakras governs certain energies in the body and influences who we are, how we feel, and what we do. When activated by kundalini energy, each chakra becomes a source of sensual and sexual enlightenment and power.

When chakras get blocked, energy can become stuck, overflowing the chakra or unable to fill it sufficiently. These imbalances show up in our lives in different ways. For instance, if the throat chakra becomes swollen with energy, we may talk too much and say the wrong things. If the throat chakra becomes depleted of energy, we may have trouble communicating and telling people how we feel, and people may misunderstand what we say. For the proper flow of kundalini, the chakras must be open and healthy.

Kundalini yoga is a complex and esoteric discipline and a yogi, or practitioner of yoga, could spend years studying and working with it. We encourage study of Tantra and kundalini yoga for those who want to learn more, but for the beginner, the chakras are a good place to begin.

Each chakra has its associated sensual function, from the instinctual first chakra to the enlightened seventh chakra. Here's a closer look at each chakra: its location, its color, what it does, and how keeping it balanced will improve your sensual and sexual self.

First Chakra: Your Primal Urges

The first chakra lies at the base of the tailbone, and its color is red. This chakra, which houses the kundalini energy, is the seat of primal urges and desires in their most basic and instinctual form. Strong and intense feelings of lust and the need for sex come out of this place, as well as strong feelings of hunger, fatigue, fear, lust, anger, and the urge to fight or run.

When the first chakra is deficient, we lose touch with our natural instincts and feel separated from the earth. When this chakra is engorged, we feel ruled and controlled by our instincts. An engorged first chakra can result in violent behavior and lack of self-control.

A healthy first chakra results in a balanced perspective, a recognition of the body's needs, and the ability to fulfill those needs in a healthy way, without denial or over-indulgence. Vigorous sexual intercourse with deep penetration as well as gentle anal stimulation both engage and activate the first chakra and can serve to awaken kundalini energy.

Second Chakra: Your Inner Fire

The second chakra lies just behind and below the navel, and its color is orange. This chakra contains *agni*, our internal fire, and is the seat of consumption and digestion.

It is the "taking-in" chakra. Everything we eat comes to this place to be burned up by *agni*, and everything that happens to us comes into this part of our bodies. The second chakra takes these experiences and incorporates them into who we are. You know that feeling of getting butterflies in the pit of your stomach? That's the second chakra saying: "Something more stimulating than usual is coming into the body for processing!"

Source of All

Agni is the Sanskrit word for the inner digestive fire behind the navel, which is thought to be responsible for heating the body, digesting food, and processing experience.

When the second chakra is deficient, we may gain weight, feel bloated, removed from our lives, unable to process the things that happen to us, as if we have erected a wall and can't take anything in. When the second chakra is engorged, we may lose weight; feel an insatiable desire for experience; and become impulsive, practicing immoderate thrill-seeking experiences like binge drinking, drugs, spending or gambling binges, or taking risks at dangerous activities like driving too fast or practicing extreme sports without sufficient experience.

A healthy second chakra results in balanced intake, a healthy digestion, and an openness to new experiences. Spicy foods can also stimulate a sluggish agni, and cold foods can calm an overactive agni. You can balance the sexual aspect of the first chakra by taking your partner into yourself and receiving your partner's sexual fluids while embracing your partner with your arms and legs, fully accepting and taking in another's sexual and sensual energy.

Third Chakra: Meeting the World, Chest Forward

The third chakra is located in the solar plexus, just beneath the rib cage. Its color is yellow, and this is the chakra that leads you through life. Just as the second chakra governs what you take in, the third chakra governs what you give out. When you send your personality out into a room, when you encounter new experiences and take control, when you behave proactively and make your presence known, you are acting from the third chakra.

When the third chakra is deficient, you may feel an inability to project, a lack of personality, or fear of new experiences and places. In extreme cases, you may experience paralyzing fear of leaving your home, a condition called agoraphobia. When the third chakra is engorged, you may become too intrusive and controlling, always getting into other people's business and trying to control what they do.

Oracle Wisdom

The body is a sacred garment.

—Martha Graham (1894–1991), U.S. dancer and choreographer

A healthy third chakra results in a balanced placement of yourself into the world and an ability to do what is necessary in your life without trying to control other people or situations. You can balance the sexual aspect of the third chakra by synchronizing deep, slow breaths with your partner. Dancing erotically or dressing to make yourself feel attractive will also help energize the third chakra, as you consciously "put yourself out there."

Fourth Chakra: All You Need Is Love

The fourth chakra is the heart chakra, and its color is green. It is located in the chest, in the heart's vicinity, and governs the emotions—those feelings that surface in our chest in reaction to experiences, people, beauty, ugliness, and even our own thoughts.

When the fourth chakra is deficient, you may feel unable to love or feel emotions, which may lead to feeling flat and unaffected by the world. When the fourth chakra is too full, you may feel ruled by your emotions and react strongly to things that wouldn't normally affect you so dramatically—for example, weeping at a TV commercial or laughing hysterically at something that isn't really all that funny.

When balanced, the fourth chakra allows you to love freely and feel emotions without fear or excess. To activate the fourth chakra's sexual component, you can engage in sexual touch with someone for whom you feel great love, while gazing into each other's eyes.

Fifth Chakra: Communication Station

The fifth chakra is the throat chakra, and its color is sky blue. This chakra governs communication. This is where you express your ideas to the world: the interface between what you think and what you say.

When the throat chakra is deficient, you may feel unable to express yourself clearly. People may misunderstand you, or you may feel frustrated at not being able to articulate your ideas. When the throat chakra is engorged, you may find yourself dominating conversations and talking too much, too fast, and with no real purpose.

A healthy throat chakra will encourage clear communication. For a really good fifth chakra workout, spend the evening kissing. Hit the chakra right on the mark by kissing that little hollow at the base of your partner's neck where the neck meets the collarbone.

Sixth Chakra: Intuition Central

The sixth chakra is sometimes called the third-eye chakra because it is located in the center of the forehead, where some ancient cultures believed a third eye existed—the eye of intuition and psychic ability. This chakra's color is a deep indigo blue, and it governs your intuitive ability and that sense of knowing something is about to happen before it happens. This is the chakra that helps you to perceive reality beyond the physical world.

When the sixth chakra is blocked, you may feel a lack of intuition, which can feel somewhat like driving blind, because we are so accustomed to the subtle nuances of intuition that we don't realize how much we rely on it. A sixth chakra that is too full can make you so intuitive and sensitive that you feel bombarded by the world and have a hard time enduring too much stimulation. You might feel like everybody is yelling!

A healthy sixth chakra helps your intuition guide you and your responses to people and situations, but still allows you to stay grounded in the physical world. Making love with your eyes closed can help energize the sixth chakra. Use your intuition, rather than your sense of sight, to feel and to let your partner's needs and your own sexual flow rise up and reveal themselves.

Oracle Wisdom

Buddha Dakini is a Tibetan air goddess with supernatural powers, which she lends to those who follow her. She grants wholeness through ultimate understanding. She is dark blue, and she understands truth. We like to think of her as the goddess of the sixth chakra.

Seventh Chakra: Universal Unity

The final and ultimate chakra, the seventh chakra, is sometimes called the thousand-petaled lotus chakra. This is the center for enlightenment, the final destination of kundalini energy, and the ultimate source of all knowing. The seventh chakra is located at the crown of the head, and its color is purple.

A deficient seventh chakra can cause you to focus all your energy on materialism and the mundane without giving any thought to spirituality. This can make you feel imbalanced and leave you with a sense of desolation, wondering what purpose there is to life and "what does it all mean?" A seventh chakra can hardly be too full of energy, for when kundalini bursts forth into the crown of the head, you see and realize the ultimate unity of all sentient beings and perceive the great flow and pulse of energy throughout the universe. You recognize how we are all one in a great out-pouring flow of ecstasy. This, of course, is the final goal of Tantric sex.

Tone your seventh chakra by making spiritual enlightenment the goal of your sexual pursuits and by learning, refining, and practicing sacred sexuality. (We *love* that kind of homework!)

Can You Be *Too* Sexy?

The more we get in touch with our senses, our chakras, and our inner energy flow, the easier it is to learn to love our bodies. In fact, living open to the sensual world can help us see how alien it is to live apart from the world, stuck in our own heads, criticizing ourselves. The goddesses of mythology understood this, and so can we.

Imagine Artemis, running through the forest, her bare feet pounding the dry leaves, the wind against her face, the rustle of trees and cool shadows of leaves and birds in the branches above her head, the scamper and dash of animals all around her. Imagine Aphrodite, wading through the ocean, holding her silk gown above her knees, sand between her toes, the sea spray on her pale skin, the smell of salt in the air and sun on her golden hair. Goddesses understand the pleasures of the earth and of the senses, and you can understand these pleasures, too.

It doesn't matter what your size or shape is. You are unique. Nobody else is like you. You may resemble other people or share similar traits, but you are the only you. You have a miraculous mind, an individual spirit. And yet you are also a part of the world and everyone and everything in it. You are one link in a great chain of being that links you with all human beings, all animals, all the growing things, the rocks and stones and mountains and oceans from the beginning of time.

Initiatress of Love

Think about who you are, and all the things that have made you: your child-hood, your life experiences, what you take, what you give, whom you love, how you move, what you know, what you feel, what you believe. Touch your own hair. Feel the muscles in your shoulders. Cup your breasts in your palms. Run your fingers over the dips and curves of your own face, around your own waist and belly and buttocks, down your thighs, up your calves. See how beautiful you are and how good it feels to appreciate your own body?

You are pure energy, taking this physical form for a while. And here you are, a goddess, like other goddesses before you, and unlike any of them: all your own, a thinking, feeling, sensual human in a thinking, feeling body capable of sight, hearing, touch, smell, and taste. See how amazing you are, how sexy? Who cares what anyone else thinks. Some people may see your beauty and sensuality, and others may not. What matters is that *you* see it, because the moment you discover and even just catch a glimpse of your own sensual beauty, you are a sex goddess. We see it in you. We see it in every woman we meet. We know it's there. Find it, even just for a second, every day, and you'll have begun your journey into the passions and pleasures of sensual love.

The Least You Need to Know

- Your body is more than the sum of its body parts. It is one part of who you are, but it is not the whole you.

- The body contains a flow of energy and whirling pools of centralized energy called chakras. Get in touch with your chakras by using sexual contact to energize and balance them.

- The first chakra governs instinct; the second governs what we consume; the third governs what we present to the world; the fourth governs our emotions; the fifth governs our ability to communicate; the sixth governs our intuition; and the seventh governs our ultimate enlightenment.

- You are sexy right here, right now, and become even more so as you awaken to the sensuality of the world around you and of your own body.

Chapter 6

Your Vagina: The Yoni Blossom

In This Chapter

- ◆ Your vagina (just say it!)
- ◆ Yoni symbolism in myth, art, and literature
- ◆ Yoni types
- ◆ The joys of self-pleasuring
- ◆ Yoni yoga

You can look in the mirror and see your face, your hair, your body, your breasts, your hips … but it isn't very easy to see your vagina. Yet this part of the female body has long been revered as the source of all life, even as creator of the universe. Intimately knowing and understanding your yoni, as it is called in the Kama Sutra, is essential for any sex goddess who wants to get the most from her body, mind, and spirit. The yoni is both sacred and worldly, symbolic and practical, and every woman's yoni is a little bit different in size, shape, color, and sensitivity.

Whether you have fully examined your yoni while squatting over a mirror, proudly pierced your yoni for decoration and stimulation, keep in touch with your yoni daily, shave it or don't shave it, give it a name, or try not to look down there unless you absolutely have to, your yoni is an important part of your body, as well as your identity. Not only can your yoni be a source of pleasure and the gateway to life for you personally, but it also links you to sex goddess traditions throughout history.

To know your yoni is to love your yoni!

Good Morning, How's Your Vagina Today?

The Western world is an interesting place when it comes to talking about sex organs. We think about them a lot, and we certainly enjoy them, but a lot of us don't feel comfortable talking about them much, or even thinking about them in too much detail. Although symbolic representations of the male and female sex organs were an important part of spirituality, not to mention daily life, in ancient India, twenty-first-century America prefers to keep its sex-organ business—both symbolic and actual—politely veiled and behind closed doors.

But perhaps this trend is changing. Although some of us may still hesitate at saying or hearing words like "vagina," "clitoris," "penis," and "testicles," it doesn't take long to get into a new mind-set in which these words seem natural. Anyone who has seen Eve Enzler's groundbreaking play *The Vagina Monologues* has probably had the experience; upon hearing the repetition of the word "vagina" for a while in the first scene of the play, of slowly coming around to the point where, by the end of the play, the word seems completely natural. Some women say that after seeing this play, they finally don't balk at the word anymore.

Issues like the legalization of homosexual marriage and adoption have also brought sex talk into the open, as what someone does behind closed doors has suddenly become relevant to what they get to do in the world, such as filing their taxes under a different category or becoming a parent. The climate is changing.

> **Initiatress of Love**
>
> If you've never taken a close look at your yoni before, use a hand mirror or put a full-length mirror on the floor and take a look. Use your hands to explore, so you can see all the visible parts. You'll see that it's pretty interesting down there, this mysterious and sensuous opening seductively nestled inside layers of soft, fleshy folds.

Eve Enzler's play *The Vagina Monologues* took an interesting approach to female sexuality. It chronicled the "vagina stories" of a cross section of women from our culture. Each of us has our own vagina stories, of course. But have you thought about yours?

How do you feel about your vagina? Are you comfortable looking at it, touching it, talking about it? Are you self-conscious when somebody else looks at it, touches it, talks about it? Do you feel like its very existence has a political component, as evidenced by the large body of feminist literature on the vagina, or in such pop-culture phenomena such as *The Vagina Monologues*, or in such political issues as pro-choice and laws governing which genders may or may not touch you there? Or maybe you see it as wholly personal?

The more comfortable you get with your own personal source of all, the more comfortable you will become with your sexual self and the more easily you will understand how your yoni can give you pleasure. Respecting your yoni is an important way to respect and honor yourself, and to be with partners who respect and honor you, too.

Beyond Taboos

Keeping your body and your yoni healthy is another way to respect your personal source of energy, life, and pleasure. All grown women should have a gynecological exam and pap smear once a year to monitor for health problems. Use protection during sex if you aren't sure your partner is free from disease, and also to protect against pregnancy if you don't want to become pregnant. Honor your body like a true sex goddess, and don't neglect your sexual health!

Your Personal Source of Creative Energy

Obviously, the vagina is linked with the reproductive process, taking in the male essence so the body can generate new life, then releasing that life, after it has incubated for a while, into the world to be nurtured.

Symbolically, the vagina can also be a source of creative energy. Just as it plays a role in creating life, it can also play a role in creating pleasure and positive creative energy in your life. Many sex goddesses have used this creative energy in their art. Georgia O'Keeffe, an American painter, is most famous for her large, close-up paintings of flowers that open like beautiful symbols of the yoni blossom. Farther back in history, yoni symbols pervade many different cultures and traditions. The horseshoe was a stylized yoni symbol used in many ancient cultures to signify entrances and exits. The mandorla, an almond-shape symbol, also called the *vesica piscis*, or vessel of the fish, is and was considered a yoni symbol in many different cultures around the world, as almonds have long been seen as symbols of the female genitalia as well as maternity charms.

It's no coincidence that the vesica piscis was associated with the salty sea smell the ancients associated with the female genitalia. One Hindu goddess was called "a virgin named Fishy Smell, whose real name is Truth," and in some ancient traditions, fish were eaten on Friday to celebrate the ancient love goddess aspect of the mother goddess, who often appeared as a mermaid.

In Tantra, the yoni is the source of all creativity, and female orgasm is the source of universal energy. In Hindu mythology, on a yoni-shape island called Jambu grew a life-giving rose-apple tree and a diamond seat or *vajrasana*, a symbol of a cosmic clitoris and source of creative goddess energy. (Check out the section later in this chapter on the vajrasana yoga pose!)

In the British Isles, ancient Irish Sheila-Na-Gig female figures with prominent gaping yonis used to decorate churches in Ireland and all over Europe prior to the sixteenth century. Similar figures adorned Indian temples. These figures were typically emaciated, and this emaciation coupled with the gaping yoni symbolized both birth and death, or the entire life cycle.

To help you both visualize and physically experience the yoni's creative power, try the following meditation, to tap into the power of Yoni, the Indian goddess of the female essence.

For this exercise, you will be making the yoni sign with your hands. To do this, hold your fingers together with thumbs apart and place your hands together touching index fingertips and the tips of your thumbs. The space in the middle of your two hands represents the shape of the yoni and was an esoteric and secret symbol.

1. Lie on your back on a firm surface, knees bent, feet on the floor. You can do this exercise clothed, partially clothed, or naked, depending on what makes you comfortable.

2. Make the yoni sign with your hands. Place your hands, holding the yoni sign, on your lower abdomen or rest them on your pubic bone, as low as possible while still remaining comfortable. (If you are only comfortable making the sign and resting it on your stomach, that's fine, too. You need to be comfortable to do this exercise.)

3. Close your eyes and begin taking long, slow, deep breaths. With each breath, imagine inhaling a bright, sparkling stream of energy that flows down into your first chakra, at the base of your tailbone. Do this for a few minutes.

4. While continuing to inhale this bright stream of energy, with each inhale, slowly rock your pelvis forward and squeeze the muscles of your pelvic floor. With each exhale, slowly rock your pelvis back and release the muscles.

Oracle Wisdom

I said to myself—I'll paint what I see—what the flower is to me but I'll paint it big and they will be surprised into taking time to look at it—I will make even busy New Yorkers take time to see what I see of flowers.

—Georgia O'Keeffe (1887–1986), U.S. painter

5. Visualize your yoni as a beautiful white lotus flower. Feel it blossoming out of your first chakra, petal by petal, unfolding to absorb the sparkling energy flowing down your spine and into the flower's center.

6. Continue breathing in and out, visualizing the energy stream flowing into the lotus flower in your first chakra. If you want to, you can touch your body in whatever way feels good. You don't have to keep your hands in the yoni sign. You may experience waves of pleasure or even have an orgasm, or you might not. Just keep feeling the energy flowing down into you, and let it vitalize and energize your first chakra.

7. When you begin to get tired, gradually stop the hip movement you are making, and imagine the sparkling energy settling quietly down into your first chakra … ready to be awakened at your bidding!

> **Oracle Wisdom**
>
> Masturbation is a primary form of sexual expression. It's not just for kids or for those in-between lovers or for old people who end up alone. Masturbation is the ongoing love affair that each of us has with ourselves throughout our lifetime.
>
> —Betty Dodson, author and sexologist

Experiencing pleasure generates positive energy, so think of getting more intimately acquainted with your yoni as one way to improve the energy balance in the universe! We cannot embrace ourselves as sex goddesses until we embrace unreservedly the yoni blossom, the source of all.

Yoni Types

Every woman's yoni is different, but different traditions have actually classified certain yoni types. The Kama Sutra describes three types of yonis and three types of lingams (as the Kama Sutra refers to the penis), and which go together best. These are as follows:

♦ The deer or doe yoni is common in petite women. Narrow and shallow, the deer yoni matches best with the hare lingam, which is about three inches when erect.

♦ The mare yoni typically belongs to sturdily built women with a strong, charismatic personality. It is full and lush, and fits best with the bull lingam, which is about four inches when erect.

♦ The elephant yoni belongs to tall, large-boned women with calm, tranquil personalities. The deepest of the yonis, this yoni best matches the stallion lingam, which is about six inches when erect.

Flying Solo

Just because you don't have a sexual partner around or available doesn't mean you can't experience sexual pleasure. Part of becoming comfortable and intimately acquainted with your own body is learning how to pleasure yourself. The more you understand about what you like, the better you'll be able to enjoy sexual contact with a partner!

Sometimes self-pleasuring can be intense and emotional. The more in touch with our bodies we become, the more we release things we have buried inside us. Many of us are taught, as children, to stuff our feelings and emotions deep inside us because they are "inappropriate." Instead of focusing on our emotions, we are taught to focus outside ourselves.

It takes practice to let ourselves focus within and totally on ourselves, and doing so can bring up all kinds of emotions. You might begin crying and not know why. Chances are, you're connecting with and releasing something suppressed deep within you. This is a healthy process of release, and you will feel better afterward. As masturbation guru Betty Dodson once said, "Seeking sexual satisfaction is a basic desire, and masturbation is our first natural sexual activity. It's the way we discover our eroticism, the way we learn to respond sexually, the way we learn to love ourselves and to build self-esteem."

Oracle Wisdom

To love deeply in one direction makes us more loving in all others.

—Annie-Sophie Swetchine (1782–1857), Russian French writer

Then again, self-pleasuring is sometimes light, joyful, and fun. It feels good, it helps you know yourself better, and it trains your body to tap quickly into pleasure mode so that sexual interaction with another is easier and more intimate.

Ancient Masturbation Wisdom

According to ancient sacred texts, self-pleasuring for men is a lot different than self-pleasuring for women. Many Eastern sacred practices discouraged men from releasing their vital essence (in other words, ejaculating) for "no good reason," and claimed that excessive masturbation would deplete the man's vitality. Making love with a woman, on the other hand, would allow a man to be revitalized by the female essence, to balance out the loss of semen. Men were encouraged to self-pleasure up to the point of ejaculation, but no farther, due to the "health risk."

For women, however, the story is completely different. The same traditions believed that, while a man had only so much vital essence to spare, a woman's vital essence is replenished with every lunar/menstrual cycle. No matter how much a woman self-pleasures, it only increases her skill and understanding of her body, and even pleases the deities believed to live within a woman.

This concept stands in interesting contrast to the more "medical" Western view that a man's semen is being constantly manufactured, whereas a woman's supply of eggs is set from birth, limited, and the older she gets, the older they get. This view casts a shadow on female fertility in our culture and is the source of the notoriously ticking "biological clock" we are so often told we should worry about.

Oracle Wisdom

Anahita is the Persian goddess of sacred sexuality who rules over water and fertility. Her name means "Without Blemish" or "Immaculate One." In ancient Persia, she was associated with religious orgies and sacred sexual practices.

The difference is all about procreation. The Western view says that men can continue to impregnate young women well into old age, although a woman's optimal window for pregnancy begins to close as she grows older (though new methods of in-vitro fertilization are changing this biological reality, allowing women to become pregnant well into their 40s). The Eastern view of sexual rejuvenation has nothing to do with pregnancy; it is only about using pleasure to achieve spiritual transcendence. In this view, it is the woman who is continually generating new vital essence, while the man's sperm eventually gets "old."

But back to self-pleasuring. In ancient times, women had many options of self-pleasuring. They could touch themselves, fantasize, or touch each other. Today's sex toys are nothing new. In Japan and China, it was traditional in households where a man had many wives to have a replica of the husband's lingam made of tortoise shell or wood, which his wives could use in his absence for self-gratification. The principle wife would "play" the man to satisfy the other wives, while all along, the husband's lingam was, at least symbolically, involved in the act.

Beyond Taboos

Some ancient texts encourage women to use natural things like vegetables and fruits as artificial lingams for self-gratification, because these contain more vital life essence. However, medical professionals no longer recommend this because of the possibility of introducing bacteria and other harmful substances into the body. A sterile sex toy, such as a vibrator or a dildo designed for this purpose, is preferable, and these are easier to come by than ever before.

So even in ancient times, sex goddess self-pleasuring was a fine art women were encouraged to practice. (We're happy to do it with or without the ancients' approval, but it's nice to know they are with us!) "Masturbation" or mutual pleasuring between two women was encouraged, as it strengthened the vital essence of both women. Such practices were common, natural, and acceptable in the East, because groups of women often lived together with a single husband who was frequently gone and couldn't keep everybody happy all the time.

Initiatress of Love

Some women are more visual and like to see erotic pictures or imagine erotic scenes of their lover's body. Some women like to imagine complex fantasies played out step by step over the course of hours. Some are more verbal and enjoy reading erotic material. (*Herotica* is one series written for women. Find more information on erotica, as well as sex toy sources, in Appendix B.)

According to Tantric thought, female sexual bonding circulated yin essence between two women, making them softer, more compassionate, and even more physically feminine, with clearer skin and brighter eyes. Sexual bonding between men was considered of a lower order and unhealthy, while sexual bonding between women was a bit like maintaining sexual physical fitness. (It hardly seems fair, but we're just reporting.)

Learning Your Body

Now that everybody is on board with self-pleasuring, you may be wondering, "But how do I do it?" (Or maybe you are already doing it, in which case, we will wait for you.) Every woman's body is different, and every woman's mind is different, so the way you self-pleasure might well be completely different than the way other women do it.

Self-pleasuring for some women doesn't require any kind of artificial lingam. Many women can reach a blissful orgasm through fantasy and touching themselves. Because every body responds differently to touch and fantasy, the best way to learn how to pleasure yourself is to practice, practice, practice! The more you do it and the more things you try, the more your body will open up to your own touch and your own fantasies and reveal to you what really works.

In ancient India, self-pleasuring, as well as lovemaking itself, was an act that tapped into the transcendent, erotic power of the ever-erect Shiva joined with the transcendent female force, Shakti. During self-pleasuring, especially when using any kind of artificial lingam, sex goddesses can mentally focus on this erect Shiva power as a fantasy. Or you can imagine yourself with any sort of idealized lover—your favorite movie star, your favorite rock star, your favorite Renaissance poet ... whatever thrills you! You can fantasize about someone you know, you can imagine yourself with a man or a woman, or with both! Nobody has to know what your fantasies are about. They are only for you.

As for the touching part, the options are endless. Some women are so sensitive to breast stimulation that this alone can bring on orgasm. Other women enjoy blunt or more direct clitoral stimulation, and for some women, penetration with some sort of artificial lingam works best. You can experiment with water in the bathtub, standing up, sitting, or lying down. You can romance yourself with candles, incense, and silk sheets. Try it in front of a mirror, or in complete darkness. The point is to try it, and practice it often.

Beyond Taboos

Fantasies are great aids for self-pleasuring, but according to Eastern mysticism, negative fantasies that involve perversion (harming, victimizing, or subjugating others, thus encouraging base thought rather than transcendence) can harm the psyche and cause psychological problems. Transcendent fantasies of pleasure, connection, and ecstasy will only enhance vital energy.

Many women won't always reach orgasm during self-pleasuring, and that's fine, too. Sometimes, your body just isn't going to respond that way. You may get excited to spend an evening with yourself in this way, but after a while, you may get tired and decide to go to sleep before you "finish." Nothing wrong with that—any kind of pleasuring attention you lavish on yourself is good and will increase your vital energy and your sexual fitness.

Breathing can also be an important part of self-pleasuring. As in the exercise earlier in this chapter, rhythmic breathing in synch with rocking, pulsing hip motions can intensify the experience and concentrate energy in the first chakra.

Try not to be frustrated if it takes you a while to get the hang of what you like. The more you do it, the easier it gets. Just keep trying different things, but don't put pressure on yourself. The point is pleasure. If self-pleasuring brings up negative or guilty feelings, you need to work through these feelings before you can become comfortable with it. We strongly encourage you to see a counselor to get to the root of these issues, because a sex goddess needs to feel completely at home with her body.

Third-Time's-the-Charm Exercise

Some books about Tantra also encourage a self-pleasuring technique that involves bringing yourself close to orgasm, then stopping and internalizing the energy, and then doing this several times before actually moving into the orgasm. Some people dispute that this is actually an ancient Tantra technique, but regardless of that, it definitely intensifies the orgasm once it happens, so you might enjoy trying it.

This exercise is for after you are already good at getting yourself to orgasm whenever you want. It also works just great with a partner, so don't feel you have to limit this exciting and pleasure-intensifying technique to self-pleasuring. Here's how you do it:

1. Set aside at least an hour of privacy. Lock the door. Set the mood with candles, dim lighting, silk sheets, or whatever you like.

2. Begin pleasuring yourself as you normally would, but incorporate deep rhythmic breathing with the rhythm of your hips, exhaling as you rock your hips inward, inhaling as you rock your hips outward. Touch yourself in whatever way you like.

3. When you feel you are getting very close to orgasm, stop moving completely, take your hands off your body, and immediately visualize your sexual energy rising upward from your first chakra into your abdomen, your heart, and all the way to the crown of your head.

4. Feel the energy intensifying as it gathers and swirls in the crown of your head. You may feel dizzy or different, suddenly connected to the universe.

5. Once the energy is out of your first chakra and in your seventh chakra, begin again. Bring yourself to the brink of orgasm, then stop, hands off, and visualize the sexual energy rising up through your body and into your seventh chakra, revitalizing all the chakras along the way: your abdomen, your solar plexus, your heart, your throat, your forehead, and finally, the crown of your head.

6. Once the energy is out of your first chakra, begin again. Do the whole thing over. But this time, finally, allow yourself to reach orgasm, which will likely be very intense and vibrate through your entire body and through all your chakras. Let yourself shake, writhe, even scream if you feel the urge! Pure ecstasy.

7. Afterward, take as long as you need to rest and relax, feeling the transformation throughout all your chakras and the balanced tranquility suffusing your body.

Yoga for Yoni Health

One of our favorite ways to stay healthy and strong is yoga. Designed to balance the body in preparation for meditation, yoga revitalizes internal organs as it stretches and strengthens muscles. It also helps calm and center consciousness, and it can tone and prepare the body to awaken the senses and make sexual pleasure more intense.

One yoga pose specifically beneficial to the yoni, called *vajrasana*, helps energize and strengthen the first chakra and the yoni. You may remember the word *vajrasana* from earlier in this chapter. It means "diamond seat" and can be used to refer to the cosmic clitoris. This pose, also called kneeling pose, is the classic pose for sitting in Zen meditation. *Vajra* can also mean thunderbolt.

This yoga position increases circulation to the feet, helps repair fallen arches, aligns the spine, releases tension in the diaphragm, and stimulates the first chakra, which energizes the yoni. Here's how to do it:

1. On a yoga mat, carpeted floor, or on grass or sand, get down on your knees, with your knees and heels together.

2. Take a deep breath, exhale, and gradually sink down to sit on your heels.

3. Keep your spine straight and place your hands on your knees.

4. Breathe slowly and deeply, imagining you are breathing from your first chakra, in and out.

5. Stay here as long as is comfortable or as long as you desire, breathing slowly and deeply from your first chakra.

Beyond Taboos

Some people find *vajrasana* too painful for their knees. If your knees hurt in this position, put a cushion, pillow, or folded blanket under you, over your heels, to increase the knee angle. If this is still uncomfortable, sit with your legs crossed, then slide one or both hands, palms up, underneath you so you are sitting on your hand(s). In this position, your hands bring energy to the first chakra instead of your heels.

For more information on yoga and lots of different yoga poses that increase vitality, check out *The Complete Idiot's Guide to Yoga, Third Edition*, by Joan Budilovsky and Eve Adamson.

Before we move on to the next chapter that celebrates your beautiful breasts, we would like to emphasize one more thing about your beautiful yoni blossom: Pay attention. As you go through your day, remain mindful of all the parts of your body, including your yoni. Whenever you sit, be aware and remember that you are sitting on a blossoming source of creative energy. When you touch yourself or come into communion with someone else, honor this sacred part of you as an entrance to your inner sanctum.

Although we always advocate treating all parts of yourself with respect, we would also like you to remember how your sexual energy is anchored at the base of your spine and spreads like a sun through this essential and elemental part of you. You are connected with all of life, and the chain connects right there, in that miraculous and multi-foliate center: your yoni.

The Least You Need to Know

♦ We are trained from an early age to feel uncomfortable about calling sexual organs by name, but the more comfortable you become with words like "vagina" and "clitoris," the more you will feel yourself opening to the pleasures they have to offer.

♦ Many ancient cultures from all over the world celebrate the yoni, or symbolic representation of the vagina, as the entrance and exit to life and the source for universal feminine energy.

♦ Eastern cultures traditionally consider female self-pleasuring as a healthy way to increase the female essence.

♦ The Kama Sutra describes three different yoni types: the shallow and delicate deer, the lush and full mare, and the deep and cool elephant. Each type best matches a corresponding type of lingam, or penis.

♦ The more you practice self-pleasuring, the more you will learn what you like and how your body responds to self-touch.

♦ Yoga and meditation can also help you know yourself and your body better.

Chapter 7

Your Beautiful Breasts

In This Chapter

- ◆ What do your breasts mean to you, and to your partner?
- ◆ Does size really matter?
- ◆ Breast appreciation at any age
- ◆ Breast health check
- ◆ Sex goddesses nurture life

To be a woman is to have breasts. Large, small, or somewhere in between, breasts come in different shapes, sizes, degrees of firmness, and height. Some turn up; some turn down. They change as we age, growing miraculously from a flat chest just as puberty gets ready to kick in, getting fuller during pregnancy and early motherhood, and continuing to change as we reach each new life stage.

A sex goddess and her partner can both enjoy her breasts in many ways, but breasts can also be a source of worry for women. Are they too small? Too big? Are they full enough, or too flat? Have they "dropped" or gotten stretch marks? Are they still desirable, or are they *ugly?*

Should we make them bigger or smaller through surgery? Will that make us more desirable? Are they healthy, and how often should we check for lumps? What happens when, due to surgery, our breasts become scarred or even removed?

Author Meema Spadola wrote a book called *Breasts: Our Most Public Private Parts.* Indeed, breasts are largely public. There they are, for all to see, if not bared than at least evident, most of the time, beneath our clothing. We can admire the breasts of other women as they walk down the street in a way we could never admire their other sexual organs. We can feel them when we hug someone who has them, and the memory of cuddling against the breasts of our mothers fills many of us with warmth and comfort.

So what does that mean for the bearer of the breasts, the sex goddess whose breasts are so much a part of her sexuality as well as her inner nurturer? Let's take a closer look at your beautiful breasts.

The Meaning of the Breast

The breasts of a sex goddess can mean many things, both to her and to her partner. In traditional cultures, breasts were the sustainers of life, nourishing children and symbolizing the nurture of all life. Ancient fertility statues, such as the *Venus of Willendorf* (believed to be one of the first human statues ever found and dating back as much as 24,000 years B.C.E.!), depicted women with huge breasts and pregnant bellies, symbolizing fertility.

Venus of Willendorf.

But this doesn't mean a sex goddess should reserve her breasts for breast-feeding! Who cares if that's what they are "for"? Breasts can also be a great source of beauty and pleasure for the sex goddess as well as for her partner, even if she never has children. For many women, the breasts, and especially the nipples, are an intense erogenous zone. For many men, breasts are an endless source of fascination, and just looking at them fuels desire.

Just as every sex goddess has a unique relationship with her body, so does she have a unique relationship with her breasts. What do your breasts mean to you? How do you feel about them? Do you remember when they first began to grow? Do you remember how they have changed throughout your life?

Oracle Wisdom

The Siberian goddess Khotun, also called Milk Lake Mother, was the nourisher of all people and animals. Khotun lived in a lake of breast milk beneath the Tree of Life. Her giant breasts overflowed the lake and formed the Milky Way. Khotun presided over childbirth and gave strength to the mother.

You and Your Breasts: A History

One of the keys to a healthy and pleasurable relationship with your breasts is to know them well. Think about your relationship with your breasts throughout your life. What has contributed to your positive attitude toward them, and what has contributed to any breast negativity?

Most women can think of at least a few stories related to their breasts, even if you've never considered telling them to anyone. Think about your stories. If you like, you can write about them in a journal. Here are some cues to help you remember the story of *your* breasts and your evolving relationship with them:

- When did you first notice your breasts were growing? Do you remember? Was it in the bathtub or shower, or while getting dressed? Or did somebody, such as your mother or a sibling, point it out to you?

- Did the emergence of your breasts change the way people (parents, friends, siblings) reacted to you?

- Do you remember buying your first bra?

- When you were a child, were you curious about your own breasts? Did you touch them?

- When did you first become aware of your breasts as sexually sensitive?

- How have your romantic/sexual partners throughout life responded to your breasts? Do you remember specific comments, reactions, or interactions?

- If you have been pregnant, how did your breasts change? How did they change after pregnancy?

- Did you breast-feed? Was it difficult at first? Do you remember trying to get it right? Or how did your breasts react when you decided not to breast-feed? Remember how it felt. Was it an easy or difficult decision, and what influenced it?

- If you did breast-feed, remember how it felt: the tingling sensation of the milk "letting down," the flow of milk, the nipple stimulation of nursing. Think about how nice that was!

- How do you feel about your breasts today? How do you feel about their size, shape, and firmness right now?

- How are they different than they were 10 years ago?

- Do you dress to enhance or downplay your breasts? How do you feel about the way your breasts appear to the world?

- What role do your breasts play in your own sexual pleasure?

Oracle Wisdom

Just as the luminous swathe of stars known as the Milky Way suggested the stream of nourishment emanating from her breasts, so it was as if the earth were encircled by waters that, falling as rain, impregnated her so she could give birth ... the vessel holding water or milk was, therefore, a paramount image of the goddess herself ... many vessels have raised breasts and are decorated with meanders and zigzags signifying the movements and patterns of water, and symbolizing the Sky Mother whose rain falls as milk from her breasts.

—Anne Baring and Jules Cashford, from *The Myth of the Goddess: Evolution of an Image*

Breast Man?

Breasts also mean a lot to our male partners, and for some men, the breasts are an intense focus of pleasure. Others enjoy the breasts of their female partners, but not particularly more than any other part of their bodies. Ask your partner how he feels about breasts in general, and your breasts in particular. Does he remember the first time he saw them? What does he enjoy about them? This is also a good time to tell your partner what *you* enjoy about what he does to them, or what you would like him to do, if you haven't already discussed the subject.

In esoteric Taoism, a woman's breasts (as well as the saliva from her mouth and the moisture generated in the yoni from sexual excitement) are a source of a special regenerative "medicine" that can benefit one who drinks from the breast. Called White Snow, Essence of Coral, or Immortality Peach Juice, this liquid comes from the Double Lotus Peak (the breasts), but it is not breast milk; it's a separate, subtle fluid that flows during periods of sexual excitement. According to the book *Sexual Secrets: The Alchemy of Ecstasy* (see Appendix B), drinking this vital breast nectar helps to fortify and rejuvenate a man, strengthening his internal organs and replacing the vital essence lost during ejaculation. Even if nothing appears to be coming out of the breast during sexual stimulation, the "nectar" can exist purely on an energetic level and, according to esoteric Taoist and Tantric lore, will revitalize the man who sucks on it. Sex goddesses who love attention to their breasts might point out to their partners the physical and spiritual benefits of this particular practice!

According to *Sexual Secrets: The Alchemy of Ecstasy*, some yogis (practitioners of yoga) have reported producing milklike breast secretions, and there have also been reports of men suddenly producing milk for breast-feeding a baby when the baby's mother dies. The book goes on to state that this phenomenon illustrates "that within man, woman lies latent."

From monthly self breast-exams for health to touching your breasts for self-pleasuring, the sex goddess takes a hands-on approach to her breasts. But does it matter how big they are?

> **Initiatress of Love**
>
> Many men enjoy stimulation of their own breasts and nipples because this area of the body contains many nerve endings. Sex goddesses can ask their partners if they enjoy this kind of contact. Or just try it and see how he reacts. A little caress, a little lick …

Breast Size and the Female Ego

We've all heard the stereotype that "size matters" when it comes to the male genitalia, even though size is more a matter of individual fit than objective measurement. But what about breast size for women? Much in the same way that culture has conditioned men to be unduly concerned about the size of their penises, society has conditioned women to be unduly concerned about the size of their breasts.

Measuring Your Breast Prejudices

How do you feel about the size of your own breasts? Do you think they are too small, too large, or just about right? Does your breast size bother you? Maybe you have considered breast augmentation or breast reduction surgery. If so, what are your reasons? Health? The feeling that you would look better with breasts of a different size or shape? Or because someone else thinks you need it?

Maybe you saw a picture of yourself and didn't like the look of your breasts, or someone commented on your breasts being too small or too large. Maybe you feel like people look at your breasts and not you. During lovemaking, some women even feel that when their partners pay attention to their breasts, they forget that there is a woman attached! Other women are happy to take all the breast attention their partners can spare but may still be concerned about how their partners are judging their breast appearance.

Initiatress of Love

Many women have had the experience of talking to a man who keeps talking back to them, but insists on talking to their breasts rather than their faces. Whether or not a man is really staring at our breasts or is just too shy to make eye contact, we may never know, but the experience can be disconcerting. If this experience bothers you, the next time it happens, consider a direct but nonconfrontational comment: "I'd love for you to look into my eyes while we're talking. It makes it easier for me to understand what you mean and helps us communicate better. I really appreciate connecting with you this way. Thanks."

You may even find yourself scrutinizing the breast size of other women. (Who isn't fascinated by all the body types, shapes, and sizes of other women in the locker room at your gym, dance, or fitness class?) Notice your attitude or thought process when you see a woman with very large or very small breasts, or particularly nice breasts, or breasts that you think might contain implants. Do you have automatic preconceptions?

We can tell you until we're blue in the face that the size of your breasts doesn't matter, but until you embrace your sex goddess nature that allows you to love your body in its unique incarnation, you probably won't believe us. Part of becoming comfortable in your own skin (and with your own breasts) is getting used to your body: how it looks, how it feels, how it responds. A sex goddess knows that every body is beautiful and sexy, no matter how large, how small, how tall or short, and no matter the breast size and shape. Let's practice seeing your body in all its beauty, right here, right now!

Love-Your-Breasts Exercise

This exercise can help you to get more comfortable with your body in general as well as your breasts in particular. The more you do this exercise, the better it works. Find some privacy in a room with a mirror and, if necessary, a lock on the door. The bathroom or the bedroom is a natural choice.

1. Turn the lights down or off, and light two candles. Put them on a table or the sink, in front of the mirror.

2. Take off all your clothes to the waist: shirt, bra, camisole, or whatever you are wearing. If you feel comfortable, take off *all* your clothes.

3. Stand in front of the mirror, bathed in candlelight, and look at yourself. Just look, as if you were surveying a beautiful work of art: a painting or a sculpture of a goddess. Just for now, don't look at "you," with all the baggage that contains. Just look at the goddess, there in the mirror.

4. Look more closely now, specifically searching for beauty. Look at the curves of your body, the flow of your hair, the subtle flicker of candlelight in your eyes. See the shape of your cheekbones, the undulation of your shoulders and arms, the dip of waist or rise of hip. And look at your breasts.

5. Notice how beautiful your breasts are. Maybe they are round and full, or small and taut. Look at their curve and the way your body holds them, tight against the chest or blooming out to either side or draped below the breastbone like ornamental pendants. Notice the dark island of the areole and the rise of the nipple.

6. Cup your breasts in your hand. Feel how they fill your hand, overflowing or not quite full. Press on them, move them, hold them, and cradle them. Feel their weight and the texture of the skin. Move your fingers over the areole and the nipple, feeling the changing textures, the tiny ridges and bumps. Are your nipples soft or erect?

7. Close your eyes, but keep holding your breasts, and concentrate all your attention on the way they feel, rather than how they look. Let yourself enjoy the sensation of your own hands on your body and notice everything you can about the way your breasts feel—the shape, the weight, the movement. Let your hands explore.

8. Feel your goddess energy stirring in your first chakra and rising slowly through your lower abdomen, stomach, and solar plexus into your chest, where it expands and blossoms within each breath. Let yourself feel this goddess energy

Initiatress of Love

Breast size and nipple size have nothing to do with degree of breast sensation, nipple sensitivity, or ability to breast-feed.

pulsing inside you and expanding your awareness to recognize the beautiful goddess within you and the beautiful goddess you are on the outside, too.

9. Open your eyes and look at yourself again in the mirror. There you are, sex goddess, in all your glory, your breasts the sustainers of life and bestowers of pleasure. Doesn't that feel good?

Three Cheers for Breast Appreciation

As we grow, our breasts change. Some of these changes are due to hormones during adolescence, pregnancy, childbirth, and menopause. Some are due to lifestyle, such as rapid weight loss or weight gain. Some are genetic, such as shape, size, loss of skin elasticity, and the particular way the breasts tend to drop as we mature.

But breasts are beautiful, useful sources of pleasure throughout our lives. Let's look at how breasts tend to grow and change.

The Adolescent Breast

Little girls don't have breasts. They don't need them! They would just get in the way of all that tree-climbing and jump-roping. But once the first hormonal changes of puberty start to stir in a young girl's body, one of the first things that happens is that flat chest starts to change.

For some girls, breasts grow quickly and look mature at a very young age. For other girls it takes longer, and for many women, breasts never get all that big. Adolescence is no picnic, and the intense hormonal changes girls experience during this time can contribute to strong emotions and feelings of sensitivity and vulnerability, making breast issues seem all the more potent.

Teenagers who develop large breasts at a young age may feel as if people look at them in a more sexual way before they are ready for it. On the other hand, teenagers who don't develop noticeable breasts may feel as if people *don't* look at them in a sexual way. No matter what other people think (and what other people think is often nothing like what we *think* they think, so why worry about it?), the teenage sex goddess (including the virgin sex goddesses) can also learn to love her breasts and her body.

Remember that who you are radiates from
every corner of your body, mind, and spirit.
Body size? Breast size? Who cares? They
are your breasts, and it's okay to love them.
Anyone who doesn't appreciate your beauty
clearly doesn't get you and isn't worth worrying
about, but chances are that the more confident
you become and the more you begin to appreciate your own beauty, the more others will see
it, too.

Oracle Wisdom

The beauty of the world
… has two edges, one of laughter, one of anguish, cutting the
heart asunder.

—Virginia Woolf (1882–1941),
English novelist

The Grown-Up Breast

After adolescence, you and your breasts reach maturity, and your breasts will finally
settle in at their natural size and shape. As you become more sexually experienced
and comfortable with what you like, you will probably also become more comfortable
with your breasts, both in how they look and how they feel.

During this stage of your life, when you are also experiencing menstruation, you may
notice that your breasts change throughout your monthly cycle, becoming more delicate, sensitive, and even painful before your period starts. Some women who tend to
have lumpy breasts may notice a monthly increase in lumpiness and tenderness during
this time. About a week after your period ends, your breasts will return to their normal, nontender state. This is the best time to do a monthly breast self-examination
(see the section later in this chapter on how to do this).

During ovulation, about two weeks after your period ends (or two weeks before it
starts), your breasts may be more sensitive to touch and you may enjoy breast stimulation more. But every woman is different, and every woman's breasts experience hormonal changes differently. The better you know your breasts and your body, the more
comfortable you will become with these cyclical breast changes.

You will probably also know at this point
what kind of breast stimulation gives you
pleasure and may also have become adept at
doing it yourself as well as sharing what you
enjoy with your partner. This stage is the full
flowering of the sex goddess, where body and
mind become better integrated. Let yourself
enjoy yourself and your beautiful, unique
breasts!

Oracle Wisdom

Ava was young and
slender and proud. And she had
It. It, hell; she had Those.

—Dorothy Parker (1893–1967),
U.S. writer

The Pregnancy Breast

When you become pregnant, your breasts go through many changes. In the first trimester, they may become very sensitive and even painful to touch. Throughout pregnancy, the body sends more blood to nourish the breasts as they prepare for breast-feeding (whether you plan to breast-feed or not). You will probably notice that the veins in your chest and on your breasts will become larger and darker blue.

By the end of pregnancy, your breast size will probably have increased noticeably. You and your partner may both enjoy the novelty of your "new breasts," but enjoy it while you can, because the change is usually only temporary (although some women do retain a larger breast size after pregnancy). Or you might find your increased breast size uncomfortable and look forward to getting your "regular breasts" back again!

If you gained a lot of weight or gained weight quickly during pregnancy, you may also notice some stretch marks on your breasts. Keep them moisturized with lotion throughout pregnancy, but avoid putting lotion on your nipples if you are preparing to breast-feed because lotion can clog the milk ducts. Sometimes, stretch marks are genetic and you may get them no matter what you do, but this is all part of what makes you and your breasts unique.

> **Oracle Wisdom**
>
> Mother Water is an Indian creator goddess, also called the Mystic Mother. According to one version of her story, she created the waters of the Great Sea, or primordial waters from which all life evolved, from her breasts. Another Indian goddess, Khir Bhawani, is the milk goddess who presides over springs from which water appears and flows out of the earth.

Toward the end of your pregnancy, you may even begin to produce colostrum, the clear and potent immune-boosting and nourishing fluid designed for newborns during the first day or two of life, before your milk "comes in." After you give birth, the hormonal changes in your body will signal your breasts to begin producing milk. If you can't or decide not to breast-feed, you may experience a painful fullness in your breasts for a few weeks, but your body will soon signal your breasts to "turn off the milk supply" and this discomfort will quickly diminish.

Pregnancy is a lovely time for the breasts; it really is. Your body is bringing forth life, and your breasts are preparing to sustain that life. Some sex goddesses never feel more beautiful than during this "fertility goddess" time, and many men find their partners more irresistible than ever before.

The Breast-Feeding Breast

If you do decide to breast-feed, congratulations! Breast-feeding is good for your baby, good for your breast health, and once you get the hang of it, it feels really good, too!

The breast-feeding breast gets full, then deflates slightly when your baby (or a breast pump) empties it. Every few hours, you will be able to feel your milk "letting down," which feels like a tingling, somewhat sharp but not unpleasant sensation in your breasts as the milk glands push milk into the channels leading to the nipple. Sometimes, the sound of a crying baby will be enough to signal this response.

Breast-feeding can be hard to get the hang of at first. A newborn doesn't really understand how to breast-feed correctly. If the baby latches on to the end of the nipple, your breasts can quickly get chapped and sore. Most hospitals and birthing centers now employ lactation consultants to help train you and your baby in efficient, pleasant, and pain-free nursing. Don't give up on breast-feeding right away—seek out a mentor or professional to help you and your baby adjust and thrive on breast milk.

Once you and your baby learn how to breast-feed, you will probably find the process very enjoyable. Breast-feeding feels good. Nature made it that way, so we would do it! For women with particularly sensitive breasts, breast-feeding can be an erotic experience, and there is nothing wrong with this. We can care for and nurture our babies while experiencing pleasure during breast-feeding, all at the same time.

Another perk of breast-feeding is that during sexual excitement, breasts tend to produce more milk. This can make sex novel and fun, as breast stimulation can result in milk squirting before and during orgasm. Rather than feeling self-conscious about this natural function, many breast-feeding sex goddesses and their partners fully enjoy the way the breasts release their milk in the throes of passion in an almost ejaculatory response.

Revel in your body's new physical response to arousal. Have fun with it! Someday, after your breast-feeding days are long over, you and your partner can recall with fondness the way you were both able to bring your body to such heights that it overflowed.

The Aging Breast

As you age, your breasts will experience changes. After a certain age, breasts "drop," sitting lower on the chest than they did at a younger age. (In some cultures, breasts aren't considered attractive until they drop.) As skin and breast tissue naturally and gradually lose elasticity, your breasts will change in appearance. But they won't be any less beautiful, just better seasoned!

The glands used for milk production begin to shrink because they are no longer needed. This process is triggered by signals produced by changing estrogen levels associated with menopause. As glandular tissue shrinks, it is replaced by fatty tissue, making breast changes easier to spot and also somewhat reducing breast size.

As the sex goddess approaches menopause, she may feel temporarily put out by the changes in her body, in the same way the changing hormones of adolescence cast the female body into transition. Yet the transition out of the childbearing cycle is also empowering. Because your breasts no longer function as milk-producing glands, they become solely and completely a source of pleasure.

> **Initiatress of Love**
>
> Even if you never experienced pregnancy, childbirth, or breast-feeding, the post-reproductive breast is still newly and wholly your own, no longer subject to the reproductive processes of biology that happen to a woman's body whether she chooses to use them or not.

Learning to love your breasts at every stage of life is an important part of appreciating the sensually evolving nature of your own body. Keep looking in the mirror. Keep touching and holding your breasts, and stay in tune with the instrument of your body. The longer you play it, the more skilled you will become.

Breast Health

One of the most important things you can do to keep your breasts healthy is to perform a monthly breast self-examination, at about the same time every month—about a week after your period ends. But let's face it: Lots of us know we *should* do it. But how often do we really *do* it? According to Imaginus.com, an independent source of information on breast health, 96 percent of women are aware of the importance of doing a monthly breast self-exam, but only 29 percent of women actually perform self-exams on a regular basis. Why don't we do it?

Some women say they are afraid of finding a lump. Some say they aren't sure they know how to do it, some forget, and some just don't feel comfortable touching their own breasts! We say sex goddesses are tuned in to their bodies and know how to keep an eye—and a hand—on the way it changes. In that spirit, let's imagine a breast self-exam fit for a sex goddess. Try it today! Even if it's not the week after your period ended, you can still practice.

The Sex Goddess Breast Exploration

Do this breast exploration about a week after the end of your period, and do it every month. Because breast tissue changes somewhat throughout your cycle, doing the breast exploration at the same point in your cycle every month will give you an idea of what is normal.

One of the key elements of the breast exploration is to establish a baseline of what is normal for you. Everybody's breasts have a sort of bumpy texture and a ridge of tissue along the outside edge. We all have our individual shapes and textures, too. The more you do this breast exploration, the better able you will be to notice when something changes and the better you will know your breasts. And why *shouldn't* you know about your body—your most intimate, vital possession! Look for breast changes, and alert your doctor if you find any.

Some women prefer to do the breast exploration in the shower because the water makes the skin slippery and easier to navigate. Or you can use lotion or massage oil.

1. As in the previous exercise in this chapter, find a private spot with a mirror and a door that locks, if necessary. Take off your shirt and stand in front of the mirror. Put your hands on your hips, and take a good, long look at your breasts. Notice their symmetry and shape, and look for any swelling, lumps, discoloration, or irregularity.

2. Do your breasts look the way they usually do? If you notice any unusual dimpling, bulges in the skin, puckers, changes in the shape or position of your nipples, or any kind of rash or redness, give your doctor a call.

Initiatress of Love

If you mark significant dates of your menstrual cycle on a calendar (we do it, albeit in "code" so dinner guests hanging around the kitchen won't feel uncomfortable noticing that today is the first day of their hostess's menstrual cycle), you can add this one, too. Mark the date. Sex Goddess Breast Exploration: SGBE for short! No one will know what it means unless you tell them.

3. Raise your arms over your head. Look again for changes.

4. Run your hands gently over your breasts, then take each nipple between your finger and thumb and squeeze gently. Look for any discharge. (If any fluid comes out and you are not breast-feeding, give your doctor a call to ask about it.)

5. Lie down comfortably on a bed or the floor. Relax and deepen your breathing. With your right hand, feel your left breast by holding your fingers together and pressing gently into your breast to feel for lumps, hard spots, and other changes. Move in circles around your breast, covering the whole breast.

6. Feel from your collarbone to your navel and from inside your armpit to your cleavage.

7. Repeat on the other side, feeling your right breast and right side with your left hand. Be sure to feel the whole breast, both at the surface and deeper down, by pressing more firmly.

8. Sit up and repeat the last three steps again while sitting. Your breasts may feel different depending on your position.

Beyond Taboos

Be sure to give your doctor a call if you did notice any changes in your breasts. In most cases, lumps are benign, but you should have them checked out by a professional. As always, if you are worried about a possible lump or change in your breast and your doctor does not give serious attention to the issue, by all means get a second opinion!

9. Put your hands together in a prayer position and place them between your breasts. Breathe deeply and visualize a protecting pink light emanating from your chest.

10. Keep breathing deeply, and imagine the pink light spreading throughout your body, down your arms and legs, and into the crown of your head. This is your goddess energy, working to keep your breasts and your whole body healthy and sound.

11. Sit for a while, enjoying the feel of the pulsing pink light beaming out from your chest. When you are ready, open your eyes, put your clothes back on, and go on with your day!

The Breast: Universal Nurturer

As you begin to pay more attention to your breasts, remember that they represent something sacred, ancient, and everlasting: the power of the feminine to nurture, nourish, and sustain life. This applies whether you have children or not, whether you breast-feed or not, and even if you never plan to parent, or if you don't have a sexual partner right now, or if you have had breast tissue surgically removed for health reasons or a breast augmentation surgery for cosmetic reasons.

Your breasts, no matter what they look like or what they have experienced, are an integral part of your body, your sexuality, your self-concept, and your connection to all of life. We hope that as a sex goddess, you will continue to honor, appreciate, and love your breasts, as you let your partner honor, appreciate, and love them, too.

Your breasts are a nurturing—and sexy—part of you. The more you know and love your breasts, the more you will enjoy and appreciate them. Respect the power of the breast and its connection with mythologies in every culture, and you'll soon see how you, too, are linked to sex goddesses since the beginning of time, as if each of you were a star in the great spinning wheel of the Milky Way.

The Least You Need to Know

♦ Breasts can represent many things—passion, pleasure, fertility, and nurturing—both to those who have them and to those who appreciate them in a partner.

♦ All breasts are beautiful in their unique way, and neither size nor shape and firmness impact breast sensitivity or nursing ability.

♦ From adolescence through pregnancy and breast-feeding to post-menopause, breasts experience many physical changes.

♦ A monthly breast self-examination can increase the chances of discovering a health problem, such as a breast lump, early enough to be effectively treated.

♦ The breast is an integral part of the whole sex goddess being. Knowing and loving your breasts will make you more comfortable with your sex goddess self.

Part 3

Prepare Yourself for Love

Sensuality is the foundation of sexuality, and what could be more pleasurably sensual than awakening every sense—sight, sound, smell, touch, and taste—in your prelude to passion? As with any venture that is worthwhile, preparation makes all the difference when it comes to shaping experiences you'll always remember (and relive in your dreams).

These chapters blend ancient and modern methods to prepare your body, mind, and spirit for expressing the whole of your spiritual sexuality—giving and receiving sexual pleasure. You are the sex goddess of your lover's—and of your own—fantasies, and it's your time to shine. Let the foreplay begin!

Chapter 8

Do You *Feel* Sexy Today?

In This Chapter

- How sexy do you feel?
- Do you have to feel sexy to initiate sex?
- Expressing your sexual nature every day
- Sex-drive fitness

Right here, right now, ask yourself this question: Are you "in the mood"? Feeling sexy can sometimes be elusive. You might wake up feeling sexy one morning, and by late afternoon you are feeling as unsexy as you've ever felt. Does it have to do with what you eat? How much you sleep? What you are wearing? Or something more?

In this chapter, we'll explore what makes you feel sexy and how you can feel that way more often. Sex goddesses learn how to tap into their sexuality all the time, whether or not they plan to have sexual communion with a partner. Your sexuality is a part of you, so why stifle it? Consider all the ways you can let it emanate from you, to give you that glow of desire. Once you've mastered that, feeling sexy won't seem quite as elusive anymore.

Calibrating Your Desire Meter

Feeling sexy isn't the same thing as wanting to have sex ASAP, but they are linked in some ways. When you have easy access to your inner sex goddess, you can be more receptive to the signs that your partner is in the mood, and you can feel more comfortable spontaneously initiating sexual contact yourself. But feeling sexy is much more than an inroad to initiating sex. It's an attitude fueled by self-esteem, sensuality, and desire.

How is your desire? Our sexual moods certainly change, sometimes from one moment to the next, and it's easy to slip into, or out of, sex goddess mode. Sometimes you feel geared up for a truly sacred sexual encounter, sometimes you just feel like some pleasurable fun, and sometimes you just don't feel like it at all! That's all natural and normal.

Initiatress of Love

Regular yoga classes can really prime your body and mind for sensual awareness. Tantric yoga centers more directly on how to use sexual energy for spiritual enlightenment, and other forms of yoga will also help make your body more toned, flexible, strong, and balanced and will give you an inner confidence and serenity that will help you to feel like your sexiest self. Look for yoga classes taught in private studios or at health clubs in your area.

But where is your baseline? How do you feel most of the time these days? Take this quiz to see how well you are expressing your inner sex goddess in your daily life.

1. When you wake up in the morning, what do you usually do first?

    A. Think, "Oh no. It's morning again."

    B. Think about what you have to do today and when you might get some time with your partner, or all to yourself.

    C. Notice the way the sun hits the curtain and the silhouette of the leaves, or the way the air feels.

    D. Nothing like beginning the day by reaching for your partner ... or yourself!

2. Your partner sends you an erotic e-mail or instant message while you are at work. What do you do?

    A. That would never happen to you (or, if it did, it would probably make you uncomfortable).

B. Smile but ignore it. You have work to do!

C. Fire back a quick but suggestive e-mail or instant message hinting at what is to come when you next see each other.

D. Who needs coffee? It's time for a cyber-sex break!

3. What would you most like to receive as a gift from your romantic partner?

A. You could really use a new: vacuum cleaner/blender/microwave/dishwasher.

B. Jewelry is always romantic.

C. A romantic getaway where the two of you can spend some quality time alone.

D. Sexy lingerie or maybe even something to act out a fantasy.

4. How often do you pleasure yourself?

A. Never! You aren't quite sure how to do it. (If this is you, see Chapter 6!)

B. Once in a while, if you haven't had sex for a long time.

C. Several times a week. It helps you sleep better.

D. Every day, and sometimes you let your partner watch … or help!

5. What is your favorite way to make your bedroom more romantic?

A. Turn off your computer.

B. Clean up the room and light some scented candles.

C. Romantic music and sheer fabric draped around the bedposts or windows.

D. All the above! Plus massage oil, red silk sheets, and nothing in the room except things that contribute to intimacy.

 **Initiatress of Love**

A clean room is a sexy room. Keep your bedroom clean, clutter-free, and empty of anything having to do with work. To promote stress-free, uninhibited sexual communion, your bedroom should be a haven of intimacy, not a storage closet or part-time office.

6. How do you feel when you look at yourself naked in the mirror?

A. You don't know, and you're hoping you don't really *have* to look at yourself naked in the mirror to find out.

B. You have your figure flaws, but you like certain parts of your body.

    C. You love the way you look in the mirror because it's *you*.

    D. Looking at yourself naked in the mirror makes you want to make love with your partner right here, right now—or at least pretend your partner is there! How could anyone resist you?

7. What's the most unusual place you have ever made love?

    A. Um … the bedroom?

    B. The kitchen.

    C. The car.

    D. Outside, in a secluded area like a beach or while camping, or even in public!

8. If your partner asked you to act out a sexual fantasy, what would you do?

    A. There is something wrong with wanting that! You wonder if your partner is dissatisfied with you.

    B. Depends on the fantasy. If it interests you, too, then why not try it?

    C. As long as nobody gets hurt, then sure!

    D. You're already a pro at the art of role playing the sexual fantasy.

9. During sex, what is a silk scarf best used for?

    A. You aren't sure about using any props during sex.

    B. For draping around your body.

    C. For blindfolding one of you while the other uses touch in surprising ways.

    D. For tying your partner's hands to the bedpost so you can do all the attention-giving. Next time, it's your turn.

10. Which of the following would you choose *instead of* an extended erotic encounter with your partner?

    A. Twenty bucks.

    B. A paid vacation day.

    C. A trip to Europe.

    D. Nothing beats the pleasure and intensity of an extended erotic encounter.

Give yourself one point for every A, two points for every B, three points for every C, and four points for every D. Add up your score. Here's what it means:

1–10: Somewhere inside you, a sex goddess lies, sprawled on a chaise lounge, snoring delicately, waiting to be awakened. For whatever reasons—stress, a busy schedule, too many other responsibilities, lack of a sexual partner, or simply a drifting away from your sexual nature (you don't often "feel like it"), you have lost touch with the sensual and sexual side of yourself, let alone the sexual-spiritual side. But if you want to awaken your inner sex goddess, you can! Start by practicing the techniques in the last section of this chapter on sex-drive fitness.

11–20: You appreciate the sensations and power of a sexual connection, but it just doesn't occur to you very often to put forth the effort. Who has the time? Whether you have sex once a day or twice a year, chances are you aren't enjoying it as much as you could if you were to open up to the sensual pleasures and desire-awakening resources out there in the world. Let your inner sex goddess claim a larger portion of your efforts, both mental and physical, and watch sex turn from an occasional pleasant diversion to something much, much better.

21–30: You are sensually awakened and sexually excited. You appreciate the sensual world and the sensations of sexual contact, and you enjoy the experience of life with the true fervor of a sex goddess. You also have a good sense of balance, and although you revel in your sexual side, you also pay attention to the other sides of yourself. You are a well-rounded and grounded sex goddess who can live well in the world but still be transported into physical and spiritual ecstasy.

> **Oracle Wisdom**
>
> The Scandinavian goddess Menglad lived in a land of giants in a castle surrounded by fire and guarded by a fierce giant. The god Svipdag heard of this beautiful fire goddess and searched nine worlds to find her, then fought his way through flame and foe to enter the castle. Seeing the great effort he had put forth to reach her, Menglad happily accepted him as her husband.

31–40: You are smokin'! You not only access your inner sex goddess on a regular basis, but you are also sensually heightened and full of self-confidence. You go girl! Just remember to eat and sleep and keep the other areas of your life in balance and perspective. Remember, being a sex goddess means much more than having a lot of sex. It means embracing your sensuality, your relationships, and your spiritual development, too. When sex brings all these aspects of life together, you will know you truly are a sex goddess among sex goddesses! (Aphrodite would be proud of you.)

How did you do? If you already feel sexy all the time, great! But most of us don't. Feeling sexy is an attitude and a lifestyle. Immersing yourself in the ways of the sex goddess can up your desire as well as your courage and willingness to initiate sex when you want it. The two keys to feeling sexy are to have more sex and to live in mindful sensuality. Here's how.

Initiating Sex

It's one thing to feel like having sex, but it's another to get up the nerve to ask for it. How do you initiate sex when you get the urge? Or do you just hope your partner will notice? Part of cultivating your inner sense of sexiness is learning to feel comfortable initiating sexual contact, but for those of us who aren't in the habit, it's easy to feel awkward or embarrassed about it.

Why do we feel so embarrassed to ask our partners for sex? It's not embarrassing to announce you are hungry or tired. But for several centuries in the Western world, women have been taught that it isn't proper to want or ask for or even enjoy sex, and although these attitudes seem old-fashioned to us now, their effects linger.

Initiating sex can be as easy as a seductive glance or a frank request. It can also be a fun and creative pursuit! To get you started in your quest to be more comfortable, and even innovative, in initiating sex, call on Aphrodite for inspiration. Notorious for her lusty desire, Aphrodite went out and got what she needed whenever she needed it ... and who would dare to deny her?

Oracle Wisdom

Myths about Aphrodite, the Greek goddess of love, beauty, and sensuality, abound with sensual detail. Notorious for her many affairs with both gods and mortals, Aphrodite is often depicted draped in filmy, gossamer scarves that may or may not cover her body. Sacred to Aphrodite were red flowers like the poppy and the rose, and the red apple, as well as the dove, swan, and swallow. Born of sea foam, Aphrodite remained always awakened to the sensuality of the world and the gods and mortals in her presence.

To kick your own inner Aphrodite into overdrive, try these initiation strategies. Let these be a springboard for your own imagination. We're sure you can think up hundreds more!

- With your partner, decide on a sign—something you could do in a public place, such as a hand signal or secret word—that means "I want you now." Then use it ... often!

- Grope your partner from behind, when he least expects it. You don't have to *say* anything.

- In a crowded public place, whisper in your partner's ear, very softly, almost imperceptibly, "I want you inside me right now." Or mouth the words from across the room.

- In the middle of a busy day or when both of you are feeling stressed, stop what you are doing, look your partner directly in the eyes, and say "I love you."

- Trace the edge of your partner's ear lightly with your tongue. Flick your tongue over your partner's earlobe, then pull on it gently with your lips.

- Slow dance.

- Meet your partner for dinner and, in the middle of the first course, inform your partner in a whisper that you aren't wearing any underwear. (Then see if you make it through dessert without leaving the restaurant in a hurry!)

- Fill your bedroom with a dozen or more lighted candles, then take your partner by the hand and lead him into the room. Close the door. (Just be sure to put the candles in places where they won't get knocked over or catch on to curtains or other flammables.)

- Forehead to forehead, look your partner in the eyes and tell him what you love most about him, or what you most appreciate that he has done for you today.

- While you are cooking dinner, picking up the living room, making the bed, or sitting on the couch reading a book with your partner in the room, spontaneously and without saying a word about it, take off all your clothes (or just your blouse) and then go back to what you were doing. (You may not get to finish!)

- Sometimes nothing is more provocative and passionate than a soulful, full-body embrace.

- Write a letter describing things you would like to do to your partner—where you would like to put your hands, what you would like to put into his mouth, where you would like him to touch you, exactly what you would like to be inserted into where and for how long. Give it to your partner, or slip it into his pocket for him to find later. Or just keep it for yourself and read it over a few times when you are in the mood, to give you inspiration.

- Brush your lips against his ear. Run your finger over his lips.

♦ Video record the two of you making love (if you both agree). The next time you feel like initiating sex, just pop in the videotape or DVD, take him by the hand, and sit down together to watch it.

Beyond Taboos

Some people are hesitant to record themselves having sex for fear the video could fall into the wrong hands. If you're concerned about this, don't feel pressured to do it. Some video cameras can project an image onto a television without actually recording it, which can be a fun way to watch yourself, or you and a partner, without actually recording anything.

♦ While you are cooking dinner, ask him to come into the kitchen for a minute to help you with something. When he does, kneel down, unzip him, and get him, well … ready for dinner!

♦ Cuddle. Look sweetly into your partner's eyes. Synchronize with his movements. Breathe together.

♦ Sometimes, there is nothing like the direct approach. Push your partner up against a wall, look him directly in the eyes, and say, "Take me now" or "I demand that you satisfy me" (or something even more colorful, depending on your inclination!).

Express Yourself

Part of feeling prepared to initiate sex is to feel open to sensation all the time. You can express your inner sex goddess by increasing your *mindfulness* and tuning in to the sensual world around you. Let yourself feel sexy, open, and sensual every single day, whether you plan to have sex or not. This kind of daily attention to your sensual well-being is what keeps your inner sex goddess forward in your mind and actively involved in your life.

Source of All

Mindfulness is a meditation technique for being completely tuned in and focused on what is happening in the present moment, rather than letting your mind dwell on the past or linger ahead in the future. To be mindful means to focus on the right-now. What does your body feel like right now? What does the air feel like? What do you see, hear, smell, feel, taste, *right now?* It also means being aware of your thoughts as they come and go in the present moment, even those about the past or the future, but noticing them and then letting them go rather than engaging them.

When you eat a meal, try to taste every bite, notice the aroma, the texture, the bloom of flavor on your tongue. When you walk outside, feel the sun or breeze, notice the color of the sky, the way the leaves rustle, the shapes and colors of buildings, the flash of cars going by or the flutter of birds. When you meet or talk to people, notice everything about them—the texture of their skin, the sheen of their hair, the flecks of color in their eyes, the way they move their hands, the shape of their bodies, their hips, their chest, their legs. Of course, you don't want to make people uncomfortable by staring. Just let these impressions sink in subtly as you talk and interact with people. Let the sights, sounds, and perceptions you get from other people drench you in mindfulness.

The way you react to other people is also a part of the sensual experience of knowing someone. Look other people in the eye when they talk to you and really listen. Answer them with kindness and frankness. Touch people's arms or hands when you talk to them (when it's appropriate). Really look at them, really see the sensual delights of other bodies, even those you have no intention of becoming involved with. Be generous with your hugs and kisses, arm-holding, and hand-squeezing. People are miraculous constructions of vibrating energy and flesh! A sex goddess notices that.

Remember, too, that although a sex goddess is open and free with her sensuality and may be inclined to touch other people often in friendship and appreciation, such actions aren't always welcomed. Not everyone is open to the touch of others, or to physical contact from those they don't know very well yet. A sex goddess is sensitive to these cues, too.

Also remember that touching others isn't always appropriate, such as in the workplace. Be aware of when you can express your appreciation for others physically, and when you are better off keeping communication at an (also) appropriate verbal level. (Even if you don't mean it as sexual harassment, you don't want to be accused of it on the job!)

Being mindful of the sensual world is a big part of enjoying sexual contact as well as enjoying life itself. Here are some more ideas for living the sensual life of a sex goddess every day:

♦ Dress in a way that feels good. Wear soft pleasing fabrics, clothes that make you feel beautiful, and colors you love.

♦ Pamper yourself; primp; touch your body, your face, your hair. Enjoy your rituals of hygiene, whether rubbing yourself all over with lotion or brushing your teeth. Notice how each of these rituals feels.

◆ Keep your skin soft with scented lotions, your hair smooth with a great conditioner, and your hands and feet well moisturized with nice oils.

◆ If you can afford it, get a pedicure every few months. Soft, touchable, well-manicured feet are a pleasure, and it's nice to know you can kick off your shoes and have nothing to hide!

◆ Wear perfume or essential oil in a scent that you love. Know that you smell great.

◆ Touch your own body whenever you get the chance, and not just for self-pleasuring, but for the sensual experience. Feel your own softness, curves, textures.

Initiatress of Love

According to a study reported in a recent issue of *Redbook* magazine (April 2004), masturbating to the point of orgasm more than once a week boosts your antibody levels by 30 percent, which could make you more resistant to viral infections.

◆ Keep fresh flowers in your home where you can see them every day.

◆ Open the windows as often as possible.

◆ Sleep on supersoft sheets—satin, flannel, soft cotton, or whatever makes you want to sink into your bed and stay there for hours. Change your sheets at least once a week. Clean sheets feel even better!

◆ Cover your furniture with fuzzy, silky, velvety, or furry throws and pillows.

◆ Paint at least one room in your house red. How about the bedroom? Red fuels the passions. Or if this seems like a bit too much, try a red comforter on the bed, which gives a similar effect but with less commitment than a paint job!

◆ Let your home and your body be altars of sensuality, and open yourself to all the beauty the world has to offer you.

Sex-Drive Phys-Ed

It's a simple fact that the more you have sex (or pleasure yourself), the more you feel in the mood for sex. If you rarely have sex, your body gets out of the habit of expecting and anticipating it. You may have more difficulty having orgasms, and the idea of initiating sex may never even occur to you!

You can increase your sex drive and inner feeling of sensuality just by practicing some regular habits, in addition to the sensuality techniques described in the last section. Just as you exercise to keep your muscles in shape, so you can practice sexual physical fitness to keep your desire muscles primed for action.

Beyond Taboos _____

Unresolved tensions and arguments will affect how sexy we feel. Check in with yourself every day: How do I feel mentally? Emotionally? Physically? Spiritually? Are there any unresolved tensions or stresses that would prevent me from giving my full attention to being in the moment with my partner? Find them and breathe through them. Talk to your partner about them, or even a therapist if you can't clear them on your own.

Your personal physical fitness plan could include any or all the following. Adapt yours to suit your own personality, body, and desires:

◆ Have more sex. The more you have it, the more you feel like it. Tell your partner it is part of your new fitness plan. We're pretty sure he'll be glad to be your workout buddy.

◆ Pleasure yourself more! We suggest at least three times a week if you aren't having regular sex, and at least once a week if you are. It's good practice, not to mention fun and healthy!

◆ Get a massage at least once a month. Having someone touch you all over and get deep inside your muscles when you know it won't lead to sex is a supremely relaxing and deliciously erotic experience—with no performance pressure! A monthly massage can get expensive, but many massage schools offer inexpensive massages so their students can practice. See if a massage school in your area offers this service.

◆ Take a bath at least several times a week. Recline in rich mountains of creamy bubbles or water transformed into soft slickness by bath oil. When relaxing in the bath, never miss an opportunity to touch yourself, and don't forget that a faucet shooting out a stream of warm water can do more for you than fill up the tub.

◆ Take a yoga class. Yoga primes your body, mind, and spirit for mindfulness.

◆ Pretend you really are Aphrodite, or any other goddess you've read about, and act accordingly in your daily life. Be brash, outrageous, and seductive.

◆ Use fantasy in your daily life whenever possible. Whether you have a big meeting, a tedious chore, a difficult conversation, or nothing much at all to do, pretending you are someone else or somewhere else can help you get through it with creativity, humor, confidence, and style.

◆ Sex is never just a physical act, although we can pretend it is. Stay closely bonded with your partner, holding hands, talking, and sharing. Intimacy begins in the heart, not in the genitals.

The Least You Need to Know

◆ Determine your baseline level of desire, then increase it by focusing on your inner sexiness, whether you plan to have sex that day or not.

◆ Sometimes women feel awkward about initiating sex, but there are many creative ways to let your partner know you are in the mood. Or just say so!

◆ Express your sexual nature by immersing yourself in the world of your senses. Dress, groom yourself, and design your home around sensual pleasures.

◆ Strategies for increasing your sex drive include more frequent self-pleasuring, more frequent sex, regular massages, and other sense-enhancing and arousing habits and practices.

Chapter 9

Rituals to Do Before the Loving

In This Chapter

- Ready, sex ... go!
- Preparing yourself for love
- Breathwork training for better sex
- Pre-coital meditations and other rituals

Sometimes you just know that today, or tonight, or in the morning, you are going to have sex. But why make it a regular experience when you can make it something extraordinary? Many ancient cultures understood the importance of preparing the mind, body, and spirit for sacred sexual union.

You, too, can engage in some of these ancient—and not-so-ancient—rituals and practices to prepare you for the most intense and illuminating sexual experience. From attitude adjustments to extended meditations, pre-sex rituals can get you ready. This chapter will help you explore the rituals that work best for the sex goddess who is *you*.

Getting Ready for Love

Why get ready for love? Why not just do it? Well, sure, that works, too, but in the practice of sacred sexuality where sexual union becomes a ritual of coming together and rousing spiritual energy to awaken the chakras, preparation can help set your intention, prime your body, and stir the energy of the first chakra for facilitating the best possible experience.

Even if you aren't sure you are going to bond sexually with your partner that day but just want to be ready, even if your plans for union aren't necessarily ritualized *this* time, even if you are thinking about suggesting that the two of you act out a particular favorite fantasy or you have planned a candlelit dinner and just want to see what transpires, ritualized preparation for sexual union is relaxing, rejuvenating, and will fuel your inner sex goddess to be ready for love should the sudden urge, or opportunity, strike.

You can prepare yourself for love in many ways. Although some rituals focus on the body and other rituals focus on the mind, for a more complete, full-self sexual experience, you should keep both in balance and equally primed.

Preparing the Body

It is important to prepare your body for sexual communion to be fully ready and engaged in the experience. The first rule of preparing the body is cleanliness. A clean body has nothing to hide and nothing to fear in full and uninhibited expression. In ancient India, practitioners of Tantra, as well as other forms of yoga and of *ayurveda*, took cleanliness very seriously.

> **Source of All**
>
> *Ayurveda* is an ancient Indian science of holistic health that encourages specific lifestyle and health practices according to an individual's dosha, or type. Therapies include individualized diet, massage, yoga, and hygiene practices to balance the body's energies and maintain or improve health and well-being on all levels.

The body was cleaned; inside and out; anointed with perfumes and oils; and wrapped in clean fabrics in preparation for love, for yoga exercise, or just for the day (or night) ahead. Some cleanliness rituals even involved pouring water through the sinuses, swallowing long strips of gauze and pulling them back out to clean the stomach, churning the stomach muscles to clear the abdomen and lower intestine, and learning to suck up water with the muscles of the rectum to give oneself a natural enema.

Many people still practice the personal hygiene rituals established by these traditions, but we won't insist you do anything quite as drastic. Instead, here are some lovely cleansing rituals to help prepare your body for close intimate contact with another body:

- Take a long, luxurious bath in scented oil or bath salts. Or add half a cup of sea salt, a cup of milk, or a tablespoon of olive oil to your bathwater.

- Or take a hot shower and scrub every inch of your skin with a body brush. Gently clean your yoni and rectum with a moisturizing soap, but don't use douches, because they can upset the vagina's delicate balance and make you more prone to yeast and other vaginal infections.

- After bathing or showering, cover your skin in lotion to seal in moisture. Put an extra layer on your elbows, knees, and heels. Don't forget your yoni. An unscented hypoallergenic lotion like Lubriderm will help keep this delicate skin moist.

Initiatress of Love

If your tub is big enough, it's a fun and sensual experience to take a bath together as preparation for making love. A bath together is also a nice way to clean up afterward while basking in the glow and staying in touch.

- Use body spray or scented powder all over, for a soft perfumed scent.

- Scrub your nails to get them perfectly clean. File them so they are smooth with no rough edges. Polish them if you enjoy that, or rub them with a lemon peel to give them a natural sheen.

- Cover your hands and feet in moisturizing cream or petroleum jelly and put on gloves and socks for 15 minutes. Uncover to soft, touchable hands and feet!

- Fill the sink or a pot with steaming water. Drape a towel over your head and steam your face for 10 minutes. Breathe the steam in deeply to clear your sinuses. You can also take a cue from an ancient ayurvedic sinus cleansing technique called *neti* by pouring salt water into one nostril and letting it drip out the other nostril, then gently blowing your nose (kissing is easier if your sinuses are clear!) and drying the nasal passages by breathing through your nose. Many people still practice neti and believe it can reduce or eliminate colds, sinus infections, and nasal allergies.

- Put petroleum jelly or vegetable oil on your lips.

- A light fasting period can make your body feel lighter and more energetic and it can purge toxins and that feeling of heaviness. Try eating and drinking only fruits, vegetables, juices, and herbal tea for 6 to 12 hours before making love.

◆ Stretch! Reach your hands up to the sky, down to the ground, side to side. Stretch out your arms, shoulders, back, thighs, hamstrings, and calves. Do a few sit-ups to make your stomach feel nice and tight, a few push-ups to prime your arms, a few squats to activate your leg muscles. Your body will feel more ready to engage in active lovemaking and creative positions. (Nothing kills the mood like a pulled muscle or a cramp!)

◆ Choose carefully what to wear. A silk nightgown? Black lace teddy? Red satin camisole and panties? Leather?

◆ Consider dressing up, just for fun, in a costume that fulfills one of your fantasies. A Greek goddess? An Egyptian queen? A billionaire socialite? A fluid modern dancer?

Feeling clean, soft, and sexy? Great! Now consider priming the inner you. One of the best ways to do this is through structured breathwork.

Breathwork Training for Better Sex

In yoga, *prana* is the essence of life, the universal energy. When we breathe in, we take it into our bodies, and when we breathe out, we release it back into the universe. Ancient yoga systems like Tantra instruct yogis to practice breath control and deep breathing to bring more prana deep into the body because prana is what animates, energizes, and unifies our bodies and spirits.

Prana is life, and the deeper and better we breathe, the more life we will have within us, the better our bodies will work, the less we will be subjected to disease and aging, and yes, the more unified and intense our sexual communion will become. In Tantra, opposites are really two sides of the same thing and becoming enlightened to this unity is the ultimate realization. When you and your partner breathe together and come together, you become one instead of two.

> **Source of All**
>
> **Prana** is the Sanskrit word for universal life-force energy that animates all physical matter and that moves in and out of the body with the breath. **Pranayama** is a traditional yogic system of breathing exercises designed to maximize prana in the body for ultimate physical, mental, and spiritual health and balance.

The practice of bringing prana into the body is called *pranayama*. Many yoga teachers teach pranayama exercises, but you can also do them on your own as preparation for sacred union with your partner, or even with your partner before and during sexual contact. Try these two exercises, one just for yourself and one for the two of you together, to begin infusing your body more deeply and meaningfully with the life-force energy of the universe.

Bhramari: Humming Breath

Also called bee breath, bhramari means "she who roams" (as a bee roams) and is an excellent pranayama technique for awakening kundalini energy in the first chakra, so this energy can then be drawn upward through the chakras during sacred sexual communion designed to draw that energy upward through the chakras.

1. Sit comfortably on the floor or in a chair with your back straight, sitting cross-legged or (if in a chair) with your feet flat on the ground.

2. Relax and take a few deep breaths. Close your eyes and mouth. Rest the tip of your tongue on the roof of your mouth, just behind your top teeth.

3. Using your right hand, close off your right nostril with your right thumb.

4. Inhale deeply and slowly through your left nostril, filling your lungs as completely as possible. Try not to lift your shoulders as you inhale. Let the inhale expand your lower lungs and imagine prana flowing into your first chakra at the base of your spine.

5. Hold your breath for about three seconds.

6. Release your thumb, opening your right nostril, and close off your left nostril with your right index finger.

7. Slowly exhale out of your right nostril. As you do, keep your mouth closed but make a humming sound. Feel it resonating inside your head. Mmmmmmm, just like a buzzing bee. Keep exhaling until you feel you've completely expelled all the air from your lungs.

8. Close your right nostril and inhale slowly through your left nostril, filling your lower lungs and energizing your first chakra with prana.

9. Again, hold your breath for about three seconds, then open your right nostril, close your left nostril, and exhale again slowly and completely with a low, vibrating hum.

10. Repeat a few times, back and forth, alternating nostrils.

11. When you are ready to stop, sit quietly for a moment and feel your body.

Oracle Wisdom

In an ancient Phoenician creation myth, the universe began with the existence of time, from which sprung two forces: desire and darkness. From this division, the god of air, Aer, and the goddess of breath, Arura, emerged. In joining, they produced the cosmic egg, from which the sun hatched.

How do you feel? Any different? More energized? More excited? More relaxed and tranquil? Does your first chakra feel stimulated? Soothed? Some people feel very relaxed after this exercise and some people feel very excited, depending on what kind of balancing effect their bodies require, because prana balances the body to a state of equilibrium. Both states—tranquil and stimulated—are conducive to the sexual communion yet to come.

Alternate nostril breathing, called *nadi shodhana* in Sanskrit, is another common pranayama technique. It is exactly like humming breath but without making a humming sound.

Eyegaze Breathing

Eyegaze breathing with your partner before sex can be an intensely intimate experience. This exercise helps you and your partner to synchronize your breathing, bringing you both into harmony with each other.

1. Sit together on the floor or on the bed, cross-legged with knees touching or with legs extended, your right leg on top of your partner's left, your partner's left leg on top of your right, or any other way that feels comfortable and allows you to look into each other's eyes.

2. Hold hands and take a few deep breaths.

3. When you are both ready, look into each other's eyes and begin to breathe. Try to synchronize your breathing so you inhale and exhale together, at the same time and at the same speed.

4. Without giving any directions but just by looking, try to gradually make your breaths slower and longer, deeper and fuller. It isn't a contest; the point is to do it in unison.

5. Keep looking into each other's eyes, keep breathing. Continue for about five minutes. When one of you is ready to stop, squeeze the other's hand gently.

Eyegaze breathing can get very intense because most of us aren't used to looking directly into someone's eyes for more than a few seconds, but the emotional and spiritual connection this exercise generates is powerful and conducive to new heights of sexual communion. We suggest practicing eyegaze breathing often!

Get-Ready Rituals

Now you may feel toned, inside and out, but you can do even more to prepare for a really special encounter. You've primed your body and your breath, but meditations and affirmations can help set your mind in the right direction. You can also arrange and adorn your lovemaking space to be most conducive to a heightened sensual experience. And let's not forget a little fun with food! Aphrodisiacs and other fanciful fare can make an erotic prelude to love.

Relation Meditation

Meditation is a powerful tool, and not just to increase the intensity and focus of sexual union. Almost every culture in the world uses some form of meditation in one way or another, whether they call it prayer, *TM* (transcendental meditation, a technique based in the Hindu tradition), *zazen* (the Zen Buddhist word for sitting meditation), mindfulness, ecstatic dancing, whirling (a Sufi tradition), or something else. Many people today continue to meditate on a regular basis for the wonderful centering, grounding, and mental de-cluttering effects as well as a focus for spiritual pursuits.

Source of All

TM, or transcendental meditation, is a meditation technique popularized by the Maharishi Mahesh Yogi (1957–1998) and practiced worldwide. It is a type of **mantra** meditation, in which a word or phrase is repeated as a point of focus. **Zazen** means "sitting meditation" and is the primary type of meditation practiced in Zen Buddhism. A **mandala** is a circular design meant to help the consciousness focus on a single point, represented by the center of the circular design.

In the ancient traditions of sacred sexuality, meditation also played an important role. Sex itself is a kind of moving meditation, but solitary focus prior to sexual communion can help you clear your mind of the constant mental chatter that could distract you from total and complete focus on your beloved and on the sights, sounds, and sensations of sexual union.

Meditation can also help you set your intention, your heart, and your body in the right direction so you feel mentally and spiritually prepared for that important focus on the experience of sex. For some people, meditation is simply sitting with mindful attention, without engaging any thoughts, feelings, or anything else that isn't in the present moment.

Other people prefer using techniques to help maintain the focus, like repeating a *mantra*, gazing at a focal point like a *mandala* or a candle flame or another object, or visualizing certain scenarios, whether they are about sex, compassion, love, sensuality,

Initiatress of Love

You can learn more about meditation by taking a class or reading a good book about the subject (check out *The Complete Idiot's Guide to Meditation, Second Edition,* by Joan Budilovsky and Eve Adamson; see Appendix B).

rising kundalini energy, spiritual enlightenment, or something totally unique and personal to you.

To get you started on a meditation that can help to focus your mind and spirit on sacred union with another human being, try either or both of the following two meditations. Have your partner read the meditation you are using out loud to you while you practice it, or record your own voice reading it and play it back whenever you need it. Both these are visualization-type meditations.

Heartlight Meditation

This meditation is perfect for generating compassion and feelings of love, encouraging intimacy, and prompting the spirit to perceive its oneness with another.

1. Sit comfortably on the floor with your legs crossed or on a chair with your feet on the floor.

2. Close your eyes and breathe deeply.

3. As you breathe, imagine you are taking in little wisps of glowing light with every inhalation. Imagine the light moving into your body and finding its way to your heart.

4. Try to slow and deepen your breathing so each inhalation is at least five seconds long. Imagine the light flowing into your heart and growing in size with each long inhalation so that with every breath, the glowing light grows.

5. Imagine the light expanding beyond the boundaries of your heart and slowly, gradually filling your chest.

6. Now the light moves up and down until it fills up your hips, shoulders, hands, feet, and head.

7. With your next inhalation, imagine the light expanding beyond the boundaries of your body. Your heart is still its center, but now the light forms an aura around you.

8. Keep breathing, as if you were filling up a giant balloon. With every inhalation, the light continues to expand, beyond your body and out into the room, slowly filling the room little by little, with every exhalation.

9. Now imagine the light expanding, just as brilliant and glowing as before, beyond the boundaries of the room to fill up your entire home. Imagine it moving beyond your home to encompass your neighborhood, your town, your city, and moving beyond your city to encompass the planet.

10. Imagine your heartlight moving beyond the boundaries of the planet and out into the universe, growing and expanding with your heart at its center until it encompasses all of space. It is glowing, pulsing, with gentle waves of light moving like circles on a pond from your heart outward, bringing you into ultimate communion and unification with the entire universe.

11. Stay here for a few minutes, imagining this glowing heartlight that connects you to all existence.

12. Imagine the light slowly receding back through space, over the planet, back over continents and oceans and your own state and city and neighborhood, back through your home and room and body, and gradually back into your heart, taking with it the love it received from the universe and mingling it with the love that already lives within you.

13. When you are ready, open your eyes and feel that love connection inside you. Are you ready to share it?

To vary heartlight meditation, do it before self-pleasuring to help in your fantasies. Or do it during sexual communion, imagining your inner light growing to merge with the expanding inner light of your partner until you are encompassed together in a single pulse of light.

Oracle Wisdom

Amaterasu is a Japanese sun goddess and ruler of the light. According to Buddhist myth, Amaterasu was violated and hid away in a cave, taking all light with her. The world was cast into darkness and despair. Eager to restore order, the gods and goddesses tried to persuade Amaterasu to come out, but she wouldn't. Finally, a goddess called Heavenly Alarming Female decided to dance wildly outside the cave in a raucous striptease. The laughter and cheers of the gods caught Amaterasu's curiosity and she ventured out of the cave. The other deities drew her out, and light was restored to the world.

Sensuality Meditation

This meditation primes your five senses for love. Consider it a sensory warm-up exercise. It will help awaken all your senses to experience sexual communion. It isn't easy—you will probably find your mind wandering, but when this happens, just bring your attention gently back to the sense you are focusing on at that moment.

1. Sit comfortably on the floor with your legs crossed or on a chair with your feet on the floor.

2. Close your eyes and breathe deeply.

3. As you breathe, imagine filling your body with invigorating and revitalizing prana that flows through every part of you like a great river full of little tributaries.

4. Bring your attention to your eyes. Imagine you are breathing from your eyes. As you breathe from your eyes and fill them with energy, look around you. Notice everything you can see: the colors, textures, shapes, sizes of things. Take in all the sights you can see, ignoring any impressions from your other senses. Try not to judge or get distracted by what you see. Stay in the present moment of your seeing.

5. Bring your attention to your ears. Imagine prana flowing in and out of your ears. Imagine you are breathing from your ears. As your ears become energized with life-force energy, notice everything you can hear. Close your eyes to tune out your vision and concentrate everything on what you can hear. List the different sounds in your mind. Birds? Cars? Refrigerator hum? Radio? People talking? Lawnmowers? Furnaces? Keep listening in total mindfulness for a few minutes.

6. Bring your attention to your nose. Pay attention to how it feels to breathe in and out of your nose, and imagine prana flowing into your nasal passages. What do you smell? Keep your eyes closed, and tune out what you hear. If it helps, hold your ears closed with your hands and concentrate fully and totally on what you can smell. Something cooking? Candles? Perfume? Dust? Even if you think you can't smell anything, keep noticing the sensations coming into you from the world through your nose.

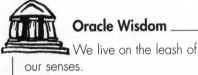

Oracle Wisdom

We live on the leash of our senses.
—Diane Ackerman (1948–), U.S. poet

7. Open your mouth slightly and begin breathing in and out through your mouth. Imagine prana flowing into your mouth and swirling around, activating your taste buds and electrifying your tongue. Try not to pay attention to sight, sound, or smell; instead, notice the tastes on your tongue. Do any tastes linger from the last thing you ate? Do you taste minty from toothpaste or gum? Notice the taste of your own saliva, even the taste of the air as it comes in and out of your mouth.

8. Close your mouth, keep your eyes closed, keep your ears covered, and imagine that prana has begun to suffuse your skin from every pore. Imagine breathing in and out of your skin so prana flows into you from every square inch. Your entire body breathes prana in and out. Now bring your attention to everything you feel against your skin: your clothes, the ground beneath you, the air around you, the hair on your scalp, the feel of your arms against your body, the places where your feet and legs intertwine or touch. Notice absolutely everything you can feel with your skin.

9. Relax, keep breathing, and let your awareness unfocus and blur, lulling you into a tranquil and relaxed state of consciousness with all your five senses fully awakened and idling, waiting for the sight, sound, smell, taste, and touch of another human being.

Just Say So: The Power of Affirmations

Affirmations are positive statements you make to yourself that help set your intention and guide positive energy in your direction. Affirmations are psychological tools that help you stop thinking negatively and start acting positively to bring the things you want and need into your life. They also help you become more aware of how you may be sabotaging your own efforts toward happiness, and many of us believe they actually help guide the flow of universal energy in your direction, drawing to you those things you desire.

Few things are easier than affirmations. Just say them out loud or think them, once or several times each day. Some people like to repeat affirmations several times first thing in the morning, periodically throughout the day, and several times before going to bed at night. You can say affirmations whenever you want and on whatever schedule, but say them! Then sit back and watch change happen, both in your life and in your own mind.

Here are some affirmations we like and use:

- I love who I am.

- I am beautiful.

- I am a sex goddess.

- I am a living, breathing miracle.

- I am always in the right place at the right time.

- I accept and love myself as I am right at this moment.

- I deserve love.

- I am loved.

- I already am my perfect self.

Initiatress of Love _____

Affirmations aren't just for you. You can say them to your partner, too, before, during, and after sexual communion. Some examples of affirmations for your beloved:

- You are amazing.
- You are perfect.
- You are incredible.
- I am all yours.
- I want you.
- You are my love.
- I couldn't love you more at this moment.
- You are a sex god!

Prepare Your Space

The last aspect of ritual preparation for making sacred love is to ready your lovemaking space. We've already mentioned that it's very important to keep your bedroom clean, uncluttered, and free of anything distracting or related to work. No pictures of your parents staring at you, no piles of unfinished reports, not even that stack of magazines you really need to go through.

Your bedroom should be a haven and a shrine to love. Red and pink are colors of passion and affection, so touches of these colors can warm up and intensify your bedroom. Soft, touchable fabrics, rounded soft shapes, and flowing lines add to a sensuous and seductive mood. Low light, candles, incense, and flowers add ambience. Also add a source of soft romantic music, be it New Age; classical, jazz; sacred music from India, Asia, Africa; sounds of nature; or anything else that speaks to you of sensuality and communion.

Beyond Taboos _____

Don't place one side of your bed against a wall! According to feng shui, the ancient Chinese art of placement, arranging a bed against a wall symbolizes resistance to having a partner, because access to one side of the bed is blocked. A bed placed so someone could get in from both sides symbolizes the desire to attract and willingness to keep a lover.

Also remember to keep your lovemaking space sacred and honor it by never using that space to have arguments. Let only loving energy and passionate lovemaking release their energies into your bedroom. Save your difficult times for other areas of your home.

Eat to Love, Love to Eat

Not everybody agrees that there really is such a thing as an aphrodisiac food, or a food that stimulates the sex drive. Aphrodisiacs, named for our patron sex goddess Aphrodite, are basically foods that in some way symbolize different components of sexual union, or that stimulate the body in a way that resembles sexual excitement. In the East, everything is symbolic, so foods that resemble a lingam or a yoni are natural aphrodisiacs.

Because we agree that symbolism has a strong impact on the mind, we like to play with (and eat!) aphrodisiac foods. Some examples of foods traditionally thought to be aphrodisiacs include the following:

- ◆ Soft, juicy fruits, such as bananas (lingam-shaped), melons (like luscious breasts), peaches (their soft cleft looks like a beautiful buttocks), and pears (like a woman's hips).

- ◆ Oysters, which resemble the soft, moist, inner flesh of the yoni, and also have a visceral, salty taste like the yoni.

- ◆ Ginseng, which means "man root," and in its root form resembles the body of a man. Try it in tea.

- ◆ Hot chili peppers, which both resemble a yoni and cause increased respiration and sweating.

- ◆ Wine, champagne, and other sources of alcohol can help people relax and break down inhibitions, but too much alcohol may hinder sexual performance.

- ◆ Traditional to ancient India were drinks made from milk, honey, and licorice. Try some warm milk with honey or some licorice tea.

Beyond Taboos

Although it isn't commonly available, Spanish Fly, a once-famous aphrodisiac, is actually made of powdered beetle parts. Although it irritates the urethra giving the impression of sexual stimulation, it is actually toxic.

Just because a food isn't technically an aphrodisiac doesn't mean you can't use it during sex! Beyond the old stand-bys, such as whipped cream and chocolate syrup for slathering on and licking off of various body parts, only your creativity will limit you. (However, keep all sugar out of the yoni, as this can contribute to infections.)

Why not pour some champagne into a belly button, drizzle honey over a nipple, drip Drambuie down the small of the back, or turn a lingam into a sort of erotic banana split? And if using each other's bodies as serving platters isn't your style, consider eating a whole meal in which you can only feed each other. Now that's erotic.

The Least You Need to Know

- ◆ To prepare the body for sexual communion, practice meticulous hygiene, use subtle scents, and stretch your muscles.

- ◆ Disciplined breathing exercises, called pranayama in Sanskrit, prepare your inner body for sacred sexuality and help awaken desire.

- ◆ Meditations and affirmations help prepare the mind for enlightened love.

- ◆ Prepare your lovemaking space by keeping it clean, sensuously decorated and scented, dimly lit, and free of any nonamorous distractions.

- ◆ Whether or not aphrodisiacs work physiologically, they certainly do have a psychologically suggestive component. Sexually suggestive food can be part of a pre-sex ritual, and using food during lovemaking can be fun and creative, too.

Chapter **10**

Foreplay: A Preview of Ecstasy

In This Chapter

◆ Kissing 101

◆ Kissing beyond the mouth

◆ Touching all over

◆ The fun of ritualistic foreplay

◆ Getting in touch with your inner Shakti and Shiva

You can prepare, bathe, meditate, light candles, and clean your bedroom all day, but once you and your partner begin touching each other, chances are you won't be ready for sudden and immediate penetration. And why would you want that, anyway? Part of the intensity of sacred sexual union is that nobody is in a hurry and passion unfolds at its own pace.

The Kama Sutra spends a lot of time talking about how a woman must be fully aroused and ready before her partner enters her. The yoni blossom should flow with nectar and open fully, like a blooming flower. The Kama Sutra even counsels that a man should not enter a woman until she begs with desire and tears in her eyes!

In other words, *foreplay matters*, and even if your partner doesn't seem inclined to spend much time on it, as a sex goddess, you can take the initiative when it comes to creative and erotic foreplay. Foreplay can mean everything from general kissing and embracing to targeted manual and oral stimulation of the yoni and lingam.

Foreplay is also everything in between, and much of the emotional and spiritual bonding of sexual union happens during foreplay. In fact, we can be in foreplay all the time, staying connected with our partner, keeping our being open to that presence and love.

But maybe you aren't sure how to go about having really effective, stimulating, erotic, enjoyable foreplay. How do you start? What is best to do? Let this chapter be your guide.

Lip Locks

The Kama Sutra suggests that all sexual communions begin with kissing. A kiss helps gauge initial interest, and can do a whole lot for escalating the level of excitement when two people come together. Kisses come in all different types, and the Kama Sutra describes lots of them. You could probably describe a few different types, too.

The mouth, in some ways, resembles the yoni, and kissing the mouth can be suggestive in this way, just as sucking on fingers evokes the lingam. According to *The Complete Idiot's Guide to the Kama Sutra, Second Edition* (see Appendix B), some types of kisses include these:

- **The Nominal Kiss.** This is a lip touch only, and an initial gauge of interest. Friends might even do this casually.

> **Initiatress of Love**
>
> Rituals, both of foreplay and of sexual communion, give us something to focus on to help us breathe through our fears and our urge to withdraw into old patterns of nonmindfulness and nonfocus during sex. Remember, there is no hurry or urgency, only a relaxing into the *now*.

- **The Throbbing Kiss.** A lip touch with the lower lip moving during the return kiss—a slight but significant move that says "more?"

- **The Touching Kiss.** In this kiss, the tongue gets into the game, brushing against the partner's lips, while each partner's hands instinctively move out to touch each other.

- **The Straight Kiss.** Lips meeting straight on, not angled as they would be for deeper tongue penetration. This can also be a casual kiss between friends, or a chaste blessing upon a lover.

♦ **The Bent Kiss.** Heads angled in opposite direction, with full lip and mouth contact, in a way most suitable for tongues to mingle and explore. In this kiss, hands move to caress faces and necks.

♦ **The Turned Kiss.** In this movie-star-style kiss, one partner takes the other partner's face in his or her hands, turning it upward to expose the mouth for a full-contact kiss.

♦ **The Pressed Kiss.** One partner presses the other's lower lip with lips or a finger. This finger-to-mouth gesture is highly erotic.

♦ **The Kiss of the Upper Lip.** According to Tantric teachings, a woman's upper lip is connected through an energy channel to her clitoris. Stimulation of one will stimulate the other. In the kiss of the upper lip, one partner pulls the other's upper lip between his or her lips. This is also a highly erotic and suggestive kiss. (You'll learn more about the Kiss of the Upper Lip in Chapter 15.)

♦ **The Clasping Kiss.** One pair of lips encloses the other's lips, both top and bottom, applying pressure.

♦ **Wrestling Tongues.** You can probably picture this one! Each tongue explores the mouth of the other partner.

Initiatress of Love

Although both men and women can be primarily oriented toward what they see or what they hear, women often like to hear words of affection, adoration, and trust as well as power during foreplay, such as "I love you," "I want you," "You're mine," "Breathe with me," or "Surrender to me." Every woman is different, so tell your partner what you like to hear. Men often like striking visual imagery, such as sexy clothing, lingerie, or erotic positions, but they also like to hear you talk during foreplay. Some men like words of power: "Kiss me!" "Lie down!" or words of surrender: "I'm yours." "Take me." And remember, sometimes your man will want to surrender to you, too!

Kissing each other's mouths often leads to kisses beyond the mouth. Kisses on the face can be tender and nurturing or romantic and erotic (or both!). Kisses may naturally move to the ears and neck (sensitive spots for both men and women), the chest, and the breasts. Kiss up and down arms and legs, and in the crooks of elbows and knees.

As we've mentioned, fingers resemble the lingam, so taking each other's fingers into mouths can be a highly suggestive and erotic experience many people enjoy. Once fingers are moistened from sucking, you may be tempted to use them to explore other areas, too, both on your partner and on yourself.

Yoni Kisses, Lingam Licks

As your mouths explore each other during foreplay, a natural next step is to apply kisses to the lingam and the yoni. Genital kissing, a.k.a. oral sex (*fellatio* when given to a man, *cunnilingus* when given to a woman), can lead to orgasm even without penetration, but it doesn't have to.

If oral sex becomes too intense and you aren't ready for orgasm, wanting to draw out the pleasure longer, stop for a moment and focus that sexual energy upward through the chakras toward the heart and head. Tell your partner if you need to stop. One or both of you can also feel entirely free to enjoy a great orgasm during oral sex! Especially for the multi-orgasmic sex goddesses, it's great to have one because it means more orgasms to come (so to speak).

> **Source of All**
>
> **Fellatio** is oral sex given to a man, specifically having his lingam sucked, sometimes but not necessarily to the point of orgasm. **Cunnilingus** is oral sex given to a woman, specifically having her yoni and clitoris kissed, sucked, and penetrated with her partner's tongue, sometimes but not necessarily to the point of orgasm.

The Kama Sutra also lists many different ways to kiss and orally caress both the lingam and the yoni. As a sex goddess, you will probably be interested in techniques for kissing the lingam, as well as yoni kisses your partner can perform on you. Here, according to *The Complete Idiot's Guide to the Kama Sutra*, are some of the lingam and yoni kisses the Kama Sutra describes.

Lingam Love

Applying mouth to lingam can thrill not only the male partner but the sex goddess as well. The lingam is a powerful symbol of the ever-erect and divinely potent Shiva, and just thinking about how it feels when inside can make a sex goddess shiver with pleasure at the very sight of an erect lingam.

Both you and your partner may enjoy lingam kisses more if you try some different techniques. Here are some of the Kama Sutra–approved lingam kisses:

- **Side Nibbling Lingam Kiss.** In this kiss, hold your partner's lingam between two fingers while kissing and gently nibbling up and down the sides. Be creative with your tongue but gentle with your teeth!

- **Outside Pressing Lingam Kiss.** Kiss just the head of the lingam with a gentle sucking.

- **Inside Pressing Lingam Kiss.** Pull your partner's lingam into your mouth, hold it firmly with your lips, and suck. Then pull the lingam from your mouth. Pull it in with a sucking pressure and suck on it again, then pull it out. Repeat as desired.

- **Kissing the Lingam.** Kiss the lingam as you would kiss your partner's mouth.

- **Lingam Tongue Strokes.** Give your partner's lingam a massage—with your tongue! Lick it all over, flicking, pressing, using long firm tongue strokes and short staccato tongue strokes.

- **Sucking a Mango.** Suck on the lingam as if it were a ripe, juicy piece of fruit.

- **Consuming the Lingam.** Take the lingam as far into your mouth as you comfortably can. (Wrapping your hand around the base can help you control how much you take into your mouth.) Caress and suck as if you are trying to swallow it.

> **Initiatress of Love**
>
> Don't be afraid to talk during foreplay. Talking helps build intimacy, and telling your partner what you like, both about him and about what he is doing, will build his confidence and make you feel closer to each other. Also, there is nothing weak or submissive about thanking your partner for giving you pleasure! Who doesn't like to be thanked for a job well done?

Yoni Worship

The yoni may resemble a delicate flower, but once aroused, it can enjoy lots of vigorous stimulation. At first, however, during foreplay, the yoni needs to be coaxed to bring forth its dew and open its petals. Oral sex is a great way to do this, and many women find they can most easily achieve orgasm during oral sex.

But how does your partner know what to do with this mysterious and many-petaled flower? The Kama Sutra has some thoughts on how lips and tongues can open the yoni, readying the sex goddess for union:

- **Pressing Yoni Kiss.** In this kiss, your partner kisses the yoni as if it were your mouth.

- **Outer Yoni Tongue Strokes.** In this kiss, your partner spreads the lips of your yoni with his fingers and brushes the outer labia with his lips and tongue.

♦ **Inner Yoni Tongue Strokes.** Now your partner can spread the lips of your yoni with his fingers and caress the inner labia with lips and tongue.

♦ **Kissing the Yoni Blossom.** In this kiss, your partner spreads the inner lips of your yoni and licks up the sides of the shaft and over the head of your clitoris.

♦ **Flutter of the Butterfly.** Little tongue-tip flicks around the shaft of the clitoris.

♦ **Sucking the Yoni Blossom.** A gentle rhythmic sucking and tongue-caressing of the clitoris.

Initiatress of Love

Music can play an important role during foreplay. It calms us, supports the romantic-erotic mood, and helps create a sacred space for lovemaking.

♦ **Kiss of the Penetrating Tongue.** In this kiss, your partner uses the tongue to penetrate your yoni, first with shallow flicks and then with deeper plunges.

♦ **Drinking from the Fountain of Life.** Drinking in the juices that flow from the yoni. Ancient Eastern traditions believed the juices of the yoni that flow during arousal contained potent sexual energy that could revitalize and replenish those who consumed it.

Finally, for the ultimate in kissing communion, try the Kiss of the Crow, a Kama Sutra pose in which you both pleasure each other orally at the same time, either while lying side by side or while one of you lies on his or her back, the other straddling them in the opposite direction. The so-called "69" position in Western culture, this pose is a highly sacred sexual pose in the East, where it was believed that the crow had mystical powers and could dissolve and combine substances. This kind of sexual communion suggests a blending of two people into a unified being.

Some people enjoy this pose, but others find it hard to give and receive oral sex at the same time, preferring to concentrate fully on one or the other. If this is you, you can both hold this position while taking turns pleasuring each other.

Reach Out and Touch ... Yourself!

For the sex goddess adept at pleasuring herself, nobody knows better what her body wants. You know your own body and what kind of touch generates a response. One of the best ways to heighten your excitement is to touch yourself.

Self-pleasuring is different when you do it on your own and when you do it as part of foreplay with a partner. Watching your partner pleasure himself or herself can be a highly erotic experience, especially for people who tend to be visually oriented. It's also instructional: Your partner can see exactly what you like.

"But it's also embarrassing!" you might protest. Sure, if you aren't used to touching yourself in front of your partner, you may feel inhibited. If your partner would like to see you do this and you also like the idea, try closing your eyes, or even tying a silk scarf around your eyes, and pretending nobody is watching.

Your partner may feel similarly inhibited about touching himself in front of you, but if you think watching this would be arousing, you might suggest it during an erotic embrace of foreplay session. Or simply take his hand, guide it to his lingam, and murmur in his ear: "I want to see …"

You can also touch yourself while you and your partner are touching each other. Four hands on your body can be even more fun than two! Caress your breasts and nipples, slide your hands over your hips, part the petals of your yoni, draw delicate circles around your clitoris with the tip of your finger. Feeling how good you feel to yourself will make you feel even better, as well as boost your confidence and glow, and that in turn will translate to your partner.

Beyond Taboos

It isn't easy to engage in extended eye contact, or to remain fully present and in the moment with our partners. In fact, in animal language, direct eye contact is actually confrontational and dangerous if one animal is untrustworthy. It is frightening enough to be with ourselves in this deep state of awareness of the present moment, but to bring another person in so deeply requires mutual trust. To move in this direction, focus on your breath and on your partner's eyes, and exchange movements that are slow and gentle.

Sensual Focus

To help fine-tune the senses, the sex goddess and her partner can work through foreplay in a complete and methodical sensory inventory. This ritualistic foreplay can help slow things down when partners are tempted to rush to penetration. It also builds intimacy. You can create your own foreplay ritual, but here is a place to start.

Work through this list at your own pace, and leave out any steps you don't care to do. Remember, it's your foreplay. This is just a guide. Keep your clothes on until you get to the step that says to take them off.

1. Define your lovemaking space. Decide if you will limit yourself to one room, and close off that room, or whether the entire home (or yard, or beach) is within bounds.

2. Collect any objects you might use: feathers, scarves, food, toys.

3. Find a comfortable space to be together. You might begin on the bed, or on some cushions or blankets on the floor, perhaps in front of a roaring fire or an open window.

4. Sit facing each other. Get comfortable. Decide who will go first on each exercise or whether you will alternate.

5. Focus on your hands first. Take turns caressing each other's hands.

6. Take turns caressing each other's face. Keep your hands on your partner's face, even if you are tempted to go lower.

> **Oracle Wisdom**
>
> At first people refuse to believe that a strange new thing can be done, then they begin to hope it can be done, then they see it can be done—then it is done and all the world wonders why it was not done a century ago.
>
> —Frances Hodgson Burnett (1849–1924), English writer

7. Take turns resting with each other's head in the other's lap for about three minutes each. While you lie with your head in your partner's lap, your partner may caress your face and hair. Close your eyes and relax as completely as possible, focusing on the vulnerable position and the pleasant sensations. Now switch.

8. Embrace in the Kama Sutra Brow Embrace, face to face with brows touching, gazing deeply into each other's eyes, for at least one minute.

9. Fill a deep pan, basin, or the tub with warm soapy water. Take turns washing each other's feet. Then, take turns massaging each other's feet with a rich lotion or massage oil.

10. With your clothes still on, stand together in front of the mirror. Embrace. Try different embraces while watching in the mirror.

11. Take turns giving each other a slow, deep, sensuous neck and shoulder rub.

12. Sit facing each other and hold each other's hands, looking into each other's eyes, for a full five minutes.

13. Give each other a scalp massage, then brush or comb each other's hair.

14. Now, undress each other completely. Don't take off any of your own clothing; let your partner do it (although you may need to lend a hand).

15. Stand facing each other and really look at your partner's body from toes to the crown of the head. Let your gaze travel upward slowly. Don't worry about your partner looking at you. Just concentrate on your own looking.

16. Now stand together, unclothed, in front of a mirror, holding hands. Look at each other in the mirror, and at the two of you together. Get really comfortable with what you see. Look for a long time if you need to.

17. Now, recline in a comfortable spot and take turns giving each other a five-minute back caress, light or firm, depending on what your partner likes.

18. Lie down together in the "spoon" position, both facing the same way, bodies slightly curled, you nestled in the curve of your partner's body with his arm around you. Lie like this for three minutes, then switch directions.

19. Staying in the "spoon" position, begin breathing more deeply. Synchronize your breathing and imagine you are both breathing from deep within your bellies. Try to inhale for 5 seconds and exhale for 10 seconds, in unison.

20. Turn to face your partner, still lying down, so each of you is lying on your side. Wrap your legs around your partner's upper leg and wrap your arms around each other. Embrace for three minutes.

21. Tilt your heads and begin kissing with parted lips. Let your tongues explore each other's mouths while your hands stroke and caress each other's backs, arms, and necks.

22. Pull apart and lie back. Have your partner massage your front—chest, belly, thighs—without actually touching your nipples or yoni. Switch places and massage your partner's front without touching nipples or lingam.

23. Switch again. This time, take turns giving each other a front massage including nipples and genitals, but without specifically focusing on these areas. Let them be just another part of the body.

24. Take turns guiding your partner's hand to where you would like to be stroked and caressed.

25. Lie back and point to a place on your body where you would like to be kissed. Your partner kisses that spot. Point to another spot, and another, until you have pointed to five spots—except nipples and genitals—on your body. Switch.

26. Lie back again. This time, have your partner very slowly lick and kiss each breast, each nipple, and finally, your yoni. Continue with this oral pleasuring for as long as you both like. If you reach orgasm, that's fine! (But not necessary.)

27. Now switch, licking and kissing each of your partner's nipples, then also his scrotum, and finally, take his lingam into your mouth, licking, kissing, caressing, and sucking on it for as long as you both like. If your partner reaches orgasm, that's fine, too! (But not necessary.)

28. You can stop here, or if you like, you can continue on to full sexual union. If you decide to continue (if one or both of you don't feel "finished" yet), be sure to read Chapters 11 through 13!

> **Oracle Wisdom** _____
>
> According to Hindu mythology, Ardhanari-Ishvara, or "The Lord Who Is Both Male and Female," was a deity formed because Shiva and his wife Devi (Shakti, mentioned later in this chapter, is one incarnation of Devi) were so deeply in love that they merged into a single being. Ardhanari-Ishavara has one female and one male breast and a tall forehead shaped like a lingam. This is the ultimate goal of Tantra: the complete merging of two opposites.

Touching Each Other

A big part of foreplay is, of course, touching each other in ways that excite both of you. Although much of foreplay involves kissing and oral stimulation, you've both got hands to work with, too. Touching each other's skin; clasping fingers; stroking curves; fingers on faces and hair, hips and thighs; and using hands to stimulate the yoni and lingam can all lead to a high level of arousal culminating in union of yoni and lingam.

Touching each other can start with a simple embrace. The Kama Sutra describes a variety of different embraces, not as sexual positions but simply as body-to-body contact. You know ... hugs! But erotic hugs usually sustain more body-to-body contact than the kind of hugs you give your parents or friends. Embraces make a lovely and intimate addition to foreplay. You'll learn more about embraces in Chapter 16. Try these:

- Embrace your partner while standing, and wrap one leg around the back of your partner's thigh while putting both hands on the back of your partner's neck.

- Embrace your partner from behind, reaching both hands around his chest. Press your fingers into each nipple and pull your hips up against him.

- While lying down, put one leg between your partner's legs and wrap your other leg around your partner. Embrace with your arms. This is called Embrace of

Rice and Sesame Seed, and it is meant to intertwine limbs so it is difficult to distinguish what belongs to whom.

◆ While your partner is sitting, straddle him and wrap your legs around him. Embrace tightly. This intimate embrace is called Embrace of Milk and Water.

◆ Other embraces concentrate on pressing one body part against the same part of your partner's body. For instance, you can press breasts, or brows, or thighs, or (while closed) yoni against lingam, moving against each other to stimulate and excite each other. Experiment to find all your many *erogenous zones!*

Touching each other can also be a more delicate pursuit, with fingers tracing and exploring over skin, curves, and crevices, supple massages with massage oil including yoni massage and lingam massage, even gentle light scratching, pinching, and biting (if you and your partner are comfortable with this; leaving scratch and bite marks on each other's bodies during sex was common practice in ancient India and a mark of possession, but it's not so favored these days!).

Fingers can caress and explore the yoni, inside and out. You can also take the lingam in your hands and using a lot of massage oil or lotion, hold, squeeze, and firmly move your hands up and down to stimulate the lingam. (Avoid scented lotions, which can irritate your partner's skin.)

Source of All

Erogenous zones are areas of the body that are particularly sensitive to erotic stimulation. The clitoris, head of the lingam, G-spot, and nipples are obvious erogenous zones, but your entire body can be an erogenous zone: face, neck, ears, chest, belly, navel, armpits, elbows, hands and fingers, thighs, kneepits, ankles, toes. The more you open yourself to erotic touching, the more of your own erogenous zones you'll discover.

Some people really enjoy anal stimulation, so if you or your partner like this, gentle anal stimulation with well-lubricated fingers or toys made for this purpose can be an exciting part of foreplay. Just be sure anything you use in this area has a flared end so it doesn't get lost in there! For many men, the perineum, that smooth area of skin between the scrotum and the anus, is a sensitive erogenous zone.

Find a rhythm to your foreplay, but keep varying it. Tease, speed up, slow down, withdraw, and hover just out of reach. Let foreplay become a dance of expectation and anticipation. Refusing to rush to the joining of lingam and yoni gives both the sex goddess and her partner plenty of time to build intimacy, enjoy a slow and intimate exploration of each other's bodies, and increase sexual pressure so that when union finally occurs, it can be of the utmost intensity, power, and pleasure.

Initiatress of Love

No matter how often we hear that we should focus on the pleasure of our partners, focusing on what pleases you is the solution to nearly any orgasmic difficulty. Without this focus on our own pleasure, we can easily get trapped in the anxiety of performing adequately for our partners, which is hardly a direct road to pleasure. The fact is that when a sex goddess is pleased, her partner is pleased as well, so focusing on your own pleasure becomes the best way to focus on the pleasure of your partner.

Shakti and Shiva, Ready for Union

According to Tantric mythology, the goddess Shakti is the universal feminine principle, and the god Shiva is the universal male principle. These two lovers came together in divine union and the result was so explosive that it gave birth to all creation.

Shiva's symbol is the cosmic lingam, nestled in Shakti's symbol, the cosmic yoni. Together, these divine sexual/sensual fully aware forces form the basis for existence. And why should your union be any different? Every sex goddess has Shakti inside her, and every sex god carries with him the essence of Shiva. These divine and perfect beings, equal and exactly complementary, were so in tune and aware that their union was as perfect as each of them.

As you engage in the play leading up to your own divine union, let your inner Shakti emerge from you and guide your actions, your expressions, your words, your hands, the movements of your body, your hips, the pulse of your yoni, that long gaze into your lover's eyes that makes you feel as if you have merged into one being. Let Shakti bring out the Shiva in your partner and experience foreplay that goes beyond pleasure, becoming a path that leads straight to an explosive and enlightened union.

The Least You Need to Know

- ◆ Kissing is an intimate way to initiate foreplay and to heighten the excitement. The Kama Sutra describes many different kinds of kisses.

- ◆ The body has many erogenous zones. Enhance foreplay by kissing, licking, biting, and sucking on necks, chests, nipples, bellies, in the crooks of elbows and knees, and the yoni and lingam. The Kama Sutra describes many techniques for kissing the yoni and lingam.

- Use your hands as well as your mouth to caress, stroke, and rub each other, searching out erogenous zones and stimulating the yoni and lingam.

- Slow down and draw out foreplay by working through a gradual list of foreplay steps mapped out beforehand. You can make your own list or use the one in this chapter.

- Shakti and Shiva represent the cosmic yoni and lingam. The lovemaking of these two deities created the cosmic egg out of which the sun was born. You and your partner can access your inner Shakti and Shiva for more sacred sex.

Chapter 11

Help Your Man Understand What a Sex Goddess Wants

In This Chapter

- ◆ Know what you want first
- ◆ No need to be a drill sergeant
- ◆ Assessing your man's attitude
- ◆ Please touch here ... but not there!
- ◆ Worship-worthy you

Your partner may be your spouse, your friend, your confidante, your life partner, but that doesn't mean he can read your mind! Sometimes it's tough to tell your partner what you like, where you like to be touched or caressed, or even how you like to be talked to and treated. But communicating your innermost desires is essential for the fully realized sex goddess. Only by asking for what you want from the man in your life will you get everything you truly wish for.

One of the difficult parts about asking for what we want is knowing what we want in the first place! You may know that you love your partner, but you may not be quite sure what it is you want from him. Do you want to be reminded of how much he wants you? Do you want him to listen more? Talk more? Be home more, or be home *less?* Do you wish he would share more, or be more affectionate even when sex isn't in the picture? In this chapter, we'll explore the many ways—both direct and indirect, verbal and nonverbal—that you can communicate to your partner about who you are, what you need, and how your relationship can become more intimate and meaningful.

I Want You to Want Me

When it comes to sex, you may know what turns you on when you self-pleasure or fantasize, but that may not be the same thing that turns you on when you are with a real, living, breathing sexual partner. For example, many women fantasize during self-pleasuring about sexual contact with other women or with more than one partner at a time, but have no interest in really doing these things. Some women self-pleasure by touching certain areas but don't get the same sensation when someone else touches those spots. Sure, knowing what you want can help you enjoy what you get a lot more, but what if you just aren't sure?

In the straightforward and comprehensive *Guide to Getting It On, Third Edition* (see Appendix B), author Paul Joannides writes:

> Be aware that a woman's understanding of her own sexuality is sometimes on a body level and may have few words. Our society wants it that way and often teaches women from day one that they aren't supposed to tell men about their sexual needs. Getting all frustrated and yelling "Just tell me" does absolutely no good. She probably would if she could, but it's a little like asking someone to tell you the meaning of life.

The fact that a sex goddess isn't exactly sure what she wants at every moment is actually a good thing. Part of the fun, mystery, and excitement of great sex is *not* knowing what each of you might be inspired to try next, or what you might both be inspired to try together, and what you might discover you really like a whole lot! Sometimes these things just happen, and you can both make it up as you go.

But every woman's body is different, and every woman's mind is different. If your partner is getting to know your body and mind, or has lapsed into some patterns that don't really work for you, there is absolutely no reason why you can't try a little re-direction. To believe that you shouldn't need to tell your partner anything at all about what turns you on if he really is the one for you is a little like believing that if you saw something happen on a movie screen, it must be true.

Initiatress of Love

In mythology and folklore, many characters appear twice, with the same name but with different incarnations or qualities. In Celtic mythology, Tristan was married to Isolt, but they had many problems and fought often. Tristan left for France, met Isolt of the White Hands, and married her. Imagine that both you and your partner leave your daily lives behind, becoming duplicate versions of yourselves without all the mundane details attached: divine, romanticized versions of your ordinary selves. Then you can slip into these alternate roles whenever you need a refreshed perspective and a clean slate for lovemaking.

Self-pleasuring does give you a lot of clues about your own body and what you will like from a partner. For example, some sex goddesses love nipple stimulation—more specifically, some love it very soft and some love more pressure. Others don't mind a little of it, but find it annoying after awhile and would never go there during self-pleasuring. How is your partner supposed to know your preference?

The same goes for other parts of your body. Maybe pressure on your pubic bone is exactly what you respond to, but direct pressure on the clitoris is too much and gets painful. Maybe you like your partner to search for your G-spot with his fingers or maybe you would rather he keep his fingers on your back or breasts and leave the yoni for his lingam to explore. These are all things you can discover about yourself from self-pleasuring, or you may already know them from experience with previous partners.

How you prefer your partner to behave during sexual communion is also largely an individual matter. Do you like him to whisper sweet nothings, or not-so-sweet nothings? Or do you prefer silence so you can concentrate on the sensations? Do you wish your partner would look you in the eye, or synchronize his breathing with yours, or try a different position other than the standard 3 you've been using for the past 10 years?

Think about the things you love about your partner and what happens when you have sex. Make a list. Then make another list of the things you think would make sex *even better*. When you know what will make your sex goddess experience even more divine, you can communicate it.

Oracle Wisdom

In the lore of the Native Americans of the Northwest, Bear Woman could change from human to bear and back again. Imagine turning into an animal during sexual communion. How would you do things differently? Let animal instinct obliterate your human logic and see what happens.

It's All in the Delivery

But wait! Nobody wants sex to become like boot camp, with you shouting orders like a drill sergeant. Your partner may want to know what you like, but most people don't like to be ordered around or told what to do. There are much better, sweeter, nicer ways to communicate your innermost desires. You know what they say about getting more flies with honey.

A male friend of ours agrees that sometimes even verbalizing the technical directions for what a woman wants is at best nonromantic, at worst embarrassing, and that *showing* a man what we want can instead become part of the sex act itself. Just imagine if you were kissing your partner's lingam and he said, "No, no, you're doing that wrong. You're in the wrong place. You never do that the way I like."

Ouch.

Yes, guiding each other toward pleasure is all about the delivery, as well as a mutual respect for each other's bodies, minds, feelings, and sensual responses. If you love to have your nipples caressed, gently guide your partner's hands to that spot. Take his fingers and move them the way you like, then make all kinds of nice noises to show him how much you like it. Why wouldn't he want to keep going there?

Some men are happy to take more straightforward direction and may even ask you for it. Great! Others may need more subtle encouragement, and you may just want your partner to continue experimenting with you to find out what feels good. Others love to be *asked*, rather than *told*, what you would like them to do. Many men would rather hear: "Would you touch my breasts?" than "Touch my breasts!" or "Please, please, would you please take me now? I need you inside me," rather than "I'm ready now. Hurry up and finish!"

> **Oracle Wisdom**
>
> If you want to build a ship, don't drum up people together to collect wood and don't assign them tasks and work, but rather teach them to long for the endless immensity of the sea.
>
> —Antoine de Saint-Exupery (1900–1944), French novelist

If you don't really know what you'd like, build sexual intimacy with your partner as you open up and explore together. You may both discover a host of ways to touch, embrace, and communicate that you never dreamed you'd love.

When describing what you like to a partner, remember to focus on what you like rather than on what your partner is or isn't doing. Instead of saying: "You don't touch me here enough," you might say, "I love it when you touch me here." In general, sexual requests are best begun with "I" rather than "You" (unless you are saying, "You are so hot" or "You are so large" or "You are as erect as Shiva. Is this the cosmic lingam right here in front of me?").

Egos are delicate (both male and female) and when you are bonding sexually, everyone feels a little more vulnerable than usual. This vulnerability is good for merging together in sacred ecstasy, but not so good for taking criticism on your technique. This is why the "I" statement is so important, as opposed to the "you" this or "you" that statement, which can easily sound like blaming. Even if you didn't mean it that way, that is how your partner might hear it. Instead, start your communications with statements like the following:

- I love it when you …

- I could never be satisfied without your …

- I most desire your …

- I like to fantasize about …

- My [fill in the blank] is incredibly sensitive to touch …

- I feel like …

- I particularly like …

- If given a choice, I really prefer …

- Actually I prefer not to …

- I want …

- I need …

- I would love to feel …

- I would like to try …

Don't worry about sounding selfish or self-centered when you talk this way. Your partner wants to please you, just like you want to please him, and this information is more valuable than gold. Why not be generous with it?

Initiatress of Love

One great way to show your partner what you like is to self-pleasure in front of him. You might also find out how much you enjoy watching him self-pleasure in front of you. Many men are visually oriented and will be incredibly aroused watching you touch yourself and give yourself pleasure, but believe us, they will also be taking notes. They want to make you feel like that, too. For more on self-pleasuring, including in front of or with a partner, see Chapter 10.

Author and relationship expert David Deida says that a man needs a woman's responsiveness while a woman needs a man's presence. A sex goddess knows that her partner cannot read her mind and knows how to respond in a way that shows she is feeling him. In the same way, if a man is present with his partner (as opposed to being distracted, thinking about other things, "going through the motions"), sex becomes a truly mindful spiritual experience with both partners totally focused on one another and the sensory experience of sexual merging.

In the Other Shoes: How He Sees You

As much as we want to bond with another human being, it's easy to overthink what we feel and what our partners do. Even sex goddesses wonder what their partners think of them, how their partners see them, how the man experiences sex. Just like women, all men are different, in mind and body. But if you are in a love relationship with a partner and you are working together for more sacred sex, we can pretty much guarantee you a few basics:

- He loves your body and he loves looking at you.

- He thinks you are incredibly sexy, especially when you act like you *know* you are incredibly sexy.

- He loves the way you see the world.

- You have a lot of little quirks he loves.

- He loves talking to you and he really loves it when he feels like you are really listening to him.

- He feels lucky to be with you.

Considering these things, wouldn't it be nice if you could return those sentiments? Your partner wants to know how you feel, and he wants to know that you love his body, that you think he is sexy, that you love the way he sees the world, and his quirks. Tell him you love it when he really listens to you, and how lucky you feel to have *him*.

Reminding your partner of these things will make him even more devoted to your pleasure, as well as more confident about expressing these things back to you. *Everybody* likes to feel appreciated, and loved, and sexy.

Oracle Wisdom _____

Damayanti was an Indian goddess of love and sexuality. She lived far away from the Indian god Nala, but both had heard about the other. Nala met a magical swan who promised to fly the week's journey to Damayanti and sing Nala's praises to her. He did, and Damayanti sent the swan back, to sing her praises to Nala. The two long-distance lovers soon fell in love, but on one trip to visit his love, Nala was overtaken by three other gods who went with him, turned themselves into Nala look-alikes, and demanded that Damayanti choose whom she would marry. Damayanti noticed that only one Nala cast a shadow and moved his eyes, so she put a flowered garland around the real Nala's neck and they were finally married.

Body Mapping

Knowing how your man feels, feeling empowered to tell him how you feel, and learning how to really listen to each other makes communicating your sexual needs much easier and more comfortable. But you can also learn each other's bodies in a more purposeful and methodical way, if you like that sort of thing.

Although manipulating each other's hands to the sweet spots during sex is a great way to communicate your favorite places, sometimes the height of passion isn't the time to express anything anybody is going to remember with much clarity later on. Body mapping is a technique you can use when you *aren't* having sex that will help each of you express to the other exactly where you like to be touched, as well as where you prefer not to be touched.

Try this exercise twice: The first time, just talk about touch. What you like and don't like in general. For example, some people love to hug but hate to have their faces touched. Some people love to have a hand on the small of their back but don't like anyone to touch their feet.

The second time, do the exercise again, but with a more erotic focus—where each of you likes to be touched, or not touched, during foreplay and sexual union.

The body mapping exercise consists of working, with your hands, along each other's bodies from head to toe with the intention of finding out where you both like, and don't like, to be touched. The point of this exercise is not to stimulate each other sexually. You'll get distracted and you'll have to start all over again later!

Oracle Wisdom _____

What this world needs more of is loving: sweaty, friendly and unashamed.

—Robert A. Heinlein (1907–1988), U.S. writer

When you touch each area, the person being touched can describe how he or she feels about being touched there. Or, if you want a more structured system, with each new spot the toucher can ask, "How's this?" The touchee can answer in one of the following ways:

- Answer "No" if you don't like being touched in that place.

- Answer "Not sure" if you aren't sure whether you like being touched in that place.

- Answer "Neutral" if you have no opinion about being touched in that spot.

- Answer "Okay" if you kind of like being touched there.

- Answer "Good" if you definitely like being touched there.

- Answer "Fantastic" or "Yes!" or "Oh yeah baby!" if your partner hits a sweet spot.

As you answer, also feel free to add more detailed information, such as "Yes, but maybe less pressure than that," or "No, I'm ticklish there and I don't like to be tickled," or "Okay, but I might like it better if you pressed harder," or anything along those lines that you think would be enlightening.

Now the exercise itself. Remember, twice through: once for general knowledge, once in the name of better sex.

1. Set aside about 30 to 60 minutes. Find a clean, comfortable space. Set the mood with candles, relaxing music, and privacy. Unplug the phone.

2. Get naked.

3. Take turns. It doesn't matter who goes first, but let's just say it's you.

4. Lie on your back. Have your partner put his hands on the crown of your head and ask you, "How's this?"

5. One at a time, your partner should move over different parts of your head: ears, hairline, eyes, nose, cheeks, mouth, chin, neck. Respond to each one.

6. Now, your partner can move to your shoulders, biceps, elbows, crooks of elbows, forearms, hands, and fingers.

7. Next, move to the chest: sternum, breasts, nipples (both around them and on them with different amounts of pressure), solar plexus, ribs, stomach, lower abdomen, and the sides of the torso.

8. Move to hips, pubic bone, and pubic hair (lightly grasping it or combing through with fingers).

9. Have your partner do several things with your yoni. Cup his hand over the entire yoni, gently massage outer lips, gently rub inner lips, stroke the shaft of the clitoris, retract clitoral hood, touch the clitoris (gently, gently!), and slide a finger just slightly into the vaginal canal.

10. Using a water-based lubricant, have your partner gently explore inside the yoni: along the front wall, all around the inner edge, and around the perimeter going gradually farther inside, back to the cervix (the bottom of the uterus, a cone-shaped protrusion at the back, deep inside the vagina). Many women have particularly sensitive spots in different places inside the yoni. Remember, this exercise isn't about moving toward sex; it's purely for information! (But it's bound to be fun, too.)

11. Now your partner can move over your perineum and around your anal area.

12. Go down each leg, knee, kneepit, calf, shin, ankle, heel, arch, balls of the feet, and toes.

13. Turn over onto your stomach, and start back at the head. Have your partner go down your body again from the backside, ending with your toes. Even if you've done some of these areas when turned the other way, they may feel different when you are lying on your stomach.

14. Now it's your partner's turn! First, have your partner lie on his back. Put your hands lightly on the crown of his head. Ask, "How's this?"

15. One at a time, move over different parts of your partner's head: ears, hairline, eyes, nose, cheeks, mouth, chin, neck. Get a response for each one, just as he did for you.

16. Move to your partner's shoulders, biceps, elbows, crooks of elbows, forearms, hands, and fingers.

17. Move to chest, nipples, solar plexus, ribs, stomach, lower abdomen, and the sides of the torso.

18. Move to hips, lower abdomen, and pubic hair. Gently pull and comb through public hair with your fingers.

19. Gently grasp his testicles and feel them. See which parts he likes you to touch, or how he likes you to touch them.

20. Move from the head of the penis in little circles all the way around and down to cover the entire surface. Find out which are your partner's favorite spots.

21. Move down to the perineum and around the anal area.

22. Do each leg, knee, kneepit, calf, shin, ankle, heel, arch, balls of the feet, and toes.

23. Ask your partner to turn over onto his stomach and start back at the head. Go down his body again from the backside, ending with the toes.

This exercise is usually quite a learning experience for both partners. And if you are both so aroused by now that you want to continue on and immediately put into practice what you just learned, then by all means do!

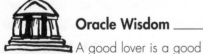

> **Beyond Taboos**
>
> Although men and women are certainly different, both biologically and as they have been shaped by culture, making blanket statements that pigeonhole each other into categories diminishes the individual. Be careful about making comments such as, "All men are ..." or "Men always ..." If you also ask your partner to be similarly aware of this destructive mode of thinking, you can learn to bond on a deeper level, not as stereotypes of your genders but as individual souls seeking union.

How to Be Treated Like a Sex Goddess

Your partner can do a lot to help you unleash your sex goddess self from within, by treating you like the sex goddess that you are. But what does that mean? Going back to what you really *want*, think beyond the basics of female desire (love, respect, and a really good orgasm). What would a sex goddess want? What would Aphrodite or Shakti or Isis want?

This is a good place to share our fantasies with each other. Fantasies can just stay fantasies or they can be something we act on with our partner. You may not want to share every sexual fantasy you have with your partner, and that's fine. Many sex goddesses keep most of their fantasies private. But maybe you want to pretend your partner's lingam is the gold phallus Isis attached to her husband Osiris. Or maybe you want to be Aphrodite, seducing a mere mortal who has no power to resist her. Or why not be Persephone, stolen away and ravished by the king of the underworld?

> **Oracle Wisdom**
>
> A good lover is a good *self* lover.
>
> —Betty Dodson, author of *Sex for One: The Joy of Self-Loving*

But you don't have to actually fantasize about being one of the traditional goddesses. If you behave like a twenty-first-century sex goddess, you are likely to get treated like a twenty-first-century sex goddess. Here are some ideas for getting the treatment you deserve and desire:

- Wear touchable fabrics and clothes that make you feel sexy.

- Walk like you own the street. Look at your reflection as you walk by windows and storefronts.

- Set up a pampering routine every day, such as a bubble bath with candles. Make it a priority.

- Always kiss your partner hello and good-bye. Add as many other kisses throughout the day as you can. Make the kisses linger. Hold on for an extra second with your lips. Make sensuous little humming sounds.

- Hold hands or walk with your arms around each other, no matter how long you've been together.

- Wear something new and different to bed. For example, trade in the flannel PJs for a long silk or satin gown. Skip the underwear. Usually sleep naked? Try one of your partner's T-shirts. Skip the underwear. Or keep the underwear but skip everything else!

Oracle Wisdom

In Roman mythology, Venus gave birth to Eros (also called Cupid), the messenger of love. This winged, cherubic figure was a trickster who used his gold-tipped arrows to make the most unlikely pairs fall madly in love. Imagine you have sent Eros to pierce your partner with an arrow so that he has no power to resist you and can do nothing but pursue you with every ounce of his being until you finally give in and allow him to taste the pleasures of your divine body.

- Never said "I want you" or "I can't resist you" or "You are the sexiest man I've ever known" to your partner? Too shy? Too embarrassed? Try it. Practice it in front of the mirror. Practice saying it with confidence. Then, when he least expects it, whisper it in his ear.

- Never said, "Tell me you want me" or "Tell me you can't resist me" or "Tell me I'm a sex goddess"? Why not? Whatever you want to hear your partner say to you, just tell him. Say it in a low, whispery voice.

◆ Back your partner up against a wall, wrap one leg around his legs, untuck his shirt, slide one hand up his chest and the other up his neck and through his hair while you give him a long slow kiss. Then pull back, turn around, and walk away (into the bedroom?). We're guessing he'll follow you.

◆ Don't be afraid to slide your hand over your sex god's pants (front, back, wherever!) whenever the mood strikes you (when it's appropriate of course!). Most men enjoy being groped.

◆ It's all right to say "I love you" first. Just don't say it until it's really true.

◆ Don't forget your female friends! A sex goddess knows how to keep in close touch with other sex goddesses, for the friendship, advice, nurturing, and emotional support they can provide. Keep that feminine energy flowing and balanced by loving your partner without losing your friends.

The Least You Need to Know

◆ To best communicate to your partner what you need and want, first figure this out for yourself. Many people aren't quite sure exactly how they want to be treated and how they like to be touched.

◆ Rather than telling your partner what to do, show him by moving his hand where you want it, demonstrate by self-pleasuring for him, or frame your desires as requests or as "I" statements rather than "you" statements, which could be interpreted as blame or criticism.

◆ Your partner already worships you. Remember this and feel more confident about returning his adoration.

◆ Body mapping is a structured technique for learning exactly where you and your partner each like, and don't like, to be touched.

◆ Tap into your sex goddess power to feel more confident, sexy, sensual, and empowered to express your innermost desires to your partner.

Part 4

Sacred Sex: Making Love Goddess-Style

Now you understand your body and its responses. It's time to share that knowledge with your partner. Maybe you're seeking new ways to explore your sexuality together, or maybe you long for a union of passion and intimacy that transcends imagination. Let the sex goddess within you connect you with the sacred sexual traditions of the Kama Sutra and Tantra or the lusty passion of Aphrodite and Isis.

These chapters share timeless secrets of lovemaking, from tantalizing techniques to positions for ecstatic union. Use your sex goddess power to enjoy intimate partnership as you've never before experienced it. Step aside, Shakti and Venus ... modern sex goddess coming through!

Chapter 12

Secrets of the Sex Goddesses

In This Chapter

- ◆ Psst … guess what Aphrodite knows?
- ◆ Secrets of yoga and Tantra
- ◆ Positions from the Kama Sutra
- ◆ Love lore from the Far East
- ◆ Sexual secrets from around the world

Sex goddesses, real and mythological, have been practicing and perfecting the art of sexual ecstasy for tens of thousands of years. We've learned a lot in that time, but as cultures appear, evolve, disappear, restructure, or move from one land to another, the sexual secrets of sex goddesses sometimes get lost, or forgotten, or secreted away along with other arcane knowledge.

Fortunately, art, literature, and historical texts have documented many of these sexual traditions and techniques from all over the world. From ancient Egypt to Greece and Rome, from the practice of mystical Judaism to the practice of mystical Sufism, from the Middle East to the Far East, sexual practices have been linked to spiritual pursuits, and sexual secrets have been variously popular, suppressed, and shared via secret networks or societies.

Books like the Kama Sutra and stories passed down orally through generations record and relate all kinds of secrets for sexual techniques, positions, and special ways to increase arousal. These are the secrets of the sex goddesses (and sometimes of the sex gods, too!). In this chapter, we'll tell you about some of them, and we encourage you to try them all!

Greek to Me

In Greco-Roman mythology, the gods and goddesses didn't have a whole lot of rules about sex, but they sure practiced it often! The magnetic and irresistible force of attraction—sometimes appropriate, sometimes not-so—seemed to govern the actions of the deities. A goddess wanted someone—god or mortal—and would do anything within her considerable magical powers to get him.

One notable aspect of Greek mythology and sexuality is the fusion between nature and the mystical. To escape predatory gods, goddesses often turned into, or were turned into, natural elements like rivers, trees, birds, or constellations. Some mystical creatures existed as essential parts of the elements, such as the nymphs or naiads who were part of water and existed within streams. These creatures often seduced, or were seduced by, wandering gods and humans, as their liquid beauty proved irresistible.

What secrets can we learn from the Greek goddesses?

- Never underestimate the power of physical attraction.
- Your sex goddess charisma is just as powerful as magic.
- Spend time in nature to enliven and invigorate your sexual energy.
- Water is an excellent environment for seduction.

Sexy Yoga

Yoga, the ancient Indian art of mastering the body through holding or moving through certain poses, is great for balance, health, strength, flexibility, and conditioning. It's also great training for great sex. That physical conditioning makes sex more pleasurable, increases endurance, and enhances the function of internal organs and the flow of life-force energy.

Yoga poses can help to activate kundalini energy (the goal of Tantra yoga). Yoga is also an excellent way to stay in shape and prepare for a night of active sex. Holding a yoga pose while practicing erotic visualizations can help to prepare both mind and body for high sexual union. You can also hold yoga positions during the joining of yoni and lingam.

Initiatress of Love _____

Ancient yoga teachings counseled that regulating the breath was of supreme importance for prolonging life and increasing vitality. One yoga breathing exercise practices retaining the breath between inhalation and exhalation. With each inhalation, imagine taking in life-force energy. Hold the breath for about five seconds, and imagine your lungs drawing that life-force energy from the air into your body, filling your body with rejuvenating energy. When you exhale, imagine expelling all negativity and tension.

Here are some poses to help get your body, and your mind, in the mood for sexual bonding. Always practice yoga in a warm room or outside on a warm day. Heat warms your muscles so they are more flexible, and a good sweat will help purge waste from your body. (Some yoga classes—notably, of the Bikram style—are purposefully conducted in a super-hot room for this purpose.) Also, take your shoes and socks off to more directly connect to the ground; bare feet don't slip as easily.

Tree Pose

Balance poses help to calm the mind, tone the body, and integrate the flow of energy up and down and between both sides of the body. Try Tree Pose to help you feel centered and calm.

1. Stand in Mountain Pose: both feet together, firmly planted on the floor, arms relaxed at your sides, looking forward, imagining yourself as firm and immovable as a mountain.

2. Slowly bring your right foot up the side of your calf until it rests on your calf, on the side of your knee, or on the inside of your thigh. You can use your right hand to help draw your knee up.

3. Fix your gaze on a spot in front of you and slowly raise your arms to either side to help balance you.

4. Bring your hands in front of your chest and put your palms together, as if you were praying.

Initiatress of Love _____

Many sexual poses in the Kama Sutra are designed to imitate the postures animals use during copulation. These include techniques such as Herd of Cows, Union of Many Goats, Union of a Herd of Deer, and Union of a Bull-Elephant with Many Females, all named for sexual unions between one man and many women at once.

5. Now slowly raise your joined hands up above your head. Balance for as long as you can.

6. While in this pose, imagine you are Kali, the Hindu warrior goddess of fertility, time, and mystery; powerful and strong with many arms extended to balance and strengthen and grasp your lover.

7. Repeat on the other side.

Yoga Shiva Pose (Natarajanasana)

This challenging balance pose, sometimes called Dancer's Pose, is named after Shiva, who is sometimes called the Cosmic Dancer. The pose also balances Shiva and Shakti energy, as you balance on one leg.

1. Stand in Mountain Pose: both feet together, firmly planted on the floor, arms relaxed at your sides, looking forward, imagining yourself as firm and immovable as a mountain.

2. Lift your right foot behind you, bending your knee, and hold your raised ankle with your right hand. Raise your left arm above you to help you balance.

3. Slowly bend forward, pulling gently on your foot to extend your raised leg behind you. Your foot should point upward.

4. At the same time, lower your extended arm in front of you so that as your leg moves up and back, your arm moves down and front.

5. Once you get good at this pose, reach both hands behind you to grasp your foot, pulling it up as far as you can comfortably.

6. As you balance in this pose, imagine yourself as the Cosmic Dancer, a sex goddess in flowing robes, glowing with light and the energy of passion. Imagine your chakras spinning, their centers opening wide to accept the flow of energy pulsing up and down from deep inside you at the base of your spine through your yoni, where it blossoms like a lotus flower, then up through your abdomen, chest, throat, forehead, and out of the crown of your head, where it holds you stable and steady with a pulsing beam of light.

7. If you lose your balance, return to the pose until it becomes too strenuous. Keep visualizing yourself as this glowing sex goddess in a graceful dance with the universe.

8. When you are ready, repeat on the other side.

*As you embody the Shiva
Pose, use erotic visualization
to get into the skin of this
powerful sex goddess.*

Butterfly Pose

This yoga pose mimics the beautiful butterfly, but also opens your hips and helps
to stimulate the first chakra.

1. Sit on the floor. Bend your knees and bring the soles of your feet together.

2. Draw your feet toward your body. If you are flexible enough, press your heels
   into your pubic bone or against your yoni.

3. Rock slightly forward to activate the first chakra, still holding on to your feet.

4. When you are comfortable in this position, keeping your back straight, slowly
   lower your chest toward the floor. The more you do this pose, the farther down
   you'll be able to get. Eventually, you may be able to rest comfortably with your
   forehead on the floor, your heels and hands pressed against your pubic bone and
   yoni.

5. If your hips are stiff, try this pose with cushions or pillows under your knees.

6. Close your eyes and visualize a butterfly fluttering through the warm, sunny,
   summer air, exploring each beautiful, silky flower, parting the delicate petals
   with its feet, plunging in and drinking deeply of the nectar, pulling out of the
   flower and fluttering on to another. Stay here in this garden for as long as it
   gives you pleasure.

> **Oracle Wisdom** _____
>
> The Indian elephant god Ganesha, remover of all obstacles, has an elephant's head on a man's body. Ganesha's consort is Siddhi, the goddess representing magical powers. The two deities, when joined in sexual union, represent the key to magical powers, which sacred sex is thought to bestow upon the participants, according to Tantra. Although Ganesha's mouth traditionally represents the yoni and his trunk the lingam, sex goddesses see Ganesha differently, with his mouth as the yoni and his trunk as the clitoris, or the woman's "secret lingam."

Tantra Secrets

The practice of Tantric yoga focuses around a balance of opposites: microcosm related to macrocosm, inner reality related to outer reality and ritual meditative and sexual acts to increase life-force energy and awaken kundalini energy so it travels through the chakras and finally reaches the seventh chakra at the crown of the head, resulting in the experience of spiritual ecstasy. Shakti and Shiva, the cosmic symbols of female and male energy united as equal but complementary forces represent Tantra's merging of opposites, which creates this universal explosive energy, the source of all creation and creativity. Practicing Tantra means learning to harness this creative energy.

You and your lover can create the perfect cosmic ecstasy known by Shakti and Shiva.

Sexual communion, specifically the internalizing of orgasm to move kundalini energy upward rather than dispelling that energy through ejaculation out of the body, was an important part of releasing the power of the kundalini. Sexual techniques designed to channel this powerful universal energy inward are part of Tantra's secrets. Here are some of the Tantric techniques and ideas described in many different sources over the centuries:

◆ Every woman contains the energy and essence of Shakti, the female principle in the universe and the cosmic yoni, but every sex goddess also contains the energy of Shiva, or the energy of the male principle. Likewise, every man contains the energy of Shiva, the cosmic lingam, and Shakti, the energy of the female principle.

◆ The best times for sacred sexual rituals are between midnight and 3 A.M., during the eighth and fourteenth nights of the new moon, and during solar or lunar eclipses.

◆ The mantras "HUNG" (pronounced "hoong") and "KLING" repeated during meditation help to awaken kundalini energy and call forth the potent, passionate, and protective power of Kali.

◆ Unlike some forms of yoga that dull the senses, Tantra teaches that supreme immersion in and ultimate sensitivity of sensual awareness leads to enlightenment.

Kama Sutra Highlights

We've talked a lot about the Kama Sutra, the Indian guide for living and loving that offers so many different types of kisses, embraces, and positions for sexual communion. Here are some of our favorite tricks, tips, and positions from the Kama Sutra. These positions for union are all meant to occur after plenty of foreplay so that the sex goddess's yoni is moist, open, and ready, and the man's lingam is erect.

Initiatress of Love

The blue-skinned Hindu god Krishna and his pale-skinned beloved Radha form a picture like the yin/yang sign when they kiss, in profile, head to head, facing each other but in opposite directions so that they kiss upside down, their faces merging into the swirled shape of the yin/yang. Try kissing like this. It's fun and promotes the balance of opposing energies.

Yawning Union

This pose is named for the woman's open thighs, which yawn to accept her lover.

1. Lie on your back as your partner kneels in front of you.

2. Rest your legs against his chest as he lifts your hips onto his thighs.

3. As he enters you, hold hands.

Full Pressed Union

This pose refers to the woman's thighs pressing against her partner's chest.

1. Lie on your back as your partner kneels in front of you.

2. Bend your legs and rest your feet against your partner's chest.

3. Your partner lifts your hips onto his thighs and enters you.

Packed Union

In this pose, the crossed legs intensify clitoral stimulation.

1. Lie on your back as your partner kneels in front of you.

2. Bend your legs and cross them at the shins. Rest your feet against your partner's chest.

3. Your partner lifts your hips onto his thighs and enters you.

Initiatress of Love

Many poses described in the Kama Sutra imitate everyday objects. Try inventing some of your own. With your partner, look around your home, your neighborhood, or a local wilderness area. Find interesting objects and shapes. See if you can make up a sexual position to imitate what you found.

Clasping Union

This union brings fully outstretched bodies together from fingertips to toes.

1. Lie on your back with your legs straight and your arms outstretched over your head.

2. Gently, your partner lies on top of you, facing you, so his feet touch your feet. He outstretches his arms so his hands touch your hands, palm to palm.

3. He enters you while you are both stretched out as long as you can. This intimate pose offers full body-to-body contact.

4. You can also do this position side to side. According to the Kama Sutra, the woman should lie on her right side and the man on his left side, both with legs stretched out and thighs pressed together.

Union Like a Pair of Tongs

In this union, the yoni holds the lingam as if it were a pair of tongs. As you squeeze your muscles around your partner, imagine you are milking the lingam with your yoni.

1. Your partner lies on his back.

2. Sit astride him, facing him.

3. Gently guide his lingam into your yoni.

4. Hold his lingam tight with your vaginal muscles, then squeeze those muscles in rhythm.

5. Move subtly over your partner, but keep the penetration deep and steady and your body mostly still.

Lotuslike Union

This cross-legged union takes hip flexibility.

1. Lie on your back and cross your legs, or put your legs in the *Lotus Position*, with each foot crossed and resting on the opposite thigh.

2. Your partner kneels in front of you, lifting your crossed legs against his chest.

3. He enters you, drawing your hips closer to him. Let him know if the position becomes uncomfortable so you can release your legs and wrap them around or leave them resting on each side of your partner.

Source of All

The **Lotus Position** is one of the most well-known yoga poses. Designed for stability during prolonged meditation, the pose imitates the shape and symmetry of the sacred lotus flower. To sit in this position, cross your legs and pull each foot, upturned, onto the opposite thigh. The position is challenging and shouldn't be rushed into, as it can strain the hip flexors. However, once you have attained enough flexibility through regular yoga practice, it's a very stable and comfortable way to sit—or to use during lovemaking!

Supported Union

In this position, the man holds the woman while thrusting. Let your partner support you and give in to the pleasure.

1. Stand facing each other.

2. Rise up and take your partner's lingam into your yoni (your partner may need to stand with his legs apart to lower himself, or use something stable to stand on if you need more height).

3. Your partner should hold on to you and support you as he thrusts.

4. If you fear losing balance, do this pose against a wall. (Actually, it's very nice against a wall.)

Suspended Union

In this union, you don't touch the ground. Imagine you are making love in the air!

Beyond Taboos

The Suspended Union is a difficult pose and not made for every couple. Don't attempt it unless you are both fit enough, you are sufficiently lighter than your partner, and he is strong enough to hold you in the position.

1. Have your partner brace his back against a wall.

2. As your partner lifts you off the ground, wrap your legs around his waist and your arms around his neck so he is holding you off the ground.

3. Move so his lingam enters your yoni.

4. Press against the wall with your feet as your partner holds your thighs and moves you against him.

Taoist Unions

In ancient China, before Buddhism made its way from India, Taoism was the dominant religion. With its origins in a matriarchal society, Taoism encourages following the Tao, or the way. Tao is a path of least resistance along which flows life energy that comes out of an interdependent weaving of the forces of nature and spirit.

In Taoism, opposites unite in a balanced equality to form the nature of reality. Yin and yang, male and female, light and dark, sun and moon (or sun and shade) are equal halves of an ultimate whole that can only be attained by fusion of opposites. Sexual communion ultimately represents this fusion of opposites between yin and yang, male and female energy. Ancient Taoist texts and Asian art depict many different sexual positions designed to intensify the energy of sexual union for the purpose of transcendent understanding of truth. Here are some of the sexual techniques and philosophies of Taoism:

♦ Taoism recognizes that every human has both male and female energy within, and counsels that sometimes during sexual union, it is balancing to reverse roles, taking turns being dominant or active and submissive or receptive.

♦ Connecting feet with hands and hands with feet during sexual union intensifies circulating energy between lovers and keeps it from escaping their bodies.

♦ In the position called Cranes with Joined Necks, sit astride your partner as he sits cross-legged and wrap your arms around his neck. Rest your head next to his so your necks touch.

Sex Secrets from Plain Girl

One tradition from ancient China tells the story of Plain Girl, a Chinese river goddess who was also a sexual initiatress. Several esoteric Taoist texts were attributed to Plain Girl and were probably written by a woman for the benefit of men, describing many secret sexual techniques for making love to women and recognizing the signs of desire.

Plain Girl writes about the Ten Stages of Loving, as recorded in the book *Sexual Secrets* by Nik Douglas and Penny Slinger (see Appendix B). The "Jade Gate" and the "Precious Gate" are common Chinese descriptions of the vagina:

1. When a woman embraces a man, it shows she wants him to pull her close and "possess her in love."

2. When a woman stretches her legs, it shows that she wants the man to gently stroke her clitoris, or the "upper part of her Jade Gate."

3. When a woman stretches her stomach, it shows she wants the man to make "short love-strokes" (shallow thrusts) inside her.

4. When a woman begins to move her buttocks back and forth, it shows that she will "soon be experiencing great pleasure."

Initiatress of Love

The seven secret disciplines of Taoism for regeneration of the body and reversal of aging were to (1) follow a particular diet, (2) practice a particular exercise plan, (3) expose the naked body to the sun and moon, (4) follow specific breathing techniques, (5) partake of certain herbal and mineral medicines, (6) practice meditation, and (7) engage in specific sexual practices.

5. When a woman raises her legs, it shows she wants the man to penetrate farther into her body, "with deep love-strokes."

6. When a woman squeezes her thighs together, it shows that "her Jade Gateway is emitting love-juices."

7. When a woman moves her body from side to side, it shows she wants the man to move his "love weapon" in strokes from side to side.

Oracle Wisdom

Legend has it that Cleopatra, a sex goddess if ever there was one, kept a large assortment of sex toys, such as polished stone or polished wood phalluses. She would call soldiers to her chambers, sometimes in large groups, to satisfy her magnificent sexual appetite.

8. When a woman raises the upper part of her body to press her breasts against the man's chest, it shows she is about to achieve orgasm, or "her zenith of pleasure."

9. When a woman relaxes her limbs, it shows she has experienced orgasm.

10. When a woman emits "a copious flow of love-juices from her Precious Gateway," she has released her vital essence, which is so revitalizing and essential to the man that he can benefit from absorbing it or even drinking it in.

Plain Girl also writes of the Eight Benefits of various sexual positions and techniques for health. These mini sexual "prescriptions" are very specific and the number of strokes are always based on the number 9, which ancient Eastern esoteric traditions believed to be a magical number, called the yang number.

These techniques were believed to cure a multitude of ailments in both men and women. Notice that all these techniques don't mention ejaculation or orgasm, although they could occur, especially in the second five, which require more "love strokes." But for these exercises, climax isn't the point. They are supposed to be therapeutic! (Of course, that doesn't mean they can't also be fun.)

1. **Concentration of Semen.** Lie on your side with your thighs open. Your partner lies next to you, between your legs, and enters you. He should give you 18 "strokes of love" (thrusts) then stop and remain perfectly still. Practice twice daily for 15 days to stop menstrual bleeding and to concentrate your partner's semen, making it more potent.

2. **Resting the Spirit.** Lie on your back with your legs extended and a pillow under your buttocks. Your partner kneels between your thighs and enters you. After 27 "strokes of love," stay perfectly still. Practice 3 times daily for 20 days. This technique will cure any chills or feelings of coldness in your lower abdomen and genitals, and will calm your partner's spirit.

3. **Benefits for the Internal Organs.** Lie on your side and bend or lift both legs. Your partner lies at a right angle to you, entering you from behind. After 36 love strokes, stay perfectly still. Repeat 4 times daily for 20 days to tone and invigorate both your and your partner's internal organs.

4. **Strengthening the Bones.** Lie on your right side with your left knee bent. Straighten your right knee. Your partner lies on top of you, resting his weight on his arms and legs (not on you). He enters you and gives 45 strokes of love. Then, you both stay still. Practice 5 times per day for 10 days to relieve congestion and to balance your partner's joints.

5. **Harmonization of Blood Circulation.** Lie on your right side. Bend your right leg and straighten your left leg. Your partner lies over you, with his weight on his hands, as if in a push-up position. He enters you and gives 54 love strokes, after which you both stay still. Practice 6 times a day for 20 days to cure vaginal pain, and to harmonize blood and energy meridians in your partner.

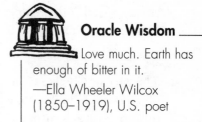

Oracle Wisdom

Love much. Earth has enough of bitter in it.
—Ella Wheeler Wilcox (1850–1919), U.S. poet

6. **Increasing the Blood.** Your partner lies on his back. Straddle him, resting on your knees. Raise your buttocks and insert his "Jade Stalk." Sink down onto him for deep penetration. Move up and down to give *him* 63 strokes of love. Or do this while squatting. Practice 7 times daily for 10 days in a row. This cures menstrual irregularity and strengthens the man's vital energies.

7. **Balancing the Elements.** Lie flat on your front, face down. Raise your buttocks slightly, placing a cushion under your hips. Your partner straddles you and enters you from behind, giving 72 love strokes, 8 times a day for as many days in a row as it takes to make both partners feel more balanced. This technique was also thought to increase bone marrow production.

8. **Adjusting the System.** Sit in a kneeling position with your buttocks resting on your heels. Lean back until you are lying down on your back, but keep your heels under your buttocks. (Don't do this pose if it hurts your knees.) Your partner leans over you and enters you from the front. He should give you 81 strokes of love, to be practiced 9 times every day for 9 days in a row. This technique can help alleviate any sexual problems and strengthens your partner's bones and entire physical system.

The secrets of the sex goddesses in this chapter only begin to touch upon the vast store of intimate knowledge available from many cultures and traditions. With plenty of practice, you may even invent a few sex goddess secrets of your own!

The Least You Need to Know

◆ The Greek goddesses and gods were often led by their lust and the single-minded pursuit of the objects of their desire.

◆ Ancient yoga traditions, including Tantra yoga, emphasize exercises to control the body and to direct, concentrate, and use sexual energy for the purpose of creativity and enlightenment. Practicing yoga poses and Tantric techniques can train the body to achieve this control and direction.

◆ The Kama Sutra shows many different creative positions for sexual union.

◆ The ancient Chinese philosophy of Taoism focuses on the bringing together of opposites to unite into a single creative force. One powerful way to unite these opposites is through sexual techniques.

◆ Taoists and other Eastern traditions believed certain sexual techniques had therapeutic value.

Sacred Sex You'll Both Love

In This Chapter

- ◆ Sacred sex: what it can be
- ◆ The Five Essentials
- ◆ How many orgasms can one girl have?
- ◆ Sexual positions for joyful unions

There's sex. And then there's sacred sex. We talk a lot about sexual union, sexual communion, and sacred sex in this book, but you might still be wondering if there really is a difference between sex for the sake of pleasure and sex for the sake of enlightenment.

Actually, there is a difference, although the boundaries sometimes seem blurred. Yet the difference isn't in the technique. The difference is in the intention, the attitude, and what you and your partner bring to the experience. In this chapter, we'll take a look at what sacred sex is really all about.

Sacred Sex vs. "Regular Sex"

Pretty much any adult of legal age can have sex if they want to have sex, either alone or with a willing partner. But having sex isn't necessarily having sacred sex. Regular sex can be a lot of different things, but it generally means getting oneself to have an orgasm because it feels good, or because our partner really wants one and wants our help. Regular sex can be relaxing, relieve tension, keep the sex organs toned and healthy, and generate calming chemicals in our bodies that make us respond to our partners in a nurturing, protective, and loving way. Regular sex is about body chemistry and physical release.

Sacred sex, on the other hand, takes the raw materials of regular sex and turns them into something divine. It is a discipline in which sexually energy is purposefully channeled to generate the most creative energy, to best activate the chakras, and to obliterate and transcend the perception of opposites. For women, sacred sex is the release of female sexual fluid, that essence of universal creative power. It is also the explosion of the divine feminine energy from within, which fuses with male sexual energy and jolts the mutual perception of the full and perfect unity of all existence, as symbolized by the full and perfect unity of two bodies.

That may sound like a tall order as you head toward the bedroom tonight, but that's what sacred sexuality, in theory, is all about. Of course, there are many ways to get to that point, and the fun is in the training. The point of sacred sexuality is exactly that: the training. Sex can be a mindful, total-immersion-into-the-senses experience of the present moment. The more you practice sex like that, the more pleasurable it is and the closer you become with your partner. You are merging with your partner when you have sex, physically as well as spiritually. Sacred sexuality is about waking up and noticing that fact.

Oracle Wisdom

One of our favorite sex goddesses had a reputation for being a prostitute, but she wasn't a prostitute at all. In fact, she was a High Priestess! Mary Magdalene was so called because Magdalene was her Priestess title. According to some sources, the anointing of Jesus' feet with oil was a ritual that signified she was married to him. Mary Magdalene was of royal blood and her relationship with Jesus made her a political threat. At a time when many matriarchal traditions were fading, Mary Magdalene essentially passed the torch of the dominant religion from the feminine to the masculine for awhile, handing the job over to Jesus for a few centuries.

Lots of things happen when we have sacred sex, and there are a lot of ways to have it, too. In the previous chapter, we revealed many different and exciting sexual techniques and positions. In this chapter, we'll examine more, including the elements to incorporate in the experience. We'll also explain what really happens at the climax of sex: an orgasm, and what to do with it (other than ride the waves of pleasure!).

The Rite of the Five Essentials

In traditional Eastern thought, all reality is made of five elements: earth, water, fire, air, and space. In Tantric practice, part of sacred sexual practice is to include symbolic ingestion of these five elements through a ritual called the Five Essentials, or Five Ms, because each of the elements begins with an M in Sanskrit.

Arrange the first four ingredients on a platter. Then get ready for number five!

1. Wine (*Madya*)

2. Meat (*Mamsa*)

3. Fish (*Matsya*)

4. Cereal grains (*Mudra*)

5. Sexual union (*Maithuna*)

This ritual is best performed at midnight on the night of the new moon. Create a romantic comfortable space with candles, incense, and soft music. You might spread out a blanket under the stars in front of a campfire, or in front of the fireplace with lots of pillows. There should be fire somewhere. In a pinch, candles will do.

Prepare your tray of food: two glasses of red or white wine or champagne, a small plate of meat such as slices of chicken, a small plate of fish such as salmon or shrimp, and a small bowl of cereal grains such as rice. If you like, you can substitute the cereal grains with a bowl of fruit, such as grapes or orange slices.

Initiatress of Love

While practicing the Rite of the Five Essentials, be sure to include something purple and something red, perhaps in the candles or the blankets or pillows, or in the lighting. Purple stimulates the woman's sexual center, and red stimulates the man's sexual center. These colors are directly linked the colors of the chakras: Purple is the color of the seventh chakra, and red is the color of the first chakra.

Sit with your partner on your right side. First, share the wine. You might intertwine arms when drinking. As you drink the wine, imagine you are drinking the nectar of the gods, who sprung from fire at the beginning of time. This honors the fire element.

Next, feed each other the meat. Think about how this and all other animals, including you, could never exist without air to breathe, and how we owe this existence to air, which is the breath of life. This honors the air element.

Now, feed each other the fish. Think about the great oceans of the world and life they support, and how the planet flows with lakes and rivers and streams. This honors the water element.

Next, feed each other the cereal grains or fruit. Think about how much we need plant foods to sustain life on this planet, and how all plant life depends on the earth for its existence. This honors the earth element.

Finally, come together. Kiss, embrace, and spend the rest of the evening in sacred sexual union. This honors the space element because the energy generated by sexual union is, like space, pervasive, ungraspable, indefinable, and all-encompassing. This is the highest sacrament of them all.

The Rite of the Five Essentials.

Positions for Concentrating Sexual Energy

Although environment and ritual add much to the experience of sacred sexuality, the positions for sexual union, according to ancient Tantric and Taoist lore, could make the difference between a mutual, intensely enlightening and reinvigorating experience and a negative experience that saps the energy and health from one or both partners.

The Kama Sutra and Taoist literature as well as many other works list hundreds of sexual positions specifically designed to prolong pleasure, concentrate the potency of sexual emissions, generate the highest possible flow of sex goddesses' fluids (for the good of the universe!), and maximize the intensity, duration, and number of orgasms. These positions have different names in different books, but the key with all sexual positions during sacred sex is to remember that energy channel connecting the first chakra to the seventh, from the base of the spine to the crown of the head. If energy can move freely through what the Taoists call this "Inner Flute," kundalini energy can be freed and sexual-spiritual ecstasy can flourish.

Here are some more of our favorite positions we've discovered from many different sources, or from personal experience.

Tiger's Tread

This position, from a Taoist text called *Sexual Handbook of the Dark Girl*, dating from the Sui dynasty between the sixth and seventh century, was thought to promote health and inhibit disease.

1. Get down on your elbows and knees. Raise your buttocks and lower your head, resting it on your arms.

2. Your partner kneels behind you and holds onto your waist.

3. Your partner should enter you in the center of the yoni and alternate five shallow thrusts with eight deep thrusts, again and again. The man should not ejaculate but should continue this rhythm until the woman's yoni begins to emit large amounts of "yin essence." Then, both partners should rest.

> **Initiatress of Love**
>
> Positions where you are on top allow you more control over where the lingam strikes inside your yoni and how much clitoral stimulation you get. Don't be afraid to touch your body, breasts, nipples, and clitoris while straddling your partner. He will enjoy watching, and that gives you stimulation in more places at once.

Splitting the Bamboo

This Kama Sutra position is evocative of a bamboo stalk split in two, but the movement involved makes the position pleasurable for you.

1. Lie on your back. Your partner kneels in front of you.

2. Place one leg on your partner's shoulder. Stretch the other one out beside him.

3. He enters you. As you wish, switch positions and put the straight leg on his shoulder and extend the other leg. Go back and forth at a pace that pleases you.

4. If you do this pose with your leg on your partner's head instead of his shoulder, it is called "Fixing of the Nail."

Swooping Shakti

This position can empower you to feel like you control the movements and motions of thrusting. As Shakti, you are taking your turn in the dominant role. Shiva can have his turn later! Doing squat exercises can really help you last longer in this position.

1. Have your partner lie down on his back. Stand with your feet on either side of his waist.

Oracle Wisdom

Shakti is the female principle but was also known as the goddess of lust and destruction, an active force to Shiva's passive power. Shakti energizes the universe with her creative power and sits by Shiva's side as his equal.

2. Squat down, lowering yourself onto your partner's lingam.

3. Move up and down several times so the lingam rubs the inside third of your yoni.

4. Now sink down deeper onto the lingam until it penetrates deep enough to touch the back wall of your yoni. "Swoop" back up, stroking the lingam with the muscles of your yoni.

5. Continue to swoop up and down, back and forth, for as long as it gives you both pleasure.

Yab-Yum

This unusual sounding position is a Tantric classic. Yab and Yum are the Tibetan terms for father and mother, and are equivalent to the Taoist yin and yang. This position is designed to efficiently circulate male and female energies between partners and encourage the flow of sexual energy up and down the channel of the chakras, increasing the spiritual experience of sexual communion and the full-body orgasm (see the next section for more on the full-body orgasm).

1. Your partner sits cross-legged on the ground.

2. Straddle him, wrapping your arms around his buttocks.

3. Lower yourself onto his lingam, taking him inside you as he holds your buttocks in his hands.

4. Lean forward and place your foreheads together, touching each other's sixth chakra or third-eye chakra, the center of intuition.

5. Imagine sexual energy flowing in waves up through the chakras and down, up and down.

6. Move in rhythm with each other and feel the energy flowing between you, drawing you closer until the lines that distinguish you from each other start to melt away in the unifying experience of ecstasy.

Initiatress of Love _____

Sometimes the regular old "missionary style" position can feel just right. Just because you *know* a lot of sexual positions doesn't mean you always have to run through *all* of them every time you meet in sexual union. The classic position in which you lie on your back with your thighs open and your partner hovers over you and enters you while you gaze into each other's eyes is conducive for emotional bonding and intimacy, and it is much less physically demanding on you.

Hiding in the Crevice

This is a great position for when you are both tired but want to be very, very close.

1. Lie down on your stomach, legs outstretched.

2. Your partner lies on top of you, also face down, with his legs to either side of your legs and his arms twined around yours.

3. He enters you from behind but remains outstretched over you. Your buttocks massage his lower abdomen. Stay stretched out like this, gently moving back and forth together. Continue as long as you like.

The Work of the Man

The Kama Sutra describes nine methods of penetration called "The Work of the Man." These are designed to excite both men and women. They include the following techniques, all of which you can use in a variety of positions.

- **Moving Forward.** The lingam moves straight in and out of the yoni, from the front or the back.

- **The Churning.** Your partner holds his lingam with his hand and churns it inside the yoni in a circular motion.

- **The Pierce.** As you lie down, your partner enters you at an upward angle, stimulating your G-spot.

- **The Rub.** Elevate your hips so your partner enters you at a downward angle, stimulating your lower vaginal area and perineum.

- **The Press.** When your partner enters you, he presses his lingam against the inside of your yoni with steady pressure and without thrusting, for an extended period of time.

- **The Strike.** Striking or slapping the vulva with the lingam.

◆ **Blow of the Boar.** Rubbing one side of your yoni with the lingam.

◆ **Blow of the Bull.** Rubbing both sides of your yoni with the lingam.

◆ **Sporting of the Sparrow.** The lingam moves up and down with increasing speed inside the yoni, usually resulting in somebody climaxing!

The Kama Sutra goes on to describe techniques for the sex goddess playing the dominant role and sitting astride her partner. She can engage in any of the nine actions described earlier, but in an active role where she manipulates the lingam and does the rubbing and thrusting. She can also squeeze the lingam with her vaginal muscles ("The Pair of Tongs"), turn in a slow careful circle while the lingam is in her yoni ("The Top"), or rock back and forth in a turning, swinging motion ("The Swing"). The Kama Sutra advises that when the woman is tired, she can rest her forehead on her partner's forehead until she is ready to resume, or they can switch places and the man can be on top for awhile.

Oracle Wisdom

Personally, I like two types of men—domestic and foreign.

—Mae West (1892–1980), U.S. actor

Orgasms 101

After all these positions and penetrations, we all know what happens. Sex proceeds to orgasm, if we're lucky. But what is orgasm, exactly? We've talked about orgasm in some of these chapters and we'll talk about it some more in later chapters, but let's look at the basics of female orgasm.

An orgasm is a series of involuntary muscle contractions in the yoni accompanied by intense feelings of pleasure and ecstasy. Some orgasms are more intense than others and some last longer than others. Some women can have multiple orgasms during one lovemaking session, and some women just have one.

Beyond Taboos

Some women have trouble having orgasms, and many women have trouble having orgasms other than during self-pleasuring. If a woman never or rarely orgasms, it's usually because she hasn't yet learned how to give herself an orgasm through self-pleasuring so she doesn't know what kind of stimulation works. Or she knows what works, but isn't quite prepared to communicate this information to her partner, or has communicated it but her partner didn't listen or understand. The solution for many women is to practice self-pleasuring more regularly and to work on being more open and communicative with her partner about what feels good.

Not everybody agrees that there are different types of orgasms, but many women believe that orgasms are not all the same. Here is a primer about the basic types of orgasms many women describe:

- **Clitoral orgasm.** This orgasm happens through direct or indirect stimulation of the clitoris. This is often the easiest and first type of orgasm women experience.

- **G-spot orgasm.** The so-called G-spot is a spongy area of tissue loaded with nerve endings, located on the inner wall of the vagina on the other side of the urethra. Stimulation of this area by the head of the lingam or by the fingers often results in orgasms that may be preceded by the feeling that you need to urinate.

- **Cervical orgasm.** Your cervix is the cone-shaped mouth of the uterus located in the very deepest part of the yoni. Typically, the front third of the yoni is most sensitive to touch, while the deeper parts are more sensitive to pressure than to actual touch sensations. In some women, the cervix itself is highly sensitive and stimulation of the cervix or very back of the vagina can trigger a deeper, slower, longer orgasm.

- **Breast orgasm.** Some women have extremely sensitive breasts and nipples. Stimulation of the breasts or nipples alone can lead to a pleasant orgasm.

- **Mental orgasm.** For many women, the brain is the most powerful and seductive of the sex organs. Fantasy, talk, visions, and ideas alone can cause some women to reach orgasm.

- **The full-body orgasm.** This orgasm is the essence of sacred sex. In this orgasm, sexual energy is directed away from the genitals and up through the chakras so the entire body contracts and pulses in ecstasy when orgasm is finally achieved. Your entire body may contract or spasm, you may shake or even yell and scream. This full-body orgasm is a taste of spiritual ecstasy because the orgasm has expanded far beyond the genitals to encompass the whole being.

Beyond Taboos

Some men and women protest that they do not want to redefine orgasm, worrying that it won't be any good without male ejaculation. In fact, it may be better. Full-body orgasm without ejaculation can be one of the most powerful experiences a human being can have.

For men, the full-body orgasm happens by inhibiting ejaculation and redirecting that emission upward in the body. For women, this isn't necessary. Orgasm in the yoni can pulse through the entire body like a wave. No need to suppress a thing! Just envision the energy moving upward through the body.

Heighten the intimacy of spiritual sexuality by using mirror vision. Watching your pleasure can help you and your partner connect to the moment and stay within its power.

Sacred sex, when it comes right down to it, is a highly individual matter. You can practice ancient techniques, or you can invent your own. The point is to be totally present with your partner, notice every touch, every shape and color and movement, every aroma and taste, and become so focused on the experience of joining with another person that you discover there is very little difference between you. This ultimate realization of your deep spiritual connection with another being is what sacred sex is really all about.

The Least You Need to Know

♦ Sacred sex is different than "regular sex" because it focuses not on simple release or pleasure but on mastering the sexual energy for spiritual purposes.

♦ The Five Essentials is a Tantric ritual that puts the lovers in touch with the five elements: drinking wine for fire, eating meat for air, eating fish for water, eating cereal grains for earth, and joining in sexual communion to represent space or the cosmos, which is pervasive and all-encompassing in its powerful mystery.

♦ Many traditions describe various sexual positions for maximizing pleasure and life-force energy, and the various methods of penetration.

♦ Many women claim to have clitoral orgasms, G-spot orgasms, cervical orgasms, breast orgasms, mental orgasms, and/or full-body orgasms.

Chapter **14**

The Glow: Coming Together

In This Chapter

- ◆ What is a sacred union?
- ◆ Rituals to honor your yoni and his lingam
- ◆ Channeling sexual energy for maximum pleasure
- ◆ Connecting body and soul
- ◆ Secrets to a blissful union

What is so sacred about coming together? You don't have to be a lifelong pupil of some of the sacred texts of sexuality such as the Kama Sutra to know the answer. You only have to be open to feeling the vital connection. You know it's sacred because it's electric when you unite. It's ineffable joy.

A sacred union is beyond the physical union of your genitals. It's a union of two spiritual beings. You feel it all over and all through your body, from your perineum to your crown, from the glow inside you to the tips of your fingers. The energy of a sacred union ripples through your bodies and out into the universe. Two beings experience unity. There is sacred power in the merging.

Recognizing that every union can be sacred is the first step in honoring the ecstasy that the body offers us. Next comes a mutual exploration of physical and spiritual connection. How can you turn a sexual encounter into a sacred experience? Let's consider.

Beyond "Insert Penis Here"

A sacred union is more than just one moment—the moment of penetration or the moment of orgasm, those "goals" we are so fixated on in our conquest-oriented culture. A sex goddess knows that sexuality can be more than a leisure or recreational activity. It can become a way of sacred meditation, as each partner moves toward full, present awareness and mindfulness.

The previous chapters have shown you what sex goddesses through the ages have known about honoring their bodies, exploring pre-loving rituals, initiating intent, and heightening desire. All are vital in leading up to this moment of union. Still, the moment of union, when bodies merge, containing each other, holding each other, and urging each other toward ecstasy, is so delicious it's beyond words. Yoni encompasses lingam, lingam enters yoni. Such a step can feel so important that it is as if everything was leading up to that moment of ultimate, intimate joining. For this reason, in sacred sexual traditions, both yoni and lingam have been given a special status, symbols of creation, of life, of death, and of transcendence.

The Sacred Flowering Goddess

The yoni, or vulva, represents a portal to enlightenment. The word *yoni* in Sanskrit means "sacred space," and indeed, in many cultures, the vulva was believed to have magical powers. In the Kama Sutra, the yoni is honored as the gateway of birth from the spiritual plane into physical form—from a soul without a body to flesh and blood. Other names given to the vagina in the East include Valley of Joy, Great Jewel, Pearl, Lotus Blossom, Moist Cave, Ripe Peach, Enchanted Garden, and Full Moon.

In Hindu art, the yoni is shown as a lotus flower in full blossom. The lotus is pictured in the arms of many Hindu goddesses, such as Sarasvati, who is usually shown carrying a book, a lyre or drum, a rosary, and a lotus. Sometimes she is depicted seated on a swan or a lotus petal. In modern times, the flower imagery in Georgia O'Keeffe's earliest paintings prompted New York art critics to label them as an expression of female sexuality, a label she never fully embraced. Yet many people through the years have responded to their erotic quality.

> **Initiatress of Love**
>
> *Kama* means "pleasure" or "sensual desire" in Sanskrit. It is the name of the Hindu god who represents the sexual nature in man. *Sutra* means "short bites of wisdom," or "aphorisms."

In orgasm, the yoni becomes the sacred lotus blossom.

Goddesses are often associated in art and poetry with flowers or fruits—peonies, roses, pomegranates, peaches, and melons. Often draped in leaves and flowers or wearing flower crowns, as Italian painter Sandro Botticelli depicted Pallas Athene in his work *Pallas and the Centaur* or Demeter in *Primavera*, goddesses were a link between the sensual realm of nature, as represented in the unfolding, yonilike petals of flowers, and the sensual realm of the body, with its own flower of sacred flesh.

Modern artists such as Judy Chicago have used the female genitalia as a motif. In *The Dinner Party*, she gathered goddesses and important women in female history around a triangular table with 13 place settings. The plate at each place is an image of female genitalia in a style reflecting the goddess or historical figure's sensibility and time.

Oracle Wisdom

Behold the Shiva Lingam, beautiful as molten gold, firm as the Himalaya Mountain, tender as a folded leaf, life-giving like the solar orb; behold the charm of his sparkling jewels.

—From the *Linga Purana*, a Hindu text

Shiva's Wand of Light

Just as the flower thrives and reproduces when pollinated, so does the yoni. Shiva's sacred lingam, the wand of light, exists as a sacred complement to the goddess's sacred blossom. *Lingam*, Hindu for penis, literally means "wand of light." In the East, other names for it include the Peak, the Warrior, the Hero, the Jade Stalk, and the Magic Wand.

The lingam, wand of light.

The lingam has the power to penetrate the yoni, just as the yoni has the power to consume the lingam. This mutual joining brings both partners pleasure, as each part is designed to fit the other. Although sacred Hindu tradition makes mention of the "ever-erect" lingam of Shiva, sex goddesses can take in this image, both physically and symbolically, as a way to increase excitement, pleasure, and a sense of unity.

Although we've already discussed many ways to stimulate bodies, from embraces and kisses to oral and self-pleasuring, and although each of these ways of touch and bonding can be sacred, the joining of lingam and yoni carries with it a magnificent sacred tradition, history, and spiritual energy. The erect lingam, as it fills with blood and rises up to enter the yoni, can stimulate a sex goddess in many ways: around the edges of the yoni; along the clitoris; when penetrating just a few inches inside the sensitive inner walls of the vagina; and as passion and excitement grow, with a deep, rhythmic thrusting that helps both bodies, from head to hips to toes, move together in their own unique incarnation of the sacred sex.

Yet how do we, as modern-day sex goddesses and sex gods, honor our own and our partner's sacred bodies and honor each other's sacred parts? Designing rituals to honor the yoni and the lingam can increase your sense of the sacred nature of your union, helping you to honor, respect, and appreciate this most intimate form of communication.

The Flower and the Jewel

The following ritual can help you to appreciate the beauty inherent in both yoni and lingam, and the magical power of bringing them together. The ritual is so named because the lingam is sometimes called the *vajra*, or "jewel" in Sanskrit.

1. As a way to spark a sacred encounter, bring your lover an offering: a flower for the goddess, a jewel (or any beautiful colored stone) for the god.

2. Undress each other, then recline together but don't touch each other. Position yourself so that you can see your partner's lingam or yoni.

3. Using all five senses—sight, touch, taste, smell, and hearing—take time to see your partner's yoni or lingam with new eyes.

4. Touch your partner's yoni or lingam tenderly. Explore it.

5. Smell it. (It's vital that you honor your partner before this session or any sexual encounter by practicing the utmost hygiene.) Notice your partner's unique scent.

6. Drink it in. Taste your partner. Resist the temptation to launch into pleasuring your partner. This is not about pleasuring; it's about what *you* are feeling. It's about discovery.

7. As you explore, tell your partner what you see, what you smell, what you taste. Tell your partner how much you are enjoying it. Express your gratitude.

Mouth to Yoni

You've read a bit about oral pleasuring in Chapter 10, but as you consider the sacred nature of sexual contact, let's take another look at coming together in this special way. A sex goddess knows her pleasure points and knows how to direct her lover to maximizing her pleasure. You have a lot to work with down there—a yoni that is studded with pleasure spots and a clitoris that seems to govern them all, a sort of volcanic pleasure center! Let your lover explore your labia with his tongue, working his way up to your clitoris. Let him roll his tongue back and forth across the hood of the

Beyond Taboos

Oral sex was taboo for many couples until the free-love 1960s, but many sex surveys show that it's a vital part of many couples' lovemaking. For many women, it's the quickest way to heighten arousal and become fully lubricated. For many men, oral sex is pleasurable for its delicate pressure and precise stimulation.

clitoris, spiraling in circles, then alternating with flicks and flutters. Let him suck it. Gently press it. Too much clitoral pressure can be painful for some women, while others like a lot. Be open to your partner about what feels good.

Encourage your lover to use his fingers, too, inserting them into your yoni. Some women like to lick their lover's fingers, tasting and smelling their own scent. This is a powerful, visceral way to connect. Many women find the connection between their breasts and their clitoris and yoni are electric. The stimulation of breasts during clitoral stimulation can be lightning hot.

Oracle Wisdom

The Taoists had a sex goddess's best interest at heart when they advised men to strengthen their tongue muscles so as to maximize the pleasure of cunnilingus (oral sex given to a woman). The exercises were elaborate—that's how serious they were— but one example has the man sticking out his tongue and retracting it, a bit like a snake. He repeats this for one to two minutes at intervals throughout the day in preparation for an evening of ecstasy.

Mouth to Lingam

Of course, oral pleasuring goes both ways. We've talked about it already, and given you some Kama Sutra techniques, but the fact is that many women are intimidated about giving fellatio (oral sex given to a man) because they are concerned they won't "do it right." It comes down to two words—licking and sucking. Lips and tongues are where it's at. And the secret is to just enjoy it. Explore.

The head of the lingam is incredibly sensitive, and the underside of the head, known as the frenulum, is generally the most sensitive of all, although this can also depend on the individual, whether or not he has been circumcised (had the foreskin of the penis removed), and his personal preference. Explore it all. Lick his testicles. Vary your tongue strokes with sensuous circles, long lollipop strokes, and little flicks of the tongue.

Use your lips (not your teeth!) up and down the shaft of the lingam, varying the pressure. Take him in as deep as you feel comfortable. If you do not feel comfortable taking him in deeper, use your hand to stimulate the base of the shaft as you suck the head. Know that the pressure of his lingam on the back of your throat, combined with sucking, can be the closest some men come to experiencing heaven on earth. But if you are worried about the gag reflex, control the depth by using your jaw muscles and your hands.

You will have the most control if your lover is lying on his back. Many men are tempted to thrust because this feels so much like intercourse, but you will need to coordinate and communicate with your partner about how much thrusting you are ready for! Oral sex takes practice, and the more you get used to it, the more it feels natural, but never go beyond what is comfortable for you. If taking your partner deep into your mouth sounds fun, or even challenging, try it! But if it makes you uncomfortable, don't do it.

Channeling the Power

A sex goddess knows that the yoni and the lingam are just the beginning point for arousal; that's why we introduced the concept of oral pleasuring as foreplay in Chapter 10. Sex goddesses through the ages have known how to channel that arousal through the body in subtle ways to create a much fuller and more connected experience.

Some call it awakening the kundalini, bringing energy up through the chakras, as we discussed in Chapter 5. To create a full-body experience of orgasm, all chakras must vibrate together. For you and your partner to experience the fullest sexual energy possible, his chakras and yours must vibrate in harmony.

Sexual energy rises through the chakras.

Chakra Coordination Exercise

To help you and your partner get your chakras in tune, consider the following list of questions. Ask each other these questions, based on the unique energies and focus of each chakra. The more you understand each other, the more you will shift toward connection. These questions may also help you to pinpoint and release tensions or issues in your relationship:

- **The first chakra.** Do you feel safe? Do you feel secure? What does it feel like to go wild? Scary or exhilarating? Can you let yourself go wild? Can you lose control?

- **The second chakra.** Whom do you give your allegiance to? Are you ready to surrender and give yourself to someone? Or are you guarded? Do you feel sexually expressive? Inhibited about certain areas of your body or your partner's body? Do you ever feel jealous? What makes you jealous? Do you feel criticized? Are you too critical?

- **The third chakra.** Do you feel powerful? What makes you feel empowered? Do you feel a sense of ownership about your partner? Do you feel owned by your partner? Do you feel like your power over each other is mutual, or is it one-sided? If one-sided, are you both satisfied with the balance of power, or would you like it to shift? How do you think you appear/seem/feel to your partner? How does your partner appear/seem/feel to you? What is your overriding impression of each other, as people, as sexual beings, and as partners?

- **The fourth chakra.** Do you feel open and free to tell your partner you love him or her? How often do you say it? Does one or do both of you wish you would say it more often? How often do you feel a sense of joy in each other's presence? Do you trust your partner? What would help you to trust more? Can you think of 10 new ways to express your love to each other?

- **The fifth chakra.** How comfortable are you with telling your partner what you want and need from him or her? Do you talk often or do you hold things in? Do you wish one of you would talk more about how he or she feels? Each of you might try completing these sentences out loud, to each other: "I love you because ..." "I love it when you ..." "Sometimes I need more ..."

- **The sixth chakra.** Do you have a sense of intuition about what your partner wants and needs? Do you feel your partner has a sense of intuition about what you need? Do you feel bonded being together without speaking? Do you sometimes imagine your partner thinks or feels things but you aren't sure if you are correct? Do you ask? Hold hands and look in each other's eyes for five minutes without speaking. Feel your partner's energy. Look deep inside your partner's eyes and heart. Feel who your partner is on an energetic level. Focus all your attention, all your being, on the person in front of you.

◆ **The seventh chakra.** When in sexual union together, do you feel a spirituality, a glimpse of divinity? Or is the experience purely physical, visceral, or material? How often do you feel deeply connected to your partner on a spiritual level? Do you sometimes feel estranged? What kinds of things bring you most closely together?

Sacred Chakra Breathing Exercise

The next time you make love with your partner, start a session with sacred chakra breathing. With each chakra, you will use an essential oil that will soothe or activate the sexual energy of each chakra. Refer to the following table for each chakra. Here's how to do this exercise:

1. Sit cross-legged on the bed, across from each other, fully naked.

2. With your eyes locked together, breathe deeply with three cleansing breaths.

3. With a few drops of essential oil on your fingers, reach out and touch your partner's root chakra, or perineum (the smooth area of skin between the vagina or penis and the rectum), spiraling your fingers gently. You are doing this simultaneously. The touch in this exercise should not be sexual. The aim is to tune in to your and your partner's vibrations.

> **Oracle Wisdom**
>
> Love is the secret key; it opens the door of the divine. Laugh, love, be alive, dance, sing, become a hollow bamboo and let His song flow through you.
> —Bhagwan Shree Rajneesh (1931–1990), spiritual teacher from India, later called Osho

4. Hold your hand over your partner's root chakra as you continue to breathe deeply. You may find that closing your eyes brings you into a stronger awareness of the energy in your body.

5. Breathe deeply three times, focusing on what it feels like in your body.

6. Breathe deeply three times, focusing on the energy you feel coming from your partner's body.

7. Repeat this for each chakra. For the second chakra, put your hand on each other's lower abdomen. For the third, in the space at the base of the ribcage (the solar plexus). For the fourth, over the heart. For the fifth, at the base of the throat, in the little space between the collarbones. For the sixth, the forehead, just over the space between your eyebrows. For the seventh, the crown of your head.

8. Be sure to spend enough time on each one until you feel complete—until you feel you have received enough energetic information. Communicate about when you are both ready to move up to the next chakra.

9. Finish by sitting, facing each other, holding hands, and breathing deeply for a few more minutes, to redirect your energy toward the whole person who is your partner, and the whole person who is you, and all the ways the two of you are connected and unified.

Chakra	Location	Essential Oils
First	Perineum	Ylang ylang, basil, bergamot, sandalwood
Second	Below navel and above pubic bone	Sage, cinnamon, ginger, patchouli
Third	Solar plexus	Chamomile, peppermint, sandalwood
Fourth	Heart	Rose, orange, bergamot
Fifth	Throat	Eucalyptus, sandalwood
Sixth	Forehead	Spearmint, juniper, rosemary, spruce
Seventh	Crown	Lavender, peppermint, rosemary

All the chakras are vital to enhancing the experience of orgasm. For example, when your throat chakra is weak, you may cater to your partner's desires and not speak of your own. You may tend to fake orgasms or only have very superficial orgasms. When your sense of personal power is low (based in your third chakra), orgasm takes energy away. Men in this situation often experience premature ejaculation; women with a weak power chakra often experience headaches brought on by orgasm. When the third-eye or sixth chakra is closed, you may no longer find your partner exciting.

The Inner Goddess Channel

Another way of describing the full-body experience of arousal is coming together through what Taoists call the Hollow Bamboo or what Margo Anand in *The Art of Sexual Ecstasy* (see Appendix B) calls the Inner Flute. We will call it the Inner Goddess Channel. The idea behind it is to amplify your sexual energy, redistributing it, along with your orgasmic sensations, to your whole body. This can be done through meditation, visualization, breathwork, and movement.

One way to think of it is to imagine a symphony played with just one instrument. Melody without full instrumentation and percussion is just a song. Percussion without melody is just rhythm. A symphony without strings lacks lushness. What you are seeking are longer, fuller, whole-body orgasms, something that envelops the body, mind, and spirit, rather than remaining bound to the genitals alone.

Oracle Wisdom

The Egyptian goddess Bast, the goddess of sensual pleasure, sometimes known as the "Cat Goddess," is known for her extraordinary vision. As the daughter of the sun god Ra, Bast would ride through the sky, protecting Ra from his enemies. At night, as a cat, she magically saw through the night with her glowing cat's eye. Because of this, she is sometimes referred to as The Sacred and All-Seeing Eye. One of the oldest versions of the goddess Bast was known by the name "Pasht." Some say our English word *passion* derives from Bast.

Sacred Breathing

Synchronizing your breathing as you move toward orgasm with your partner is one of the most wonderful connections you can experience. It is very intimate. Breath is so vital to us that when you connect to your partner's breathing, you are connecting to his essence.

To practice, let one person lead through a few cycles, then let the other person lead. Go back and forth until you cannot tell anymore who is leading and who is following. You will gain the sense of "being breathed" rather than having to breathe.

Move through these types of breath and then experiment with some of your own:

◆ Slow and shallow

◆ Slow and full

◆ Fast and full

◆ Fast and shallow

Slow and full breathing can help you focus more deeply on your feelings and build awareness. Fast and full breathing can bring up a lot of energy fast. It can keep you focused on your body. It can bring up strong energy, suppressed emotions, old memories, powerful feelings. Use fast and shallow breathing when you are overwhelmed by sensation. It's the kind of Lamaze breathing women use to work through contractions during childbirth.

By practicing sacred breathing with your partner outside of the sexual experience, you will find that "in the heat of the moment," you are easily able to synchronize your rhythms, prolonging your experience of ecstasy.

Once you had tried this, practice circular breathing, synchronized with your partner, in the Lotus Position. The man sits cross-legged with the woman on his lap, her legs hugging him, with or without penetration. They gaze into each other's eyes, breathing in and out with no pauses. Feel the energy move up through the chakras, starting at the root chakra. When one center feels full, move up to the next one. Synchronize so that both partners feel full before continuing to the next chakra.

Know Thyself

The Kama Sutra was on to something in classifying the size and shape of genitals. Penises and vaginas come in different sizes, widths, shapes, and sensitivities. The way your genitals match up can determine which positions will yield the most pleasure for you. Some women experience more pleasure vaginally, others in the clitoris. We're all different. Here are some options for different kinds of sensations:

♦ Positions in which the woman lies on her back and the man enters her while kneeling between her legs are best for deep penetration.

♦ The Splitting Position can give both partners more pressure and stimulation when the genital connection is a looser fit: The woman lies on her back but keeps her legs pressed together. The man kneels before her, resting her legs on one shoulder.

♦ Side-by-side positions increase the friction, while rear-entry positions allow for deep penetration—and stimulation of the breasts or clitoris.

♦ Man-on-top positions are ideal for a man with a long lingam and a woman with a short yoni, because he can better control penetration as he thrusts.

♦ Woman-on-top positions are good for women who want more clitoral stimulation, because you can control the position and angle of entry.

Taking time to discover the ways you spark together is part of the unfolding of the mystery. It's not clinical, and it need not be a passion-killer. In practicing sexual union with higher consciousness, you are weaving yourselves together.

Sex and Astrology

Astrology can reveal a lot about how you and your partner fit sexually. Astrological signs are divided into four elements—fire, earth, air, and water. They can mix together in intoxicating ways. Knowing which one you are means you can bring a little bit of your "fire" or "air" to lovemaking and delight your partner. It may be just what he needs to ignite his sexual energy.

Element	Astrological Signs
Fire	Aries, Leo, Sagittarius
Earth	Taurus, Virgo, Capricorn
Air	Gemini, Libra, Aquarius
Water	Cancer, Scorpio, Pisces

◆ **Fire and fire.** A bonfire of love. Your passion may run out of control. Call 911!

◆ **Fire and earth.** This combination can be very sensual yet steadfast. It burns like a campfire. It's a blend of excitement and contentment. This one could go the distance.

◆ **Fire and air.** Air lets fire breathe. This combination is intense and powerful. The spark never goes out.

◆ **Fire and water.** Steam heat. A very passionate combination.

◆ **Earth and earth.** Highly sensual, very comforting. Your challenge will be to really go wild.

◆ **Earth and air.** Innovative sensuality. Your lovemaking could push the limits of pleasure if you are not too much "mind over matter." This is often a meeting of equals.

◆ **Earth and water.** Pleasure meets comfort. This relationship is like rich, dark chocolate. An earth lover delights in caressing and clasping his or her lover. A water lover really knows how to go with the flow.

◆ **Air and air.** Heady passion. Ecstasy. Could this be for real?

◆ **Air and water.** All romance all the time.

◆ **Water and water.** Deep caring. Highly sensitive, highly erotic. You may need to cloister yourself for days, or weeks, at a time.

Ultimately, sacred positions are connected positions, both physically and emotionally. Whether you are facing each other for more kissing and clasping or back to front, whether you are on the bed or on the floor, whether one or both of you are upside-down or backward, connection means a mutual flow of energy, emotion, and love between chakras, between minds, and between spirits.

Body to Body, Soul to Soul

If you'll remember from Chapter 3, *tantra* is the Sanskrit word for "weaving." In the context of the sacred sexual union, it can mean the unifying of two people, diverse in their hopes, dreams, and desires and the way they approach the world. It can mean the unifying within us of seemingly contradictory aspects. We become harmonious within. We join with another in creating a harmonious whole.

Initiatress of Love

Taoists believe that it takes seven years to know your partner's body, seven years to know your partner's mind, and seven years to know your partner's spirit. That's 21 years just to get acquainted!

But the Tantric tradition emphasizes wholeness above all. Tantra embraces everything, good and bad, and does not judge it. All experiences, unpleasant or pleasant, painful or pleasurable, acceptable or forbidden, are part of the experience. There is no duality. Every experience provides an opportunity for illumination. The goal, as always, whether it's a sexual union or otherwise, is to integrate all aspects of yourself into a whole being: you, intimately connected with all other beings and with the vibrating energy of the universe.

Although the yoni is a symbol for physical regeneration, the act of sexual union in and of itself is a spiritual and emotional regeneration. The union restores us and sustains us. It is about wholeness. It is the embodiment of the concept of yin and yang, the complement of opposing forces to form a whole.

The dance of Krishna in an embrace with his beloved Radha from an eighteenth-century Indian painting exemplifies the yin and yang dance. She is depicted right-side up, and he is up-ended, his lips rising to meet hers. The placement of their eyes mirrors that of the "eyes" within the yin/yang symbol. She is light, he is dark. Her hair is falling and flowing down; the jewels around his neck appear to be flowing upward.

This yin/yang flow is evoked in many other works of modern art, such as the embrace of the lovers in Marc Chagall's famous painting *Lovers in the Red Sky*. Their arms together form a circle, one curving down, the other curving up. Countless goddesses take on both yin and yang energy. The Egyptian goddess Bast is both sun and moon goddess. The Egyptian sex goddess Qutesh is depicted riding a lion, nude, holding a lotus flower in one hand and two snakes in the other.

In a sacred sexual union, the energies of yin and yang are rebalanced, again and again, both within each individual and between two partners. A sexual union is the union of four. Within the man there is an inner woman; within the woman, there is an inner man.

Psychologist Carl G. Jung termed the feminine element of the man "anima," the Latin word for soul. The masculine element within a woman was termed "animus." He believed these aspects resided in our subconscious and argued that both men and women explore and develop their submerged energies.

Uniting is vital, because it awakens an underexpressed part of yourself. When you and your lover climax, whether serially or in unison, you are merging not just with him but also with his inner woman. You awaken that which desires to be awakened in him, just as he touches your inner male energy, helping to awaken this part of you. He allows you to express your utmost femininity and your utmost masculinity, while you do the same for him. And so the four of you participate in this complex mix, this medley of energies, culminating in a loving and transformative explosion of understanding: We are all one.

In Hinduism, the god Shiva is worshipped as one of a trinity. He is the embodiment of pure consciousness in its most ecstatic state. He united spiritually and sexually with the goddess Shakti. The Hindus believe that Shakti gave form to Shiva's spirit and created the universe. So the creation of the world derived from an erotic act of love. The dance between Shiva and Shakti is the backdrop of all life and influences all living beings. What unfolds from this dance is the beauty of all creation, pleasure, and pure joy. The Hindus attribute all happiness to this joyful erotic dance of creation.

Shakti is depicted as playful although Shiva is depicted as creative power waiting to be expressed. This erotic dance is reflected in the nature stories from other myth traditions, such as in Greek mythology with the story of Gaia, mother earth, and Uranus, god of the sky. They are paralleled in Native American mythology, which often depicts earth mother and sky father dancing together.

In other mythical traditions, lovers assume different forms in the name of preserving their union. In another rendition of the Isis/Osiris myth, Isis turns herself into a sparrow hawk and brings Osiris back to life by fanning him gently with her wings.

Oracle Wisdom

As a body in a world, here is our choice: we can be more loving or less loving. That's it. We can relax as the entire moment's show of love's swirl, feeling open as all—a vicious rainstorm, tweeting birds, our lover's lips, a sense of worthlessness—or we can close to some aspect of experience, pulling away as if we were separate.

—David Deida, U.S. writer on spiritual sexuality

The goddess is represented in many early cultures in forms such as the spiral, the meander, or the labyrinth. These symbolized the hidden patterns and pathways of the life-force energy of the Divine Feminine. The patterns depict the life-force energy flowing through the goddess and connecting different dimensions of her being with each other and with the world. The sacred union is the path of seeing and coming to know these hidden patterns within. As we learn what lies deep within us, we can evolve to be more realized beings. The goddess knows and experiences these patterns of the Divine Feminine through union with another being; this gives new meaning to knowing in the biblical sense. When Adam "knew" Eve, they both glimpsed the sacred patterns of the universe!

Secrets to Blissful Union

The secret to attaining a blissful union is not in technique, nor is it in the position. A sex goddess knows it's the subtle dance of giving and receiving. It's a dance of intimacy, teetering between maintaining our separateness and merging together. This unfolds between two lovers in many layers, the energy rippling between them and rising.

Awakening the kundalini power in the chakras and letting it vibrate up through your body is not a momentary occurrence; it's a process. Each time two lovers come together, they are merging their energies. If a chakra is out of balance, the lovers will miss a beat somewhere. But with the techniques we give in this chapter, two lovers can enhance the vibrations of each chakra. With practice, it will seem natural to you to tap into a full-body orgasm. You will open up your Inner Goddess Channel, circulating sexual energy throughout your body. With practice, too, you will become aware during lovemaking when sexual energy hits a block within your body, and you will have breath, visualization, and sexual techniques to draw upon to work through that block, incorporating it into your lovemaking.

Does that mean you cannot or should not make love if every one of your seven individual chakras is not optimized? By all means, no! Lovemaking with mindfulness to the places in your body that don't vibrate with full sexual energy is the way to unlock those parts of yourself.

This flirtation between the preservation of individuality and merging into intimacy unfolds during the process of lovemaking. There is joy in the journey. There is joy, too, in uncovering the mysteries within. There is arousal in the questions: Will I take him inside me? Will she receive me? Do I know him, or her? How much do I give? These mysteries don't just unfold in the bedroom. They unfold in all your moments together.

Many goddesses took mortals as their lovers. Why? We think the answer lies in the mystery. We humans are mysterious creatures. There is thrill in discovery, even danger. Will this person cherish me? Will this person stay by my side? You don't know. You don't ever absolutely know. This is the enchantment.

There is mystery in a longtime union, too, only we may not always recognize it in the moments of daily life. It may seem two people are committed for life. Certainly, if they are married and have children together, own real estate and have set up wills together, they are entangled. But the true dance of intimacy continues, as an undercurrent in every day of their lives. In each moment, they choose to join or remain separate, to agree or disagree, to be together, or not be together. In this way, some people who are married can in fact be very lonely. It's togetherness we truly seek, not legal bonds.

We want to be chosen, and chosen again. During lovemaking, particularly that first moment of joining, we feel chosen again. Think of Soatsaki, the Blackfoot feather woman and sex goddess. Her lover, Morning Star, brought her to heaven by pulling her in on a spider's web. Now, *that* is being chosen.

There is mystery, too, in what we don't know about our lovers. Remember the Japanese goddess called Life-spirit in Chapter 2? Her lover, a handsome prince, faithfully visited Iku-tama-yori-bime each night, but he left at dawn. This continued over many passionate nights. She looked forward to each setting sun when she would reunite with her lover. Yet she mourned the sunrise, because at each break of dawn over the mountain, he would leave. So one night she tied a thread to her young lover's clothes. The next day, she followed the thread as it unraveled, leading her up into the mountains. There, she looked full into his face and realized he was a mountain god, something about him she had never imagined.

Initiatress of Love

Maya was the Hindu goddess of fantasy and illusion. She is sometimes referred to as the Universal Mother or the Universal Shakti. Next time you make love with your partner, open up to each other about your fantasies. Share with him a story about a time in your life you were very different from who you are now. Create a little illusion, a new dimension, a different vibration.

Climaxing Together

Rare is that moment when two people achieve simultaneous orgasms. Yet we are programmed to expect that in our culture, setting it up as the ultimate in lovemaking skill. Why? Where did this come from? If two people were able to calibrate the sexual energy in their bodies this precisely time and time again, we would feel more like robots, or computers, than human beings. There is passion in the differences, excitement in the unknown.

Instead, our take on climaxing together is that the connection remains—and heightens—when one partner or the other experiences orgasm. When you climax, he shares in the sensations you are experiencing and vice versa. You know how to heighten his experience of orgasm, and so you remain connected through his peak, and he remains connected through yours. This is our definition of climaxing together.

Both partners must develop a deep awareness of what each does right before orgasm. A sex goddess must learn what triggers her own orgasm, and her lover must be aware of her in exquisite detail.

Some of the simple techniques for delaying ejaculation, such as squeezing the base of the penis or tugging at the scrotum, are—in the Western world—based on the idea of the man having enough control to wait for the woman to reach orgasm. And they *do* work. But we hardly think that having one lover "bide his time" is the right energy. Instead, delaying ejaculation and orgasm on the part of *both* partners to allow the potent sexual energy to rise up all the way to the crown chakra teaches both partners more control over their bodies and gives them the option and opportunity, should they choose during some of their encounters, to climax together. But it certainly isn't a requirement. And if you never "learn" how to climax at the same time, so what? The point is to take the time to give and receive pleasure to each other.

Oracle Wisdom

Sex pleasure in woman … is a kind of magic spell; it demands complete abandon; if words or movements oppose the magic of caresses, the spell is broken.

—Simone de Beauvoir, French writer

The Karmic Dance

The culmination of this dance between individuality and intimacy is a spiritual union between two separate beings, bonded by their mutual love for each other and the coaxing of sexual energy up the chakras and radiating between them. In sexual union, we each decide to live fully and wholly in the present moment of togetherness. Sexual energy heightens and spreads through your body as you, step by step, allow the possibility of what you might become *together*. We're not talking about one person submitting to the other or one person having power over the other, because the trust and energy between you lets you *both* surrender to the spiritual-sexual energy that pulses between you and obliterates all distinctions. For this to work, each of you must decide you are willing, momentarily, to let go to find yourself. This is the karma of sexual union—a union like this emanates its goodness out into the world. You are still you, wholly and completely, yet something new has flowered between you and your partner, bonding you. You might just see the universe in a whole new way: not as a collection of beings and things, but as One.

This begins at the body level. Quite literally, in the sacred union, the distinctions of body parts—arms and legs, buttocks and bellies, lips and tongues—begin to blur. As you explore every crevice of each other's bodies, as you luxuriate in every finger stroke on skin, on every square inch of it, you lose the sense of yourself as a separate being. Try doing this simultaneously, letting fingers, tongues, and lips do the thinking and moving. An excellent position for this is the "69" position, called the Congress of the Crow in the Kama Sutra, in which two lovers give each other oral pleasure simultaneously.

No matter which position you choose, the next time you make love with your partner, don't hold back. When you say yes, say an absolute yes. Say yes to every touch, every sensation. Send every sensation through every chakra of your body. Surrender your whole self, body, mind, and spirit. Let yourself merge beyond distinctions.

> **Oracle Wisdom**
>
> Imagination equals Eros. I want to experience what it's like to be inside someone else in the moment when that someone is being touched by me.
> —Charles Simic (1938–), U.S. poet

The Least You Need to Know

♦ A sacred union is more than the union of your genitals. Sacred unions can change us profoundly.

♦ Oral sex is a way of honoring his lingam and your yoni. It can be a prelude to intercourse, or it can lead to climax.

♦ By tuning into the movement of sexual energy throughout your body, you can have a fuller experience of orgasm.

♦ By using techniques such as sacred breathing, you can learn how to synchronize and combine your sexual energies.

♦ Discovering how you and your lover best combine together, body to body, soul to soul, can be an exciting journey.

♦ The most intense orgasms can result from the culmination of the dance between individuality and intimacy. You are weaving yourselves together.

Part 5

After the Loving

The intimacy of lovemaking arises from the ability to extend ecstasy beyond the merging of bodies. You've built up to the passion and climax of your sexual union by integrating your minds and spirits. Even as your bodies wind down from the intensity of physical arousal, your emotions and your energies can remain in heightened states for considerable time.

These chapters explore ways to extend the ecstasy, if you desire, and suggest methods to prolong the pleasure for both you and your lover. Bask in the warmth of your orgasmic energy, and use it to strengthen your relationship as well as the essence of your femininity.

Chapter **15**

Extending Pleasure

In This Chapter

- ◆ Heightening your sensual focus
- ◆ The rhythm of passion
- ◆ Multiple orgasms for you, and for him
- ◆ Fusing sexual and spiritual energy
- ◆ Demanding your pleasure

Oh, those wondrous moments of orgasm! They are ecstasy. They are the ultimate. What we will do for them!

But are moments enough? We deserve more than that. And we can have more than that! Sex goddesses know this. They let their bodies be open to experiencing the fullest pleasure. They know how to suspend time so that moments of pleasure are expanded. They know their lover's body, his rhythms of arousal, and the ways to maximize pleasure for both. They know how to ask for more—more, more, more.

Prolonged Pleasure

Channeling the energy of your sexual ecstasy rather than letting it dissipate is one of the central principles of Tantric sex. It's difficult to define

Tantric sex. It's spontaneous, joyful, and playful. It's deeply intimate and meditative. It's about wholeness—about creating a wholeness of two people. Tantra always has wholeness as its goal, with no dualities, no differences, and no judgments.

One of the first things people think of when they think of Tantric sex is the concept of prolonged anticipation. "Oh yes, Tantric sex," they will say, "that's where you don't do it but you think about doing it and you see how long you can go thinking about doing it without actually doing it."

One common Tantric routine might look like this: Schedule a long weekend together where you will have no other demands or distractions. Spend Friday going for a long walk, just talking and listening to each other with empathy and deep understanding. On Saturday, spend the morning lightly stroking each other. Do not have intercourse. After a light lunch, spend the afternoon caressing. Imagine that you can feel every stroke and every caress you bestow on your partner. Again, do not have intercourse. On Sunday morning, stroke each other all over. After an hour, you may join, inserting the penis in the vagina. But do not launch into full-fledged intercourse. Just be linked together. Lie like this until the man's erection subsides. In the afternoon, begin with stroking, and continue for an hour. Then join, inserting the penis in the vagina, going for a long, slow intercourse that builds sensuously and gradually to *orgasm*.

Source of All

A woman's **orgasm** is a series of contractions of the muscles around the middle and front of the vagina. The contractions intensify and become rhythmic, progressing to a series of involuntary—and very pleasurable—spasms. At the onset of an orgasm, the vagina expands at the cervix, an effect called tenting, a bit like a hot-air balloon filling up. Blood fills the vaginal lips, clitoris, and vaginal walls, creating engorgement. The tissue becomes tumescent, or thick. During an orgasm, your brain waves change.

What is happening here—other than torture? At its most poetic level, you are weaving yourselves together. You are imitating the erotic dance of Shiva and Shakti, emulating the act of creation. You are creating something with your partner—a palpable third entity of "we." At its simplest level, you are heightening desire and arousal. You are slowing down the process to mirror courtship, with all its exhilarating ups and downs, moving closer and moving apart, doubting and desiring. A Tantric routine like this is tuning you into the way sexual energy flows through your body. It opens you up to a full awareness of the vast possibilities for pleasure. But perhaps most important, slowing down creates a significant shift—from performing to being.

The performing mindset limits the possibilities. It's the difference between reading musical notes written on paper and hearing the orchestra play the full symphony.

To refer to Tantric sex as prolonged anticipation is to overlook Tantra's focus on the present moment. What Tantra does is elongate the present. Practiced fully, it envelopes two lovers in a heightened awareness of the sensual. The Tantric path encompasses beauty, sensitivity, and exhilaration through all the senses—eating, drinking, tasting, smelling, and touching. It is this that holds you in the present. For the two lovers, there is no other moment.

Initiatress of Love

When one sense is highly activated, it stimulates all the others. Heighten your experience of sex through exploration of the sense of touch, smell, taste, hearing, and sight. Use essential oils. Burn candles. Luxuriate in the touch of lush silks and velvets. Prepare your sexual chamber with satin sheets—or even flannel. Luxuriate in the touch of your partner's pubic hair. Loll your tongue in his ear. Mix light touch with hard pressure. Make love in the swimming pool. Close your eyes for a moment, then open them and look into your lover's eyes.

Heightening the Sensual

One of the keys to heightened sensation is to stop thinking about whether the moment is as it should be. It is what it is. Tantra does not judge. You no longer think about who you are and how you should be. The discipline of Tantra with its prolonging of anticipation and arousal is the training for emptying your mind of old mental, emotional, and physical patterns that no longer serve you. There is no more room for them when the present moment is so full of pleasure. Focusing on the sensual takes you out of that mind-state of evaluating what is good or bad. The sensual focus keeps you in your body. You make it a journey, not a goal.

Prepare a sensual feast for your lover. Remember, he is a sex god! Gather items that will activate all five of his senses. Start with our list that follows, then brainstorm a few items of your own. Have him sit in a comfortable chair or on a cushion on the floor. Blindfold him with a soft silk scarf. His only task is to breathe deeply, trust you, and be open to all sensations. As you lead him through each segment of the sensual journey, let gentleness and calmness be your mantra. Punctuate each segment with a minute of silence, breathing deeply and in synch with his breath, before you transition to the next segment. Do them in this order: smelling, hearing, tasting, touching, and seeing, removing the blindfold for the last segment. (Sensual hint: Use your fingers to deliver the food. Let him taste your fingers along with the food.)

Smelling	Hearing	Tasting	Touching	Seeing
Essential oil such as peppermint, ylang ylang, bergamot, orange, or lavender	Tibetan chimes	Strawberry	Velvet	Prism
Spray bottle of water with scent of rose, lavender, or cedar	Tibetan singing bowl	Olives stuffed with garlic, almond, or pimiento	Fur	Orchid
Basil, cilantro, or rosemary	Maracas or gourd	Chunks of fruit such as cantaloupe, watermelon, or pineapple	Moiré or raw silk	Artwork
Fragrant jam or jelly such as apricot, rose petal, or raspberry	Small drum	Chocolate	Feather	Glow of a candle
Pine cone	Tape of water sounds	Amaretto or cassis	Rose petals	Your face

When you heighten your senses, you open yourself up to a higher dimension of experience. With practice, you will acquire a natural panoramic view of the sensations you are experiencing during sex. It will seem that the energies of your body are the sounding of many chords. You will be able, all at once, in one moment, to focus on all the sensations available to you.

Finding Your Rhythm

An orgasm can't be orchestrated. It is the natural unfolding of the energy within our bodies. This is precisely why it's so delicious. It's enchanting, somewhat mysterious. It holds great power because its energy is so untamed. We want it to last forever, because we don't know where it will go. How long will it last? How intense can it be?

But the more you know the rhythm of your own body, the more you listen to its natural percussion, the more likely you can sustain an orgasm—or build it to a peak. It's more about allowing it to happen than causing it to happen. Opening yourself to your fullest rhythms—and knowing where you are out of synch—is the secret to ecstasy.

If you were to draw the energy of orgasm, what would it look like? In many ancient cultures, the goddess is represented in wavy lines, sometimes called ideograms. These mirrored and recorded the movements of the sun, the moon, and the stars. They mimic the motion of the sea, the turning of the earth. They reflect the rhythm of life. The muscular contractions of orgasm are like the rhythmic waves of the cosmos.

To activate your sense of your own body's rhythms, you can use dancing and drumming techniques outside—and inside—the bedroom. Certainly, the goddess Eikineba of Africa knew this. She taught dancing and drumming to be used as masquerades. And we know what masquerades are all about—flirting! Are you who you say you are? Are you what you promise to be? Only one way to find out! So, too, with Hi'iaka, the supreme patroness of the hula in Hawaii. She was the sister of the goddess of fire and the goddess of dance, Pele.

Oracle Wisdom

When Kali, the Hindu goddess of fertility and time, danced with Shiva, a frenzy overtook them, and the earth shook with their rhythm. As the goddess of time, Kali had all the time in the world. She was also the goddess of mysteries, known for her creative destruction, of bringing on transformation through relinquishment of old patterns. She is often depicted standing with one foot on Shiva's leg and the other on his chest. Ancient Hindu worshipers invoked Kali to fulfill desires and receive special powers.

Tantra embraces and enhances all forms of creative expression, such as movement and dance, massage, martial arts, the fine arts, healing, and music. Deepening your understanding of the natural dynamics of music or dance can enhance your sense of orgasm. Your understanding of crescendos of sexual energy will become intuitive.

Blossom with Orgasm Energy

Loosening the sacrum and pelvic bones is essential to transforming raw sexual energy and channeling it up the Inner Goddess Channel through the whole body. Practice this pelvic rocking exercise to harness your powerful orgasm energy in ways that allow it to suffuse your entire body.

1. Kneel on the floor Japanese-style with your legs parallel, feet tucked under buttocks, and toes pointing back. Use a pillow that you have doubled over to elevate your pelvis from the floor. (This is similar to the vajrasana, or Thunderbolt, the yoga pose you did in Chapter 6.)

2. Rest your perineum against the surface of the pillow. The perineum is the space between your yoni or lingam and your anus. For men, the pillow should rest right behind the testicles. You may do this exercise together, facing, or you may do it separately.

3. Rest your hands in your lap. Let them relax. Breathe deeply, keeping your spine straight but your belly relaxed. Relax your shoulders and jaws.

4. Bring to mind a time when you first experienced a rocking sensation as a child— and it felt good. Maybe it was a carousel, a seesaw, a bicycle, or a pony.

5. Gently rock your pelvis back and forth, noticing the sensations as your yoni or lingam rub against the pillow.

6. Quicken the pace, breathing faster. Intensify your rhythm until you feel tingling in your yoni or lingam.

7. Focus your awareness on your yoni or lingam. Fully enjoy the sensations.

8. Experiment with ways to enhance your sensations, moving more slowly for a while, and then speeding up again.

9. Keep your awareness focused on the connection between your breathing and your yoni or lingam. When your breathing connects with the pleasurable sensations in your yoni or lingam, the two sensations merge, and you will feel an expansion of pleasure.

This exercise may feel like riding a horse. When riding a horse, you must meld your body with the horse as he trots, canters, or gallops. Your whole pelvic floor softens as you sink into the rhythms of the horse's sway and his weight shifts from leg to leg. You have to go with the flow.

Some restorative yoga poses also open up the sacrum. Supta Padangusthasana, or the Spider Pose, works like a massage to your hip bones. In that pose, you lie on your back with your legs extended. Using a yoga belt over the heel of your right foot, bend your right knee in, pulling it toward your armpit, hugging your chest. On the next inhalation, extend your right leg upward. Hold it. On your next inhalation, let your extended leg fall open, toward the floor.

Jathara Parivrittanasana, or reclining spinal twist, is another pose that opens the sacrum. Start by lying on your back. Bend both knees, with your feet flat on the floor. Keeping your arms extended to your sides, palms up, torso up, twist your bended knees, letting them fall to the floor. Do not arch your back. Keep your shoulder blades moving down your back. As you breathe, let your back relax. Hold for 30 to 60 seconds.

Screwing

Yes, we said screwing. A subtle half-twist of the sacrum, first one side, then the other—basically, screwing—can keep lovers connected in a state of ecstasy for a long time. If you do a lot of Latin or African dance, this subtle twist of your hips will come naturally to you. If you want to cultivate it, take your partner salsa dancing one night! The idea is for the man to "spiral" his sacrum. But it also works for the woman when she is on top. Try it out. Put one hand on your pubic bone and the other on your tailbone, just below your spine between your buttocks. Spiral left, then right. Tilt your pubic bone up as you push your tailbone forward. Your back will curve slightly, in a "C." Now tilt your pubic bone down as you push your tailbone back, arching your back slightly.

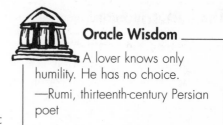

Oracle Wisdom

A lover knows only humility. He has no choice.
—Rumi, thirteenth-century Persian poet

Waves of Bliss

There are many ways to experience orgasm as there are stars in the sky. The possibilities are infinite. As you learned in Chapter 13, women can experience orgasm in the clitoris or the vagina, or deeply in the very back of the vagina (the "cervical orgasm"), or even a combination of these. Men can experience orgasm in the penis, or even the prostate. Both men and women can experience anal orgasms, orgasms with ejaculation (more about that in Chapter 17), multiple orgasms, and intense, earth-shattering, full-body orgasms.

The Night of One Thousand Hands

You can heighten your state of arousal by stimulating many of the pleasure centers. Because many women find the clitoris to be a sure-thing orgasm, stimulating the clitoris while doing just about anything else is highly erotic. The Pressing Position from the Kama Sutra involves the man pressing hard and close against her labia and clitoris. It's a variation of the missionary position, but the man is churning his lingam in the woman's yoni, rubbing up and around her clitoris. Women can play with experiencing the full range of sensations in the Pressing Position by raising their thighs and squeezing their partner between them.

Rear entry positions also allow for the man to heighten the woman's pleasure by stimulating her clitoris or her breasts. Rear entry can also stimulate the perineum and anus. Woman-on-top positions also allow for maximum stimulation of the clitoris and the perineum.

The Butterfly Pump

Women can heighten their lover's pleasure through muscular contractions of the vaginal walls. Think of it as an internal lingam massage. Focus on fluttering your vaginal muscles. Vary from gentle flutters to hard squeezes, almost like bites. This muscle is called your PC muscle, or pubococcygeus muscle. It's this simple: The stronger your PC muscle, the more intense orgasms you will have. Two positions noted in the Kama Sutra can be good for practicing your PC muscle skills: the Rising Position and the Pair of Tongs. In the Rising Position, the woman lies on her back, raising her legs straight up, above the man's shoulders. The man kneels before her, inserting his lingam in her yoni. By pressing her thighs together, she can squeeze his lingam, increasing the friction as he thrusts. The Pair of Tongs is a woman-on-top position, with the woman sitting astride the man, facing him, knees bent, pressing her thighs together and contracting her PC muscle.

Initiatress of Love

U.S. gynecologist Dr. A. H. Kegel recommended that women use PC muscle contractions to strengthen their yonis. He also developed PC muscle exercises for men to enhance the quality of penile contractions and the intensity of their orgasms.

Here are the basics of mastering the Butterfly Pump:

1. Next time you urinate, stop the urine flow midway through. This uses the PC muscle. Stop and start a few times.

2. Now lie down and insert one or two lubricated fingers into your yoni. Contract your PC muscles a few times. See if you can feel the contractions.

3. Flutter your vaginal walls by contracting the PC muscle really fast 10 times.

4. Envision your yoni as an elevator, making four stops. At the fourth, or highest, stop and hold it. Descend to the ground floor.

5. With your two fingers in your yoni, open them as if making a peace sign. See if you can use your PC muscles to push your fingers back together.

Explore. Play with this. Try pulsing moves, tightening and relaxing your PC muscle in quick, short pulsations. Try pumping moves: Tighten your PC muscle as you inhale, holding it for a count of six. Exhale, relaxing the muscle and bearing down as if you are urinating or having a bowel movement. Use visualizations such as this one suggested by Margo Anand in *The Art of Sexual Ecstasy* (see Appendix B): Imagine your yoni as a mouth sucking a ripe, juicy plum from the yoni opening to the inside, using the PC muscle. Or imagine you are milking your partner's lingam. Use rhythmic variations of breath to intensify your experiment.

The wonderful aspect of the Butterfly Pump and other PC exercises is that you can do them anywhere—at a traffic light, in line at the bank, or during a boring business meeting.

One technique for transforming your orgasm into a fuller experience is pressing on the perineum. During the moments of orgasm, you can contract your PC muscles. This recirculates your orgasmic energy up through the Inner Goddess Channel.

For men, PC exercise drills looks like this: Tweak the muscles between the base of the lingam and the anus. Try to twitch the head of your lingam. Squeeze your lingam muscles for three seconds, then relax for three seconds. Repeat this 10 times, about 3 times a day. When you can keep a tempo, you know you have strong lingam muscles.

The G-Spot

The G-spot (or Grafenberg spot) is a power spot on a woman's front vaginal wall, about two thirds the way up. Ironically, it was named after a man, Dr. Ernest Grafenberg. Pressing firmly on the G-spot with a finger or a penis can unleash a powerful erotic sensation in many women. The spot varies in size among women, but on average is about the size of a pea. It feels rippled or rougher in texture than the surrounding area. Both partners can feel it when it is highly aroused. Research indicates that not all women have a G-spot, but those who do know it's a sure thing for pleasure. The Taoists called it the Black Pearl.

With your partner, or on your own, see if you can find your G-spot with your fingers. Use the sacred breathing techniques we have drawn upon in previous chapters, synchronizing your inhale and exhale with his. Explore, spiraling your finger, then rubbing up and down. Then let your partner find your G-spot with his fingers.

Several positions allow for intense stimulation of the G-spot during intercourse, including the Level Feet Posture, Raised Feet Posture, and Refined Posture. In Level Feet Posture, the woman is lying on her back, the man kneeling. The man lifts the woman's lower torso, bracing himself against her. Her outstretched legs rest on his shoulders. Raised Feet Posture is a variation in which the woman bends her legs at the knees and draws them back. By raising the woman's hips, he can stimulate the G-spot. The Refined Posture is another variation: Instead of resting her legs on her partner's shoulders, she plants her feet on the mattress, raising her hips to meet him. Her partner lifts and supports her buttocks.

Other positions that allow the penis to reach the G-spot include using a pillow to support her buttocks or crouching on all fours and being penetrated from behind.

The exact location of your G-spot determines which positions will feel the most pleasurable to you. Women whose G-spot is deeper will not find man-on-top positions as satisfying because they won't be sufficiently aroused during intercourse. Try woman-on-top positions or the scissors position: The man lies on his right side, with the woman lying next to him on her back. Her right leg is between his thighs, and her left leg is on top of his thighs. He can stimulate her clitoris with his hand—or she can stimulate it on her own.

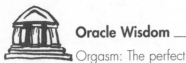

Oracle Wisdom

Orgasm: The perfect compromise between love and death.

—Robert Bak, U.S. poet

The other G-spot is the A-spot, a smooth spot located on the front wall of the vagina midway between the cervix and the G-spot. Researchers have found that 95 percent of women are massively aroused when the A-spot is stimulated. It's an excellent way to get really lubricated really fast. One study showed most women became moist within 10 minutes.

Lips That Hold Secrets

A woman's body holds many secrets. A sex goddess knows all of them in guiding her lover's exploration during a lovemaking session. Sacred sexual traditions, for example, emphasize that a woman's upper lip is one of the most erogenous zones of her body. That's because there is a nerve channel that connects her clitoris to her upper lip. It's called the Wisdom Conch-Like Nerve and is said to be a channel of orgasmic energy. It connects up from the center of her body to her throat chakra, curling over the back of her head through the center of her third-eye chakra to her upper lip. Both the Kama Sutra and the Ananga Ranga encourage men to gently nibble and suck the upper lip of their lovers. Women are invited to reciprocate on their lover's lower lip.

The shankini nadi rises through the body of a woman as a serpent with two mouths, from the yoni lotus to the upper lip. Through this conduit the Great Elixir moves.

Withholding Ejaculation

Orgasmic energy can go way beyond the genitals. From the traditions of Tantra and Tao, the secret lies in withholding ejaculation. Ejaculation is a short-lived genital release. It is fleeting. Transforming the energy, rather than dissipating it in ejaculation, can lift you to a near-psychedelic experience of orgasm of body, mind, spirit, and soul. If you have ever wondered whether there was more to ejaculation than this, the answer is: Oh yes!

A sex goddess knows that the key to enhancing her pleasure and her partner's pleasure is in moving the focus off ejaculation. She knows his orgasm will be stronger, when it comes, but by then, she will have had several intense orgasms. So the shift is: Ejaculation does not equal orgasm.

The Tao believes that withholding ejaculation leaves the man strengthened, his mind clearer, and his hearing and vision improved. His whole nervous system is energized, and blood flow is improved, contributing to a youthful, vigorous appearance.

Beyond that, there is a big payoff: Taoist master Mantak Chia and sexuality writer Douglas Abrams Arava remind us that more than 3,000 years ago, the Chinese wrote that men could achieve multiple orgasms by delaying and withholding ejaculation. According to Chia and Arava, sex researcher Alfred Kinsey found a similar phenomenon in the 1940s.

Initiatress of Love

The Taoists advocated a precise schedule for ejaculation that varied with a man's age, believing that it depleted energy reserves. A 20-year-old man was instructed to ejaculate no more than once every 4 to 5 days, while a 40-year-old man should not ejaculate more than 1 day out of every 8.

The Tao way of sex is not to let sexual energy control you. Instead, both partners control the sexual energy with conscious intent. The Taoists call the experience of moving sexual energy up through the body to the head "Riding the Tiger." There is no agenda of desires—to achieve, to release, to possess. You don't ask where it is going. You just ride.

This requires ultimate discipline, with sharp meditation skills and high sensory awareness.

Chia and Arava recommend these techniques for men:

♦ Strengthening PC muscles.

♦ Heightening sensitivity to arousal and mastering it.

◆ Staying in the moment (as opposed to dissociating or desensitizing to keep from "going over the edge").

◆ Understanding the stages of arousal. The Taoists called the four stages of erection "the attainments": lengthening, swelling, hardening, and heat.

◆ Using deep breathing to maintain control of arousal. Borrowing a bit from bio-rhythmic training, this is the skill of using breathing to reduce the heart rate.

◆ Visualizing drawing orgasmic energy up from your genitals, amplifying it, and pulling it up through all chakra energy centers.

Suspended in Rapture

Orgasm is glorious because it seems as though the universe has stopped. When the waves of orgasm ripple through the body, your brain floats away. You are weightless. You disconnect from the mundane. You are expanded. It may only be a few seconds of muscular contractions, but it seems as though it lasts forever. There is no more forward motion in time. There is no time. You exist in the joyful present.

Initiatress of Love

The classic Taoist texts suggested that it took 1,000 loving thrusts to satisfy a woman completely.

Another translation of *Tantra* from Sanskrit carries the meaning of expansion. The root word, *tan*, translates as "to expand, extend, spread, continue, spin out, weave." To tap into the energy of Tantra in sexual union is to tap into the constantly expanding energy of the universe. Think of Tantra as a cosmic weave, the interlocking threads of different thoughts, dreams, and visions of all experiences.

In this context, the orgasm can be viewed differently, through cosmic eyes. It's easy, then, to understand how vast we feel during the moment of orgasm. We feel, for a moment, so much larger than our small selves. For just an instant, we get a glimpse of our magnitude, and of our potential. The beauty of it is that it generally takes the union with another to bring us to that peak. But truth be told, even when we reach orgasm through self-pleasuring, we have achieved it through a sacred union—the union that honors ourselves and our connection to our creator.

In this respect, we'd like to reinvent the fairy tale of Sleeping Beauty. Perhaps the reason the kingdom slept for 100 years was because that first kiss between Prince Phillip and Briar Rose was the beginning of a century of Tantric sex. Imagine a whole kingdom held suspended in rapture. That's good karma.

A full-body orgasm can open you to another dimension. It's psychedelic. It's a fusion of sexual and spiritual energy. The waves of ecstasy just keep coming. Within the moment, you experience clarity. It's as though you are in an altered state, though not in the way that your senses are diminished. The opposite is true. Your senses have never functioned with more clarity.

If you are a visual person, you may see bursts of color on the screen of your mind. If you are an aural person, you may suddenly hear with pinpoint precision. A highly verbal person may hear clear directions and guidance. You may even experience a synesthesia, when a stimulus to one sense produces a sensation for another sense. You may hear colors and see sounds. The color purple may produce a scent.

When sexual and spiritual energies fuse, it is a feeling like no other. It's beyond words.

To cultivate these sensations so that you may have them more and more frequently during intercourse, start noting them in a journal. As with dreams, most everyone has dreams each night, but not all of us remember them in vivid detail. But when you start recording your dreams, you start remembering them. The same is true of the sensory experiences you may have during lovemaking. The more you bring them to awareness, the more activated they will become.

> **Initiatress of Love**
>
> Tantra originally developed in India about 5000 B.C.E. as a rebellion against the repressive moral codes of organized religions, particularly the ascetic practices of the Brahmins. At the time, many in society believed that sexuality had to be denied to attain enlightenment.

Goddess Wildness

The myth of Persephone is most often told from the viewpoint of the mourning mother, Demeter, whose grief at the kidnapping of her daughter to the underworld is so powerful that it sends the earth into barrenness. But let's not forget that Persephone goes back to her husband each year for six months. Now, Hades is one dark and dangerous dude, but it sounds like he is pretty irresistible. In the myth, Persephone must return to the underworld because she has partaken in the food of the dead—the pomegranate seeds Hades offered her.

But another way of seeing this story is that Persephone tasted passion—she tapped into her wildness. So when she returns to the underworld, it is not as captive, but as queen of the dark, dangerous, and wild. She flourishes, and has a child with Hades. Persephone's story is one of transformation from innocence to a woman coming into her power and passion. Let her story encourage you not to fear your own wildness but to cherish it. Let it encourage you to explore the mysteries in your partner and in yourself.

There is nothing more arousing than a woman who wants her pleasure; who asks for and openly seeks pleasure. Although this may seem a little self-centered, it's not. When you are focused on your own sexual needs, you are doing a great honor to your partner. You know what you want. This can fill him with gratitude—he knows how to please you—and heighten his desire. Like the Hopi fertility goddess Kokopell' Mana, who hiked up her skirts and distracted men running a race, there is nothing more riveting for a man than a woman who is making it absolutely clear what she wants.

Venus of Willendorf was big and bold. She just oozed sexuality. Imagine this goddess in sculpted form becoming incarnate and walking among us. Imagine the little swish to her hips. Imagine her breasts swaying openly as she walked naked. She would not have been heavy-footed and ponderous. As she talked to you, she would have added that little swirl of her upper body, leaning forward with her breasts. She had her curves, and she was proud of them. The same goes for the Moroccan spirit of Aisha Qandisha, with her pendulous breasts.

All in all, taking care of your own needs is something that only makes you more desirable. When you have your own creative work and your own sex life with yourself, you come to a sexual union as a mature, fulfilled woman—with so much more to give. You shed your inhibitions about deserving pleasure, because you know what you want and you know you deserve the best. You shed your inhibitions about initiating sex. Allow yourself to receive pleasure without focusing on the need to reciprocate. Just feel it. Take it. It is being offered. And learn to ask for what you want.

Extending pleasure is an extension of these practices. In the moment of union, ask yourself how good you can stand it. Ask if it can be more. Imagine yourself opening your arms to the sky, receiving more and more. Imagine a wave rippling over your body, up through your perineum to your crown, out your arms and legs. Imagine successive waves, each growing in intensity. And make noise. Moan. Scream. Sing.

The Least You Need to Know

- Channeling your sexual energy into a full-body experience is one of the central principles of Tantric sex.

- By focusing on the present moment and heightening your sensual focus, you can experience a deeper, more prolonged ecstasy.

- Opening up the sacrum through pelvic rocking, movement, dance, and yoga can open your sexual energy centers.

- There are many ways to experience orgasm. For women, it can be in the yoni, the clitoris, or the anus. Men can experience orgasm in the lingam, the prostate, or the anus.

- Both men and women can enhance their sexual pleasure by practicing the Butterfly Pump, a contraction of the PC muscles.

- Like the goddesses Persephone, Kali, Kokopell' Mana, and the Venus of Willendorf, there is nothing more arousing than a woman who announces her desire for pleasure.

Chapter 16

Embraces and Soft Kisses

In This Chapter

- ◆ After the orgasm: now what?
- ◆ Rituals for concluding sacred sexual union
- ◆ Back to ordinary life
- ◆ Keep the faith, as a whole individual and as a sacred couple

After the intense bonding and melding of selves that takes place during sacred sexual union, what happens when it's all over? Do you throw your clothes back on and get back to the office? Turn over and fall asleep?

Part of sacred sexual union is an awareness and understanding of what happens in the moments, and hours, after physical/spiritual release. With "regular sex," you may feel pleasantly tired or invigorated, and that's about it. With sacred sex, your intense physical and spiritual bond is anything but over. If you never thought much about it other than "on to the next thing," this chapter is for you.

The Aftermath

After orgasm, men's bodies and women's bodies react differently. When men ejaculate, they are incapable, in most cases, of becoming aroused again for a while. Their bodies need to replenish and rest. After ejaculating, men tend to feel very calm, serene, and safe. They feel like all is right with the world. But as for touching, cuddling, and kissing, well … for many men, that's like eating another meal after they just had dessert!

Women, on the other hand, respond differently. Although some women feel "spent" after a good orgasm, many women do not. Because they can have many orgasms in a row, women's bodies don't need to rest or collapse in exhaustion after an orgasm. They can keep going. A sex goddess may not be ready to stop, just because her partner has ejaculated, and may feel frustrated that he has suddenly moved on, mentally, to other things (including that good night's sleep!). Even when no longer sexually aroused, many women prefer to remain in intimate physical contact with their partners for a period of time following sex. The release of oxytocin in the body following orgasm fills women with feelings of affection. Following sacred sexual communion, the bond between a sex goddess and her partner is even more deeply solidified, and remaining in contact seems the most natural thing to do.

When a man learns to orgasm without ejaculation—something that is a big part of ancient rituals for sacred sex—he reacts differently. He isn't "spent" and may continue to feel extremely affectionate and physical with his partner. He may also be able to experience many orgasms in a row. However, even after ejaculation, men who have just engaged in sacred sexuality with their partners are likely to feel so much closer to them that they will enjoy extended physical contact, conversation, and sharing.

At the same time, many women feel "spent" after orgasm and are ready to roll over and go to sleep while their partners may desire more closeness. Recognizing the importance for bonding time after sexual communion is an important part of sacred sex, which doesn't end with the ending of the orgasm. Honor the sacred union by respecting the important, relaxed, serene post-orgasm time together, honoring each other and your intimacy.

Oracle Wisdom

The Mother of Ten Thousand Things is the Chinese creator of the world and all life. In the Chinese philosophy of Taoism, she represented the feminine principle, or yin aspect of all reality. Even if you don't have children, part of being a sex goddess is to honor your inner creator. All that you "give birth" to—love, ideas, words, art, relationships—makes you a mother, too. Look within and recognize your own feminine principle, your own inner Mother of Ten Thousand Things.

Ritualizing this post-sexual contact is a beautiful way to carry your feelings of closeness and unity past those moments of ecstasy. Rituals can foster that sense of safety and security that comes from intimate contact. They can bring you closer together and create a tradition in your relationship, whether that tradition is simply a series of gentle kisses after lovemaking, a certain shared favorite food, or a stylized bathing ritual.

Winding-Down Rituals

As you and your partner lie together, arms intertwined and bodies humming with the serenity that follows ecstatic pleasure, you may feel particularly close to each other, as if you understand each other just a little better than you did before, as if you barely need to communicate out loud, as if it is difficult to tell where one of you stops and the other begins. This beautiful feeling is a natural result of sacred sex and it need not end. You can prolong it for as long as you like.

A sex goddess knows the power of ritual and will probably enjoy inventing post-sex rituals in addition to the rituals she enjoys before and during sexual play. Here are some ideas for rituals to follow sacred sexual communion. Pick your favorites, or try them all! Let these get you started, then use your imagination to invent rituals and routines that suit the individual needs and personalities of both you and your partner.

Double Shavasana

After a rigorous yoga practice, it is traditional to practice a final pose called *shavasana*, or Corpse Pose. This basic pose of deep relaxation is designed to simulate the complete lack of tension in the body of a corpse, as well as the spiritual state of being freed from the physical bonds of the material world. After sacred sex, as the two of you continue to bask in the glow of your unity, a double shavasana pose can help to solidify your bond. In the esoteric Tibetan Buddhist practice, death and sex were often equated, orgasm being like death in the way that it frees the mind from the bonds of the impermanent material world. As you and your partner lie together in this pose, imagine how you have, just for a short while, escaped the material world for a higher spiritual reality that transcends the separation between bodies, even the very notion of bodies, to discover true transcendent unity.

To practice double shavasana, one of you should lie comfortably on your back, legs outstretched and relaxed, feet about shoulder-width apart, arms loosely at your sides. The other partner (perhaps the lighter partner, depending on what makes you both comfortable) lies, face down, directly on top of the first. Rest a pillow in the crook of the bottom partner's shoulder to support the top partner's head. The top partner may rest his or her legs on top of the bottom partner's, or on the sides, or with one in the middle and one on either side, whichever is more comfortable. However, there should be as much contact between equivalent body parts as possible: chest to chest, hips to hips, shoulders to shoulders, arms on arms, palms on palms.

Rest in this position as you both consciously focus on complete and total relaxation. Imagine melting into each other so completely that you are a single being containing all the balancing elements of the universe, both yin and yang in perfect harmony. Let your entire body go limp: feet, calves, knees, thighs, hips, abdomen, chest, shoulders, elbows, hands, neck, and head. Visualize becoming one with your partner. Stay here for as long as is comfortable, feeling your energies mingling and imprinting on each other.

Initiatress of Love

Many yoga poses lend themselves to two people. Try sitting back to back, cross-legged, or on your knees and linking arms for a brief period of meditation. Or lie down on the floor on your backs, feet pointed in opposite directions, the crowns of your heads touching. Lift your hips up and support them with your hands, elbows plant on the floor, in a shoulder stand. Bring your knees, lower legs, and the tops of your feet together over your heads. (Be sure you have enough spinal and neck strength and flexibility to do this comfortably.)

Oracle Wisdom

Was this the face that launched a thousand ships,
And burnt the topless towers of Ilium?
Sweet Helen, make me immortal with a kiss!

—From *Doctor Faustus* by Christopher Marlowe (1564–1593), English dramatist

The Ritual of the Nine Kisses

After orgasm, make it a tradition to give each other nine long, slow, tender, nurturing kisses before getting out of bed (or rising from wherever you may be). In Taoism, nine is the most sacred and potent number, called the Yang number, and is believed to have mystical powers. If nine kisses seem like too few, make your magic number any multiple of nine. Eighteen kisses? Twenty-seven kisses? Ninety kisses? Don't stop if you want to keep kissing! (And if it gets you started all over again, well, you wouldn't be the first couple to think you are finished and find you aren't quite …)

Hydrotherapy Ritual

After a long and strenuous session of lovemaking, we may find ourselves happily sweaty and a little bit sticky! To help transition back to the duties of your day, you will probably plan on taking a bath or a shower, so why not take one together? Even if you aren't ideally equipped with a shower containing two showerheads or an oversized claw-footed bathtub, you can still make cozy room for two. Take turns tenderly cleansing each other's bodies with soap and body brushes, sponges and hands, whether swapping turns under the shower spray or sharing a warm tub of bubbles.

Rite of Refueling

All that physical exertion can really make a sex goddess hungry! Sharing a snack and a cool drink of water or a relaxing glass of wine after sexual bonding is a nice way to relax and wind down together. Feed each other or just share food from one plate. Rehydrate with juicy fruits like pears and apples. Indulge in some really good chocolate or a plate of fine cheese and crispy crackers. And don't forget plenty of cool fresh water to help cool you down! Toast your sacred bond, toast each other, toast the beautiful night or the beautiful day. Enjoy each other's company.

Initiatress of Love

According to the Kama Sutra, after sexual communion, the lovers should cleanse themselves and then apply perfumes and scented oils to each other's bodies, embrace, and speak pleasantly to each other. They should share a drink from the same cup and feed each other sweetmeats, fruit, and other delicacies, to properly conclude their union.

Pillow Talk

Talking after sex is somehow easier, freer, and more intimate than talking at other times. When both you and your partner have lowered your defenses and feel closer and more supportive of each other, you can feel free to say things you might not otherwise say. After sacred sex, to maintain the energy between you, talk about subjects related to your experience, to positive appreciation of each other, and expressing affection, rather than bringing up unpleasant or stressful subjects like disagreements or mundane concerns like bills, to-do lists, social or time commitments, and other worries. Let this time continue to be about the two of you, basking in the warm glow of your union.

212 **Part 5:** After the Loving

To help you focus your pillow talk in a positive direction that promotes continuing sacred contact, here are some conversation starters:

♦ I think my favorite part of this experience was when we …

♦ I especially loved it when you …

♦ What was your favorite part?

♦ When we were at the peak of intensity, I experienced …

♦ This is something I love about you …

♦ Will you tell me something you love about me?

♦ Just thinking about the way you [fill in the blank] still makes my knees weak.

♦ If we could go anywhere in the world right now, where would you want to go?

♦ What do you think is the most romantic thing we've ever done?

♦ Remember when you touched me here? [touch] I really liked that. Will you do it again sometime?

♦ I love looking at your …

♦ I love it when you say …

♦ I love the feel of your …

♦ I love hearing you …

♦ What would you like to try next time?

And don't forget, humor is a powerful way to bond. Keep your sense of humor, before, during, and after lovemaking. Keep your hearts light and enjoy each other. No need to get so serious!

Ritual of Silence

Sometimes, words are inadequate to express our feelings. Sitting or resting together, holding hands or entwined in each other's arms, and making a conscious effort *not* to speak for a set period of time, such as 10 minutes or even half an hour, can urge us to focus inward rather than outward. It can help us feel rather than analyze our experience, and sense the presence and touch of our partners rather than focus on what they say or even how they look.

Together in stillness, reflect on your experience of sacred sex and how it has changed the way you feel right now, in your body, touching your partner. Don't worry about putting the feelings into words or communicating them. Your partner will "hear" you and you don't have to utter a single syllable.

After sex, as you melt into each other, having reached the blissful center of sacred union, gaze soulfully into each other's eyes. There are no words … just you and your lover.

As you lie together in stillness and embrace after sexual union, you may find your mind wandering to what you have to do next. Just as in meditation, keeping your mind directed to a single focus takes training. When you are focusing on winding down with your beloved and you find your mind straying to other subjects, gently direct it back to the object of your affection until you are both ready to transition back into your day.

Ritual of Gratitude

For some couples, gratitude after sexual union is an unspoken "given," but why not express your gratitude anyway? If you both agree to say "Thank you," sincerely and graciously and with your whole heart, you will verbalize and bring to the forefront of your consciousness the recognition that you made yourselves completely open and vulnerable, and were completely accepted by each other. You gave each other profound pleasure and a transcendent experience. You continued to forge the deep emotional connection you have together.

Whether you say "Thank you for sharing your body and your spirit with me," or "Thank you for giving yourself to me and accepting my giving to you," or "Thank you for that mind-blowing orgasm," or just "Thank you, my love," this ritual of gratitude is a lovely and comforting conclusion to the sacred time and space you have just shared.

Back to the Salt Mines

Eventually, of course, you'll need to get up and get moving. We all have things to do, tasks to accomplish, people to see, e-mails to send, things to clean, work and family relationships to maintain, money to earn, and bills to pay. Yet the miraculous thing about sacred sex is that we can take the experience with us, back out into the "real world," so we remain suffused with a certain inner tranquility we might not have felt before, and a warm, loving knowledge that out there, close by or even far away, we have someone who truly knows us because we have become a part of each other.

> ### Initiatress of Love
>
> In the ancient Eastern traditions, sex wasn't something kept hush-hush behind closed doors, or something nobody ever talked about. Sex was simply another part of life, like eating and sleeping, meditating and working, playing and creating. And like these other things, it could be engaged in mindlessly, or it could be practiced with reverence, presence, and a refined and disciplined technique that could elevate it beyond the mundane to something truly life-enhancing.

Rather than bringing your ordinary life into the bedroom, we suggest taking your attitudes about sacred sexuality out into the other realms of your life. If you eat, sleep, play, and work with the same mindful, reverent attention with which you practice sacred sex, you will be creating an extraordinary existence for yourself. That's what practices like Tantra are really all about—freeing the mind to discover what lies beyond our preconceptions and assumptions about life and work and each other. When you discard the notion of separateness and embrace the notion of unity in all aspects of your life, sacred sexuality becomes sacred existence.

Keeping Your Relationship Sacred, 24/7

Of all things to keep sacred beyond the confines of the bedroom, your relationships are the most important. Possessions, money, your job, your status—all these are cultural constructs to keep society moving along at an agreeable pace with minimal discord. But you may notice that with the regular practice of sacred sexuality, your perceptions begin to change.

In yoga, namaste is a traditional pose in which you hold your hands, palms together in a prayer position, in front of your heart. This pose means you are honoring the light in others as you honor it in yourself. That inner light you share with other sentient beings is the source of the unity sacred sexuality helps you to apprehend. It is the source of ecstasy because in this light, all difference falls away and we are all one oceanic pulse of love energy. In other words, the practice of sacred sexuality will help you to understand that love truly is the meaning of life.

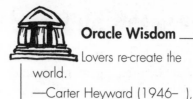

Oracle Wisdom

Lovers re-create the world.
—Carter Heyward (1946–), U.S. Episcopal priest

When this happens, the people in your life take on new significance. Sure, you love your parents, you love your kids, you love your friends and relatives and, of course, your partner. But to see these other people through the eyes of the sacred lover is to see them all as perfect beings lit from within by the universal energy that animates us all. Annoying habits don't seem quite so annoying. When a friend or a relative is kind or generous or simply happy, the sacred lover notices and feels a spark of inner joy because the practice of kindness and the feelings of happiness within one of us can ripple out through all of us.

Of all these connections, your partner—the one with whom you have made sacred sexuality a regular practice—can be your most intimate and valued link to this inner light. Together, you are exploring what sexual energy can do to your body and your spirit. This kind of high intimacy can keep you closely bonded no matter what happens in your life, if you let yourself stay in touch with it and with each other.

It's not always easy to carry that afterglow feeling with us when we head to the office or off to do errands or into the bathroom to clean the toilet! In fact, it's impractical to think you could hold on to that feeling all the time. But what you can hold on to is the *knowledge* and memory of that feeling, and the ability to get that feeling back when you next come together in sacred union.

You can keep your sacred connection strong in other ways, too. Many of these involve the power of ritual, which can shape your attitudes and refresh your commitment to each other on a regular basis. Others involve agreements you make with each other, and with yourself. Let's look more closely at some important ways to keep your relationship sacred all day, every day.

Beyond Taboos

If you are in the habit of telling other people personal things before you share them with your partner, consider re-thinking your habit. If you make your partner your primary confidante and tell him about things that happen in your life before anyone else finds out, it will help both of you to feel prioritized and closer.

Agreements for Sacred Couples

You and your partner are a sacred couple. You might not always feel very sacred, but you are. Together, balancing your energies, your yin and yang, your dark and light, you form a completed energy that can take you to new levels of understanding. Honor this bond all the time by making these agreements with each other. Tell them to each other verbally, shake hands, write them down, and sign them like a contract, or do whatever seems right to you—including change what they are to suit you—but make them and be empowered as a couple.

We Agree to Worship Each Other

In a sacred relationship where two people are working on total trust and intimacy, agreeing to respect, honor, cherish, and worship each other is important. When we say "worship," we don't mean your partner should take the place of some transcendent deity in your religious practice. But on the other hand, we do suggest that you both seek to search out, recognize, and even bow down in humility to the sex goddess and sex god within each other.

> **Oracle Wisdom**
>
> Inari is the Japanese vixen goddess invoked to maintain successful love relationships. Call on her to bless your relationship after sexual communion.

Also important for this agreement is that the worship be mutual. If you both see the inner divinity of the other, you are seeing the inner divinity within yourself as well. Remember that inner light, the one we all share? This is what you seek out in each other when you agree to worship each other. See it, honor it, love it, worship it, and grow eternally closer.

We Agree to Be Honest

Although what is "true" may seem to change from moment to moment in your lives, let your partner be the one person with whom you share everything honestly and openly. If you never have to worry about hiding anything from each other, you won't have any barriers or walls to keep you from total union, body and soul.

Honesty can be tricky. Do you tell your partner you think he looks horrible in that shirt or that her new haircut is not at all flattering? Well, maybe not in so many words—why be hurtful? The way you choose to speak to each other is a big part of honesty. But be honest about who you are, what you want, and also what you love and cherish about your partner. Sometimes, you may need to tell your partner something that might hurt. But if you build a strong bond of trust, you can talk about it and get to the reasons behind what happened. Knowing you can trust your partner to be honest with you can do amazing things for your relationship. You'll find you don't have to play games, tiptoe around each other's feelings, or be anyone other than who you really are, because you know that is the person your partner loves. Honesty is tough, but it is a powerful glue for a sacred relationship.

Oracle Wisdom

The truth doesn't hurt. Only lies hurt.

—Steven Sashen, author and teacher

We Agree to Accept Each Other for Who We Are

Isn't it funny (or maybe not so funny) how we are always trying to change other people? Truly loving someone unconditionally means loving that person for who he or she is *right now*. Sure, sometimes your partner is going to make you angry, or frustrated, or irritated. Sometimes you will think, "If only he could be like *this*," or "If only she would stop doing *that*." This agreement doesn't tell you to stop feeling those things, because we know perfectly well that you can't stop feeling those things. However, it asks you to notice when you feel those things and then consider letting them go.

Do you wish your partner would listen to you? You can ask him to listen to you, and you can also accept that he is the kind of person who is sometimes single-mindedly focused on something and you might have to wait to have a conversation until he is ready to pay attention. You wish your partner would quit telling you to put your dirty laundry in the laundry basket instead of on the floor? What if she never stops asking you that? What would happen if you just let go of the irritation you feel and accept that she likes to have a neat bedroom? Maybe you'll decide to start putting your laundry in the basket and maybe you won't, but the point is to accept your partner for exactly who she is and what he does, right here, right now.

Working to look at your partner for exactly who he or she is and loving what you see is crucial for an intimate bond. And remember, it doesn't mean you and your partner won't argue. It just means opening your eyes to who you are *really* with, not that made-up person you keep imagining your partner might transform into one day. Live in the right-now, and love will expand beyond your dreams.

We Agree to Do the Best We Can

This is a very important agreement to make. Sometimes you will hurt your partner's feelings without intending to, or even on purpose. Sometimes you will behave badly,

Beyond Taboos

If you're wondering whether you should say or do something that might hurt your partner, imagine saying or doing it, then imagine your partner's possible reactions. If you think you might be hurtful, ask yourself whether the action or words are really worth it. Maybe they still are, but at least your decision will be made with consciousness and forethought. Let love guide your actions and words.

Oracle Wisdom

The First Woman, according to Persian myth, lived inside a reed so entwined with her lover that they seemed to be a single body. Nothing in the universe existed except for this reed, containing the joined pair. At last, a god found them and separated them, keeping them apart for 50 years. When they were finally reunited, they gave birth to children who populated the world.

and sometimes your partner will behave badly. But if you agree to both try your best to be the best *you* possible at that moment, then you can also each accept the other. You can say, "I may not like how you are acting" or even "I don't like the way I am acting." Yet you can also say, "That's the best he can do right now so that's okay," or "I am doing what I need to do right now, so that's okay." This kind of mutual acceptance that each of you will try your best builds a bond of trust.

Choose not to tell your girlfriends about the confidence your partner has shared with you. Choose not to complain to your parents about things you don't like about your partner. Keep your relationship sacred in your mind and heart, whether you are together in sexual union or miles apart.

We Agree to Physical Contact Every Day

When possible, you and your partner should touch each other as much as possible. Kiss, embrace each other, hold hands, rub each other's shoulders, put your arms around each other. Our bodies are connected with our minds, feelings, and spirits, so closeness in one of these areas vibrates into the other areas, drawing us closer as a whole. The more you are in physical contact with your partner, the closer and more intimate you will feel on all levels of your life. Even when you aren't planning to have sex, let your bodies be united in touch. No matter how long you have been together, keep holding on to each other and remember your unity, your balancing energies, your divine partnership. Let touch be that string around your finger, that "reminder note" of who you are, both individually and together.

Remember Who You Are

Finally, as a fully realized sex goddess within a sacred partnership, it's important to remember who you are as an individual. This may sound contradictory to what we've

said before, because the nature of sacred sexuality is to balance complementary energies and recognize that the two of you can come together into a single unified force.
But that doesn't mean your existence gets subsumed into anyone else's! In the same
way, your partner should remember who he is as an individual.

When you are strongly bonded to someone, it's easy to feel like you are missing a part
of yourself when you are apart. Yet just as you are whole together as a couple, you are
also whole apart. The divine light in you shines in all sentient beings and each is as
individual as a wave in the ocean. We all may come from the same great ocean of
energy and we rise up as individuals for a short while before sinking back down into
the ocean, but each wave is its own completely unique incarnation for some time—for
the span of a human life.

Becoming "one" with someone else, in other words, doesn't mean you lose anything
at all. You are still you: a brilliant, shining sex goddess emanating the energy of
creativity, the source of life, the very nature of reality. You have behind you Gaia,
the earth mother; Kali, giver and destroyer of life; Aphrodite, goddess of love and
passion; Shakti, the source of all creation; Foam Woman, the Native American creatrix with 20 breasts to nurse the world; Brigid, Celtic goddess of fertility and poetry;
Devi, Indian goddess and avenger of evil; Diana, Greek goddess of the moon who
belonged to no man; Radha, Hindu goddess of infinite love and sacred partner
to husband Krishna; Mysterious Female, the Chinese creator of all life and the root
of heaven and earth from whose womb the universe was born; and a hundred thousand other sex goddesses who were and are and continue to be completely and wholly
their own beings, whether they find unity with a partner or not.

Only in finding this inner light, whole and complete on its own, can you truly bond
completely and without barriers to a partner who is, himself, also whole and perfect.
Alone, you are miraculous. Together, you can be transcendent.

The Least You Need to Know

- After orgasm, both women and men may continue to desire close contact, or
  may be ready to move on to sleep or the next thing. In sacred sex, a period of
  bonding following orgasm helps to strengthen the sacred connection.

- Rituals such as sharing food, bathing each other, or lying together in silence can
  help to structure and establish the final stage of sacred sexual union.

- Sacred sex isn't separate from your regular life, and you can carry your feelings
  of openness and your recognition of the unity of all things into other areas of
  your life, such as family relationships and work.

◆ Keep your relationship sacred all the time, whether you are having sex or not, by agreeing to always worship the divine aspect within each other, to be honest, not to criticize or hurt each other, and to keep in close physical touch that reminds both of you of the physical, mental, and spiritual connection you share.

◆ Maintaining your sense of self as a whole and perfect individual will make you better able to bond as a whole and unified couple.

Chapter 17

Afterglow: Enjoying Your Goddess Energy

In This Chapter

- Fire and rain: yang and yin energy of orgasm

- Heart energy and holding on to the moment

- Total acceptance, total glow

- Female ejaculation

- The space between you

You never want this feeling to end. And it doesn't have to. For women, it's natural that orgasms—or multiple orgasms—continue to direct and empower energy flow long after the orgasm takes place. As the energy of orgasm blooms in you, you can hold its glow, extending your pleasure and your partner's. Staying in the afterglow means remaining connected to each other—and to the ancient and natural power of spiritual and sexual ecstasy.

That said, you might ask, "What afterglow?" You might wonder if we were referring to the split-second after the man ejaculates with an ultimate groan of pleasure, then rolls over and falls asleep—snoring, to boot. The answer is a resounding: No!

The Energy of Orgasm: Fire and Rain

The Taoists describe male sexual energy as fire (yang) and female sexual energy as water (yin). As you learned in the previous chapter, male sexual energy is easily ignited, but also quickly extinguished. When he's done, he's done. Women take longer to get aroused, but experience a longer, lasting energy that builds in waves. Taoists seek to harmonize male and female energy arcs by teaching men to delay ejaculation. Some teachers, such as Mantak Chia (author of *The Multi-Orgasmic Couple* and other books), believe men have multiple orgasms, too.

A man is depleted after ejaculation. Really. There is a physiological explanation for the reason he conks out before he can mutter, "Love ya, babe." But Tantric and Taoist teachers believe that you can elongate the timeline between arousal and orgasm—and most important, between orgasm and ejaculation. It only makes sense that you also can stretch the energy out beyond the peak.

For a man, sexual energy starts in the genitals and rises, like a flame, to his heart and head. When a man ejaculates quickly, the energy never rises from his root and sexual chakras to his upper chakras. The sexual energy burns up like a rocket booster. Not allowing his sexual energy to flame out is the real secret to extending pleasure and expanding to ecstasy for men.

For a woman, her sexual energy needs to be brought *to* her yoni from the extremities of her body. That's why foreplay—and afterglow—are crucial. A woman needs to remember that the goal is to bring her partner's sexual energy out of his lingam and through the rest of his body. Translated, for men, this means: Do not move directly to go. For women, it means: Start at go. Move from there.

Understanding the differences in your sexual energy dynamic and your partner's can be the key to extending and expanding the afterglow of orgasm. If men are inherently "fire" and women are inherently "water," then your common goal is not to "extinguish" him too quickly. You want to keep him at a slow burn. Too much stoking of the fire just sends him over the edge—leaving you behind. Yet your yin (water) energy is as soothing to him as a fine-mist rain. You cool him down. You keep the fire from raging out of control.

If you'll remember in Chapter 14, we defined combinations of sexual energy using astrology's elements. One way to balance his yang (fire) with your yin (water) is to add the other elements into your lovemaking and afterglow.

The air element mixed with fire heightens desire and passion; air can rouse the sexual energy and bring you to the next level of orgasm. The air element evokes the angels, messengers, and enlightenment. Mixed with sexual energy, it is the vehicle for enlightenment through ecstasy. The air element is what we are striving for in this intoxicating mix of fire and rain, as two lovers channel their sexual energy up through their chakras, amplifying it through their entire bodies. The air element brings that energy up to the crown chakra of spiritual enlightenment. It can bring on the orgasm of the soul. You and your lover can feel orgasmic pleasure for hours afterward and still feel connected to each other when apart.

Earth mixed with fire can deepen the sensual pleasure. Think of "earth" energy as the fire pit that creates the ideal conditions for the fire, yet contains it. Think of the earthenware bowl that conducts heat to the pot of water, which boils, producing steam. "Earth" is the conduit.

Every movement can be defined as an elemental movement—air, fire, earth, water. It can define how you touch, and where you touch. Some combinations are more stimulating, while others are more harmonizing.

We have brainstormed a few key words for each element, and encourage you to add a few ideas of your own.

Fire	Earth	Air	Water
Rising	Deepening	Opening	Falling
Intensifying	Healing	Stimulating	Flowing
Creating friction	Enveloping	Expanding	Harmonizing
_____	_____	_____	_____
_____	_____	_____	_____
_____	_____	_____	_____

How can these translate into the afterglow? You send healing water love with your eyes. You send deepening earth love tongue to tongue. You emanate lightness and expansion when you are in face-to-face positions. And the fire energy? Well, that part is obvious, isn't it?

Knowing what stimulates your partner *too much* can guide you in controlling his ejaculation, allowing you—and him, too—to orgasm multiple times. Alternating shallow and deep thrusts during intercourse is a way to balance fire with earth energy, keeping things intense, but not too stimulated. Slow, deep thrusts allow the man to have the most ejaculatory control while the woman experiences the greatest satisfaction. By not moving in and out so much, the man does not overly arouse, but the woman is highly stimulated, with deep sensations along her vaginal walls—ideally the G-spot—but is also aroused by his pubic bone pressing on her clitoris.

Harmonizing moves are those in which similar body parts touch—lips to lips, genitals to genitals. To stimulate, touch lips to ears, tongue to genitals. To open and expand, switch positions. The healing energy of "water moves" keeps the flow going. Often the partner who is on top is the giving partner, bringing forth the sexual energy of the other. Long, soothing strokes are comforting. They invite your partner to feel safe. They can summon sexual energy in your partner to be expressed in a healing way. They can bring a lovemaking session to a nice close as you sink into the glow.

> **Oracle Wisdom** _____
>
> Pele is the Hawaiian goddess of the continuously erupting Kilauea volcano. Fiery, yet gentle, Kilauea rarely throws out clouds of ash or spews plumes of fire. The lava spouts into the air in fiery fountains, or bubbles out quietly to flow in rivers, gliding to the sea. When lava meets ocean, steam clouds billow. The gentle, hot lava continually changes the shoreline—as do two lovers who dance in the afterglow of love. Pele is also the mother goddess, the fire goddess, and the goddess of dance. Many of the myths about Pele revolve around her establishing a home at the Kilauea volcano and sending for her lover Lohiau to share her home.

Woman of Many Pools

Acupuncturist Felice Dunas (author of *Passion Play*) has a wonderful way of describing the way a woman is aroused. Like the energy of yin, which is falling, sexual energy in a woman pours through her body from her head to her heart, finally dropping to her genitals. That is why most women must open their minds and hearts before they open sexually. Mental and emotional connections must develop first before the body responds.

A sex goddess knows she is a fountain of seven magic pools filled with energy, starting at the crown chakra and trickling down through the third-eye, throat, and heart chakras, then spilling into the lower chakras. Like a waterfall, that enlivening, creative energy gathers speed as it falls down.

If we think of a woman's sexual energy as moving down through her chakras and a man's sexual energy moving up, then we can meet each other halfway—at the heart chakra. As it would happen, the heart chakra is the chakra associated with the water element. Perhaps these two Greek nymphs already knew that. They both connected with their lovers through water—through the heart.

Arethusa was a Greek wood nymph who ruled the springs and fountains. She was hotly pursued by the river god Alpheus until Artemis, goddess of the hunt and the forest, got wind of it. Artemis changed Arethusa into a spring on the island of Ortygia, where she was forever joined with Alpheus. These were two lovers with a water-water connection. In another Greek story, Dryope was a fountain nymph who was so taken with Hylas that she lured him into her fountain, where he disappeared.

Chakra energy rises from the lovers as their union enters full blossom.

In the Tantra tradition, it is believed that the sacred union of lovemaking causes secretions from the pineal and pituitary glands in the head, which fall as Drops of Wisdom. These Drops of Wisdom emanate from the heart chakra, nourishing and transforming the body and mind, empowering both lovers with transcendence.

Meditate together, using a chakra balancing visualization to guide you. Sit across from each other, holding hands to form a circle. As you breathe deeply, begin to synchronize your breath. Guide your energy to rise from your root to your crown. Let it fall from your crown to your root. Notice which chakras are not vibrating with as much energy as others. Direct your breath to them. Continue breathing as you direct your energy flow up, then down again. Notice the energy around your heart chakra. Visualize this energy connecting and uniting you, each time you channel your energy up, then down.

Meeting in the middle—at the heart chakra—is also the meeting of heaven and earth. Yang is thought of as the energy of heaven, while yin is the energy of earth. It is here, with the energy of love, that the sexual energy arcs of the man and woman intersect. It is why we can connect so powerfully when we are so very different.

The Energy of the Moment

Let love be the operative word in savoring the moments of afterglow. Let yourself experience the energy of a wide-open heart chakra.

Being held and caressed in no great hurry and with no particular agenda may be the most sensual experience of all. If you're not ready to let go of your intimate connection, skin- on-skin contact, simply for the essence of the experience, provides some of the most exhilarating sensations imaginable. After orgasm, spend time luxuriating in each other's touch by …

- ◆ Clasping and caressing your partner. Let your hands play. Caress your lover with your fingertips. Touch him lightly all over.

- ◆ Giving a 10-minute hand massage. Stroke and caress each finger. Clasp each finger, then the palm. Do compressions from the wrist up the arm. Rub each fingertip, each knuckle, each finger-pad in the palm. Spiral up each finger. Slide your fingers over the top of his hand. Cup your hands gently over his.

- ◆ Cuddling.

- ◆ Gliding your fingertips up and down each other's backs and torsos.

- ◆ Spooning. Lying side by side, you curl up together. The inside partner tucks his or her buttocks into the genitals of the outside partner.

Initiatress of Love

Taoists believe that sexual energy makes up about 25 percent of our life-force energy. Denying sexual energy means losing access to a vital source of energy for emotional and spiritual growth.

You'll want to bring your touch back into harmonizing (water) touch, touching like to like: lips to lips, hands to hands, bellies to bellies, genitals to genitals. This gentle touch connection may be exactly what you're craving for to prolong the experience of your lovemaking until you both relax into satisfied bliss and are ready to stop.

The Energy of Elevation

After orgasm, your skin glows. Your blood flow increases. Your hair is shining, your eyes are radiant. You are light. Practically speaking, regular orgasms can improve your cardiovascular health, enhance body tone, and relieve menstrual cramps. Really!

For a woman in the glow, her body becomes a resonating chamber. Remember, in Sanskrit, yoni means womb or abode. In those few seconds of orgasm, some Tantra practitioners believe, you are back in the womb. You have merged with your Source.

After orgasm, you can feel it in your whole body. Your fingertips and scalp tingle. Your ovaries and uterus vibrate with aliveness. In the moments of orgasm, you know just how perfect your body is. You completely accept it. It is perfect. It has just bestowed upon you a magnificent gift.

At its essence, orgasm is total acceptance, of yourself, of your lover, of your creator. Tantra teaches that the physical body is a temple, a sanctified realm that is unparalleled in any earthly temple. The body embraces all the elements of air, water, fire, and earth, and the Tantric description of it is quite poetic. Tantric teachings equated the channeling of sexual energy upward with the summoning of creative energy. It was believed the fire of love illuminated the temple of the body. Tantric teacher Saraha Doha referred to the body as having sacred rivers. Within it, the whole universe and all creation lies. "Here are the sun and moon, as well as all the pilgrimage places. I have not encountered another temple as blissful as my own body," he wrote.

Initiatress of Love

The Taoists thought love was good medicine. They referred to sex as the "human herb." If you had been lucky enough to have been born in an East Asian country in ancient times, you might have even had a Taoist physician prescribe several weeks of lovemaking to cure your ailment. He might even specify a certain position. This is taking a medically excused absence from work to a whole new level!

Contagious Ecstasy

One of the most powerful aspects of learning how to revel in the temple of the body and expand the energy of orgasm beyond the moment of orgasm is the contagious nature of the ecstasy you experience. When positive, ecstatic, blissful energy emanates from you and from your partner, it also emanates outward, toward the world and toward others. Ecstasy really is contagious, a familiar concept to ancient practitioners of Tantra.

More than a few examples come to mind of couplings with contagious ecstasy. In the Tantra tradition, the mystic Saraha, a respected philosopher and scholar in the ninth century, became the consort of a Tantric female. It is said they lived together in a cemetery, dancing in continual ecstasy. But they had a profound effect on the grieving of those who came there to bury their dead, bringing them rapture and enlightenment. According to the legend, Saraha and his consort eventually influenced the king and queen of the time, ushering in a period of joy and peace. So you see, your ecstatic reveling in the afterglow of sexual union is more than pleasurable. It's community service!

The Energy of Goddess Empowerment

As the energy of ecstatic sexual union and its long slow afterburn infuses the sex goddess with bliss, she becomes like a mirror to the world. There's nothing like the glow that overtakes the sex goddess when she is in love. You can't bottle it. You can't buy it anywhere. But when you've got it, you definitely can't hide it. Have you ever noticed how quickly your women friends pick up on the glow? They know—just know, somehow—that you are basking in the attention of a lover.

The myth of Ishikoridome-no-mikoto from the Shinto tradition of Japan comes to mind. A talented artisan and stone cutter, she was commissioned to create a mirror that would lure the sun goddess Amaterasu from her cave. Darkness had enveloped the earth for months. Another goddess, Ama-no-Uzume, was commissioned to perform a frenzied dance outside the cave. The sun goddess poked her head out to see what all the commotion was about, and she saw her beautiful image in the mirror. The darkness lifted, and there was light.

In Japan, the mirror represents a woman's soul. It reveals to a woman her deep knowing and her enchanting qualities. The mirror in this tale was called Kagami and became a symbol of purity.

When you have that glow, you have that unmistakable shine of all that is divine within you coming through. Other women can reflect your light. They can pick up on that glow you have after being with someone you love. They can't help but notice. It's infectious.

Elixir of Life

It can be incredibly empowering to realize what your body is capable of. One aspect of being a sex goddess is understanding the power of female ejaculations. Yes, women ejaculate, too. Some sex doctors call it the female prostate, a genito-urinary organ

that releases fluid when the G-spot is stimulated. Some say female ejaculate is a combination of several fluids: vaginal lubrication,
cervical mucus, fluids from the uterus, secretions from the Bartholin ducts (female
prostate), and the G-spot. In this way, the
woman mirrors the male energy arc, with one
important distinction: The woman's ejaculation
is not depleting. Amrita is one of the names
given to female ejaculate. It means the "nectar
of the goddess."

In Tantra, a woman's secretions during sex are
described as "yoni-waves," and they are believed to be psycho-magnetic. If a woman ejaculates during oral sex, when a man's lips and
tongue are buried in his partner's yoni, Tantra believes that her ejaculate polarizes and
balances his head-center energy, releasing secretions in his pineal and pituitary glands.
It is believed that this release can open up the powers of the psyche through stimulating the third-eye chakra. The Tantric texts refer to it as the Wave of Wisdom.

> **Beyond Taboos**
>
> Before scientists under-
> stood that women can ejaculate,
> too, women who were able to
> freely ejaculate were treated as
> though their bodies were mal-
> functioning. Some were instructed
> to do more Kegel exercises,
> while others endured surgery to
> correct the problem. Fortunately,
> we understand today that women
> are complex sexual beings with
> many dimensions.

Sarasvati, the Hindu goddess of fertility and prosperity, was believed to have holy
waters that flowed west from the Himalayas to the sea. In some traditions, it is
believed she discovered *soma*, the elixir of the gods. She is known as the patroness of
the Sixty-Four Arts, of which the most supreme is the art of love. Sarasvati is sometimes depicted holding a container of *soma* and the *vidya*, emblem of knowledge.

Both Tantra and Tao believe that a man can compensate for his loss of energy upon
ejaculation by drinking from the sexual secretions of a woman. They are called the
Threefold Elixirs: her saliva, her breast secretions, and her ejaculate. A woman's
ejaculate was called Moon Flower Waters, White Metal, Lotus-Nectar, or Love
Juice (we're not making this up). The *Ananga Ranga* (a fifteenth-century Indian text
on love, based on the Kama Sutra), referring to different types, describes it variously
as "love-essence perfumed like a lily that has just burst open," "hot juices with the
perfume of honey," or "a salty love fluid," according to the woman.

A Natural Woman

Although sacred sexual union can bring out your masculine side, bringing balance to
your dominant energy, an encounter of high ecstasy also brings out your feminine
side. Sometimes it's easy to submerge your voluptuous spirit, with all the many go-go-
go, do-do-do roles you play. But sacred sex reminds you again that you are a goddess.

In truth, both you and your partner are called upon to empower the feminine within. In his book *Waking the World*, Alan Chinen challenges both sexes with four distinct tasks that mark the development of a healthy feminine side. Channeling the goddess energy of afterglow toward this personal development has the effect of multiplying your goddess glow.

1. **Defying the demon.** Face your internal demons. Know your weaknesses. Examine what caused those parts to develop in you more slowly. What was happening in your family of origin? This is the key to cultivating inner peace. Goddesses who evoke this energy are Kali, the Hindu goddess of creative destruction, and Isis, who breathed her lover back into life.

2. **Reclaiming your true self.** Begin to trust your instincts. See your place in the world. This step also includes finding healing and clarity in the wilderness. It means facing your aloneness, facing your fears, charting new frontiers. Goddesses who evoke this energy are Persephone, Bast, and Isis.

3. **Befriending the goddess in others.** Collaborate, honor beauty, celebrate authenticity. Support consensus-builders. Validate the nurturers. When you see these qualities in your partner, encourage them by praising him. Goddesses who evoke this energy include Hestia, the Greek goddess who maintained the home fires. She kept not just the flame of home burning, but also the flame that symbolized the emerging republic-state. The flame of Hestia burned in all of the meeting halls of Greece. Her name was invoked in all endeavors of the state. She is the spirit of all collective endeavors—of two "me's" becoming a "we."

   Another is Sarasvati, who brings forth creation in 64 disciplines including singing, dancing, writing, painting, sewing, cooking, making perfumes, chemistry, logic, household management, martial arts, and religious rites, just to name a few. Her energy is compared to the flames of an inner sun, blazing from the solar plexus. She burns up all negativity and purifies the soul to bring about inner transformation.

4. **Awakening the world.** This is where your goddess energy spreads. Break through old customs, illusions, and constrictions. Create new paradigms. Get people to think outside the box. When you initiate change for the good of all, you change yourself, and you transform your intimate relationships. You take them to a higher level. This kind of goddess empowerment energy inspires and changes your partner.

When you are in touch with the goddess glow, you have cultivated the energy in your third-eye, throat, and power chakras. It may surprise you to read in a book about sex that you should focus on your throat, eyebrows, and belly. Why not focus on the sexual chakra? But many women struggle with trusting their intuition, expressing their needs, and coming from their place of personal power.

The afterglow makes you feel feminine and filled with gratitude for your femininity. Too often in our high-achievement, techno-swirl lives, we neglect to treasure our gifts of intuition, expression, and power. But a high ecstasy experience with your lover will remind you again and again. You feel alive. You quite literally tingle with your power and magnificence. Use the path of sexual ecstasy to open the portal to understanding. The goddess energy helps us bring the feminine face back to our understanding of the Divine, to reintegrate flesh and spirit, mind and soul.

Initiatress of Love

Symbols of Aphrodite are the red poppy, rose, myrtle, apple, dove, swan, swallow, tortoise, ram, planet Venus, and month of April. All are sacred to her. Use some of these symbols on an altar in your bedroom or meditation room when you want to draw upon your empowered goddess energy.

Dancing Together, Dancing Apart

All this talk of union may begin to sound a little bit smothering after a while, at least to some of you. But an important part of being a sex goddess is also to maintain your own power, identity, and personal space. The art of dancing apart is just as vital to intensifying the sexual energy between you and your partner as the art of connecting and coming together. This is much easier said than done, however. It's difficult to master dancing apart gracefully. The last thing you want when you are still in the glow of love is to assimilate back into real life, or to turn away from the person who has just touched you so deeply.

But sex goddesses know that this is just another segment of the erotic dance, one that can intensify your experience of desire, arousal, and ecstasy. As we are one with others, we are also one within ourselves. This dichotomy adds complexity, beauty, tension, and passion to sexual union.

Whether your partner has been your legally wedded spouse for 50 golden years or is the hot guy you just met at the technopop club downtown, you will dance apart and together many, many times over the course of your relationship.

This doesn't mean the glow subsides. It means it only gets better. Light candles when you are apart from the one you love to remind you that the glow remains. As you look at the candle flame, feel his skin on your skin, his lips pressed on your clitoris, his lingam rhythmically rocking in your yoni. You will continue to feel connected to his body.

And then, blow out the candle. This reminds you to release him as an individual—and to release yourself. This allows what the Lebanese poet Kahlil Gibran refers to as the moving sea between you. It allows your love and your passion and your shared vision for living to build. And we won't even tell you how delicious it is when you come back together as two whole, separate individuals after knowing each other so deeply. *Gasp!* The mystery is back. About two and a half days—the time it takes for the moon to move into the next constellation in the sky—is enough time to shift your energy and channel it into your self, replenishing your chakras.

Oracle Wisdom

Certainly Persephone knew all about this dance of together-apart, together-apart. She was forced to spend six months each year away from her husband, Hades, king of the underworld. Talk about a commuter marriage! We wonder if her modern-day parallel is the East Coast–West Coast couple racking up frequent flyer miles. We wonder if she wore something really sexy underneath her flowing goddess robe as she was transported across the River Styx back to the underworld.

In this practice of creating sacred space between you and your partner, you can magnify the good karma your union sends out into the world. Remember that human love is a mirror of divine love. Your giving to each other and your surrendering your aloneness send waves of inspiration out into the world.

Let the magic of your union imbue your body, mind, and spirit with your power, where you become the magician of your life. Leave behind that person whose happiness is dictated by the circumstances of the moment. Embrace and sustain the woman who vibrates with her very aliveness and can really make a difference, choosing to create her own reality.

And so linger with your lover. Stay mindful of this new level. Stay centered. Stay conscious. Know that your natural state is bliss.

The Least You Need to Know

- Male sexual energy is easily ignited, but quickly extinguished. Female sexual energy comes to a slow boil, but it builds in waves.

- Take cues from astrology's energy elements to balance the fire energy of yang and the water energy of yin.

- After orgasm, unite your energies through the heart chakra. Close your connection by balancing your energies at the heart.

- Savor the glow between you by being in no great hurry. Enjoy the simple sensation of skin on skin.

- Women ejaculate, too. Ancient sacred texts on sexuality recognized the female ejaculate as having healing powers.

- Let the space between you be as sacred as your togetherness.

Part 6

Feeling Sexy Every Day

Life is life, isn't it? There are always demands on your time and energy that draw you away from indulging your inner sex goddess. It's hard to feel sexy when you've got a toilet brush in one hand and a baby's diaper in the other! Even Gaia, first goddess and mother of all creation, had her heavenly hands full, what with the responsibility of populating the earth and all.

These chapters look at ways to stoke the sex goddess fires despite the mundane tasks of domesticity that occupy so much of our time and energy. Draw from the strength and wisdom of goddesses before you to remain a sexual person in your daily life. It's not always easy, being a goddess, but it's worth the effort!

Chapter 18

Mother Love

In This Chapter

- ◆ Sex goddess, meet mother goddess!
- ◆ Passion, pregnancy, and motherhood
- ◆ Rekindling the flames with your partner
- ◆ Sexy mama: loving your new body
- ◆ Replenishing yourself, resparking desire

So one thing leads to another and the next thing you know, it's love and marriage and a baby carriage. How does the sacred sexual connection change after children come along? Dramatically, but it doesn't have to be the end of passion. Instead, it is a deepening. The sex goddess energy transmutes to something new.

Far from being the end of passion, motherhood brings complexity, commitment, loyalty, and the kind of fierce protectiveness you can witness on any nature channel when it shows what happens should anyone threaten the cubs of a lioness or grizzly bear. Traditionally, we think of men becoming protective of their families when children arrive, but women do, too, and that protectiveness extends beyond the children to the whole circle of the family itself. Such feelings may be part instinctive to preserve and maintain the family, but they are also a function of the full flowering of the sex goddess as she fulfills her creative destiny.

Part Sex Goddess, Part Mother Goddess

When you become a mother, your sex goddess energy doesn't exit to make room for new mother goddess energy. Just as the birth canal expands during labor, so does your capacity for more love and more passion. If you have more than one child, you already know that your heart just grows larger to make room for more, and as your children grow, you only love them more.

So motherhood does not displace your sexual energy, though at times you may find the sex goddess in you is so submerged, you fear she might slip beneath the waves. Motherhood in fact can—and should—heighten your sex goddess energy. It enhances what is already there in finding newer expressions. It is not an either/or proposition; it's an "*and*," an augmentation. *I am a sex goddess.* And *I am a mother goddess.*

In Hinduism, motherhood and sexuality are not separated, as they sometimes are in Greek mythology (for instance, with Demeter and Persephone). The three Shakti goddesses—Sarasvati, Kali, and Lakshmi—represent intuitive wisdom-energy. They bring forth that energy through an erotic dance with the Hindu gods—Brahma, Shiva, and Vishnu, respectively. The energies of passion and creation are fused. Shakti is seen as the active energy of creation that moves through every being, every animal, and every material thing. The act of sex is the bringing to life of the energy of love. It brings forth what lies dormant within us, what yearns to be expressed. The ultimate of that energy is the bringing forth of a new life.

Oracle Wisdom

Another goddess who fused the energy of eroticism and creation was Awitelin Tsita, the Zuni goddess who had four wombs. Her lover was the sky god Apoyan Tachu, and they made love continuously until all her wombs were filled with children. She illustrates the principle of love, sex, and motherhood expanding to its ultimate capacity. The Zunis believed that Awitelin Tsita gave birth to the human race from these four wombs.

The Erotic Side of Pregnancy

Pregnancy can be highly erotic. Yes, yes, yes, we know about the morning sickness, the swollen feet, the heartburn, the bleeding gums. We know about the stretch marks. We know about the insomnia. And then there's that part about turning into a beached whale.

But there is a highly charged quality to the flowering of your body. Your breasts are full. Your skin is glowing—despite the morning sickness—because of all that increased blood flow. Your skin may even feel satiny. You start to feel soft all over. Indeed, your tissues are softening, thickening with fluid. Everything is more sensitive—the areola around your nipples, your labia. You are supple, if not graceful. The surging hormones that nourish, grow, and house your baby may keep you in a fog of nausea, but in the midst of it (or hopefully by the second trimester—morning sickness doesn't usually last past the first trimester), you may feel electric, alive, and vibrant.

This new expression of you as a woman may feel very fulfilling. Some women find they are really turned on by their partners during the early part of their pregnancies. As they feel their baby grow inside the uterus, they feel a deeper bond with their lovers. "We are making this," they think. It's a palpable expression of your love. It's growing every day. You may feel your uterus contract and stretch. At about the fifth month, you may feel your baby kick. Some women feel movement before that, and they describe it as butterflies or rising bubbles. And you get to carry this growing bundle of your love energy around with you every day.

Some women also find that out of necessity, they explore other ways of lovemaking—new positions, a deeper experience of oral sex. Or they get a lot more cuddling from their partners. Their partners dote on them, checking in more frequently during the day, or bringing them tea after a long day at work, setting up foot baths, and propping them up with pillows. When you're getting this kind of attention, who wouldn't want to be pregnant? And who wouldn't want to shower your lover with adoration in gratitude?

The Erotic Side of Post-Partum

After baby comes along, it will take most women six to eight weeks to be ready for intercourse again. The dramatic drop in hormones that takes place after birth may really put a damper on things, and the nights of interrupted sleep lead to exhaustion. Plus, your body has to heal before you start having sex again. Doctor's orders!

Many women experience a loss of desire after pregnancy that extends long past the medical period of enforced abstinence. For some women, the desire returns right away, but for others, it may be up to two years before they really get their groove back. Your body is working on nourishing and nurturing the baby and is telling you not to make any more babies yet! (It doesn't know about birth control.)

But most women will tell you that when your desire does finally come back, it comes back with a vengeance. A mother's desire can be stronger than it ever was before. You may wonder what on Earth happened to you. You may feel like a teenager. You may think, "What's wrong with me, am I thinking with my genitals instead of my head?"

Enjoy this time of renewed sexual vigor. The act of becoming a mother summons energy up from the root and sexual chakras, intensifying it in the power and heart chakras. It is one powerful, miraculous act to carry a child and give birth. Experiencing the intensity of love for your child is like passion cross-training—when you learn how to love this much, this strongly, this fiercely, you can turn that fierce love to your partner as well. You learn to feel with every part of your body in a completely new way. You are charged with passion, with love, with sexual/spiritual energy. You are a mother goddess, *and* you are a sex goddess. They go hand in hand. (For even more on this subject, check out *Releasing the Mother Goddess* by Gail Carr Feldman, Ph.D., and Eve Adamson; see Appendix B.)

Beyond Taboos

Many women experience post-partum depression anywhere from a few days to a few years after giving birth. Although this is normal, it is also confusing. You may feel like you have lost your former self, are consumed in baby care, or even have no desire to care for your baby. This is caused by hormones and has nothing to do with your mothering ability! The condition is very treatable, so please talk to your doctor if you feel unable to cope with your feelings after giving birth.

Deep Intuitive Wisdom

Intuition plays a vital role in sparking the erotic charge you experience as a mother. The path to motherhood, through nine months of pregnancy, is like intuition boot camp. A woman who may prefer to dwell on intellectual, rational, cognitive pursuits may find that pregnancy is deep immersion training for knowing and trusting her body. The medical world has come largely to embrace the intuitive power of a woman bearing a child in her womb. Doctors and nurses have learned to perk up their ears when a pregnant woman says, "Something just doesn't feel right." Many a woman has saved her unborn child by insisting that a doctor see her right away, only to find the umbilical cord was blocking off blood flow or the amniotic fluid was low.

Nine months of pregnancy awaken a woman's body to the collective wisdom of all women who have gone before her. She gets even more attuned to goddess energy. Pregnancy is a transformation not just of the body, but also of the mind and the soul.

It is an act of selflessness, but at the same time, an act of self-fulfillment and the ultimate creative act. It causes you to face your self-doubts as you become a parent. Childbirth itself is a lesson in trusting that your body knows what to do, in quelling the mind that is so aware of pain, so that the body can do what it must do.

These kinds of shifts can summon the deep intuitive wisdom of the Hindu goddess of transformation, Kali. Getting to know Kali means getting to know a woman coming to terms with her own awesome power. Kali was both the goddess of creation and the goddess of destruction. Represented naked with black skin, by some accounts Kali is "clothed only in space." (Something you may relate to as you lie on the delivery table and suddenly no longer care that everybody in the room can see you without your clothes!) Kali was black because, in Hindu thought, black is the color by which all distinctions dissolve. In the dark, you cannot tell the difference between objects and space. Everything looks the same. In the same way, mother and child, while finally becoming two distinct beings at the moment of birth, remain spiritually tied—for several years, the child doesn't understand that he or she is anything separate from the mother. Distinctions are dissolved.

Many of the other Hindu gods and goddess call on Kali for her fierce protective nature. She devours demons and protects mothers and children. She is the most raw, even violently protective incarnation of mother goddess energy. Although she strikes fear into the hearts of all those who would hurt the innocent—she is frequently depicted wearing the skulls of her victims, her face smeared in blood, and draped with snakes—Kali is the ultimate in calming and relieving the fears of those she protects. No one can hurt you if you have Kali on your side. And isn't that just what you want your child to feel about you?

As you get to know and embrace your own Kali energy, which you may have glimpsed for the first time after becoming a mother, you may also discover the many ways in which intuition plays a vital role in creating sexual and spiritual alchemy between you and your partner. It is a way of deeply knowing yourself and your partner, and it is also a component in the unfolding of the orchestrations between you. This deep knowing of your partner creates a bond of trust that leads to the surrender again and again, and to the relinquishment of you as maiden in favor of a vigorous and passionate embrace of who you have all become as a family: mother, father, child. Just like Isis, Osiris, and Horus—a family within which fearsome protection was a matter of course, each member acting rashly and violently to protect, rescue, and restore the others—your family has become a new "self," infused with magical power, passion, and its own new energy.

But of course, when it comes to your sex life and your passionate bond with your partner, sometimes the family recedes, temporarily, in favor of the new partner bond you are forging. (The baby has to sleep *sometime!*) As you re-see your partner with new eyes, your intuition may seem to tell you, magically, just what your partner needs next, where to touch him, how to touch him. It may also help you to feel free to *ask* what your partner wants. Intuition is a skill that comes with practice, in lovemaking sessions that prolong the pleasure, suspend time, and produce whole-body ecstasy and multiple orgasms. The more you do it, the bigger reservoir of intuition you have between you. When the bond between you is built on deep intuition, it is nearly impossible to severe, even if you take a temporary hiatus from sexual intercourse after children come along, and even if it transmutes as you shift into sex goddess/mother goddess mode. You are more than your bodies and your minds. Your souls are intertwined; your spirits move toward enlightenment in tandem.

> **Oracle Wisdom**
>
> Know that she is the life in my body, and in my soul.
> —Rumi, thirteenth-century Persian poet and Sufi mystic

Your Partner

Of course, we can give you all kinds of inspiration about your sex life post-partum, but we also know what life as a new mother is like. (Husband? What husband?) After your baby comes along, you may wonder where your partner fits into your life as you become consumed with baby care and the intense needs of that tiny creature. Your partner may wonder, too. He may feel out of the loop, even a little bit isolated from the mother-child circle.

To keep your family strong during this sensitive, emotional post-partum period, both you and your partner must make a commitment to keep your connection the priority. Your whole family rests on the strength of the bond between you. Children can take up every ounce of your energy. Little ones need so much, and their demands are so urgent. But it's vital that you commit together that your relationship will take precedence over all. No, that doesn't mean you won't feed the baby when he is hungry because you are engaged in a make-out session! But it does mean that you cannot push your partner out of your inner soul in favor of your baby. Together, you form the twin pillars of family. Together, you nurture this being for awhile before setting her free to make her own life. But the bond between you and your partner can last far beyond that time. Keep it strong. Nurture it like a garden. Don't forget to water the garden just because you are busy breastfeeding or giving the baby a bath!

Use this heart chakra ritual to seal that commitment between you, to keep each other in your hearts and to cherish and honor the heart you have built together—the heart of your partnership. It can be something to come back to any time you sense your commitment to each other is out of balance or you begin to feel far away.

1. Sit across from one another, cross-legged on pillows on the floor.

2. Take in three deep, cleansing breaths. Let the first breath take in the good energy that surrounds you and direct it deep into the energy centers of your body. Exhale, releasing all that you don't need to take on.

3. The second breath clears the mind. Direct it out from your third-eye chakra in four directions. This is the energy center of knowledge, which equips you with the wisdom of parenthood. This is the place where truth that comes from the outside gets tested against your inner truth.

4. Take the third breath in, deep down to your root chakra, lifting it up through your crown chakra. This is the energy of spirit, where lower thoughts become higher thoughts.

5. Light a candle between you. Ideally, set the candle so it is level with your partner's face. Spend a few minutes gazing into the flame of the candle, focused on that glow but aware of your partner's presence behind it.

6. Gazing into each other's eyes, each of you tap your own sternum, using your first two fingers. This mimics your heartbeat. Tap it 33 times.

7. Rest. Repeat the tapping once more, 33 times. Rest one minute. Repeat, tapping 33 more times.

8. Extend your hands to your lover, palms up. Take his hands in yours. Hold your gaze together as partners.

9. Say to your partner, "I love you with all my heart, all my mind, all my body, all my soul."

The Loving Circle

You and your baby naturally create a loving circle, with your baby's head cradled in your arms. Newborns can only see about 14 inches away—about the distance from the suckling breast to the mother's face. In those first few days, there is an intense energy circle between you. Again, this can make your partner feel apart from that special circle. Where does he fit in?

But your partner can and should be a vital part of this energetic loving circle of nourishing the baby. The two of you brought this child into the world. A sex goddess knows this change is about expansion—not contraction—of the love energy. In the early days, dedicate at least one breast-feeding session a day to the loving circle, with all three of you touching and connected. You can tuck yourself back-to-chest in the arms of your partner as you breast-feed. Let him loop his arms around both of you. This is a wonderful way to connect through touch. As your baby feeds, you two can connect about your day. Or you may breast-feed on your side on the bed, with your partner lying on his side, facing you. The baby is between you, but you remain connected through your eyes, or by twining your legs together. Another loving circle pose has your partner putting his head in your lap as you breast-feed. There are infinite variations, but the guideline is to create a three-way connection, a conduit of love through touch.

Rituals like this can be introduced into your married-with-children life at any time—whether your children are teenagers or in elementary school. Hold hands as you invoke your blessings at the dinner table. Make the loving circle a part of bedtime stories or movie night. Stage a group hug before you leave the house in the morning. It may feel silly, but it definitely will feel good.

Initiatress of Love

In Tantric and Tao teachings, breast milk was cherished as one of three sexual secretions of a woman, called the Threefold Elixirs. Known as White Snow, Essence of Coral, or Immortality Peach Juice, breast milk can be a highly erotic part of lovemaking if both partners feel comfortable with that. The ancient texts so revered the nourishing qualities of breast milk that they advised "Of the Three Peaks, this one should first receive the attention of the lover." They also believed that the flow of White Snow could be generated simply by sexual excitement, and indeed, non-nursing women can produce breast fluid when sexually excited. This may be even easier for women who have previously breast-fed.

Romance, Partnership, and Friendship

Goddesses know all about trinities, right? (Remember the maiden, mother, and wise woman of Chapter 3?) A trinity of energy exists within your partnership—that of romance, partnership, and friendship. At any given moment, if someone did a snapshot report of the state of your relationship, one part of the trinity might be more pronounced than another. When children come along, they realign this trinity of sacred partnership. The focus quite naturally moves to partnership because the imperative for working together for the good of the whole is so strong.

First and foremost, you must accept and honor that shift. You may initially mourn what seems like the draining of romance from your partnership. You may think it will never get back to the way it was before, with long, luxurious lovemaking on the fur rug by the fire. That may seem a distant memory. You may feel lucky if you get a quickie in before the kids wake up and jump on your bed.

The next step is to begin to imbue partnership and friendship with some of the same value you placed on romance. See the value both bring to your life. Express your gratitude to your partner for his role in upholding the partnership.

That said, all three aspects of the trinity of marriage must work in conjunction, and passion is a vital part of that. If one is out of balance, it will eventually cause chaos with the other two. Think of it as the three central feminine deities of Hinduism—Sarasvati, Kali, and Lakshmi—and each day you must please each of them without making the others jealous. As you learned earlier, in Hinduism, each is a Shakti goddess who brings forth energy through union with Brahma, Shiva, and Vishnu, respectively.

The trinity of Hindu goddess energy parallels that of romance, partnership, and friendship. Sarasvati represents the creative principle—among her 64 arts, the foremost is love. Therefore, Sarasvati represents romance. Kali is the energy of the transcendent. She represents transformation that takes place in the intimate dialogue between a couple—that daily dance of partnership. Finally, Lakshmi manifests the energy of the preserver. As the wife of Vishnu, Lakshmi's assignment is to bring to bear Vishnu's constant desire to preserve life. Friendship in a marriage does this. It preserves the life force of the marriage.

The energy of romance is heady. When you first fall in love, you may feel like you are walking on air. The energy of passion is fire. When you first get together, you can't get enough. You are consumed by him. You want to ravish him. After motherhood, your sexual energy may have more earth and water qualities—water because your capacity for tenderness and affection is exponentially multiplied, and earth because giving birth brings you in such a deep connection with the earth. Earthy energy can be very sexy, and this is the place to go when you really need to summon your sexual energy again.

Your skin may be your most erogenous zone. You may find the idea of a mud bath or mud mask very invigorating, as it helps to connect you to the earth. A lot of your sexual energy may flood into your hips; pregnancy and childbirth have a way of infusing this part of you with new energy. You may find the pelvic rocking exercises in Chapter 15 really awakening your newfound energy in a powerful way.

Tantric Dating

Another way to continue to connect with your partner rather than mourn the "loss" of the previous stage of your relationship is to reclaim some of that new-love excitement. Make a commitment to date each other! But first, you must agree on some ground rules. Above all, the most important commitment is that you will have a good time. Whether there are glitches with the baby-sitter, delays in traffic, or kitchen miscues at the restaurant, the most essential thing is that you are together, and you are alone. That means you have to follow a few rules:

- Don't talk about the children.

- Don't talk about money.

- Unless you have an emergency, don't call the baby-sitter. It is not an emergency if you forgot to tell the baby-sitter that the ice cubes are in the freezer. She'll figure it out.

- Compliment him.

- Touch, touch, touch. Brush against him. At dinner, take his hand across the table. Waiting in line at the movie, caress his shoulder. Touch his elbow lightly. Let there be no mistake you are *into* him.

- After the event—movie, dinner, whatever—do not rush home. Your children are already in bed, safely sleeping. So take a minute as you are walking down the street to duck under the awning of the little gift shop and kiss. Give him a deep tongue kiss. Press your whole body against his.

- Reveal something new to your partner, perhaps an event in your childhood, something that you remember from before you met. (Be sure it is something benign. This isn't the time to unearth a deep, dark secret.)

- Talk about your first impression of him, whether it was good or bad. It will either make him chuckle or turn him on (or both!). Either way, it's good. A trip down memory lane can shift your perspective when so much of your lives has become about the swirl of daily existence.

- Wear something that makes you feel sensual—a sexy fabric such as chiffon or silk; something that glitters; something that enhances your most erotic physical feature.

- Now that you feel sexy, move sexy. Swish your hips as you walk. Slide back in your chair sinuously.

Take turns planning your date night. It's a great feeling to know that someone cares so much about you that he went out of his way to plan an evening. Remember, it's more than buying tickets. Surprise him with a flower that you slip to your server, and have the server present it just before dessert. Change it up, and slow it down. Add a little mystery by scheduling a rendezvous at sunset in the park instead of just leaving from home together.

Still, we caution you about having expectations that are too high. As you adjust to the changes in your lifestyle and in your body, reactivating the dating gene may take a little practice. Practically speaking, it may be difficult to shore up the baby-sitting network or afford the high price of a good sitter (can you swap baby-sitting with other couples who would also like to start "dating" again?), and your actual nights out may be few and far between. The downside of planning "high moments" is that sometimes they don't live up to our fantasies. You may have every intention of presenting a fresh, sexy, sweet-smelling goddess to your partner for your Tantric date, only to have the baby spew oatmeal at you minutes before the sitter arrives. Your moments alone together may be rare, and you may be just aching to hear how he cherishes you, only to find out you have a very grouchy husband who is working too hard and has no intention of giving you a compliment at the moment!

Go easy on each other, and schedule little moments along with the big ones. Take the baby out in the stroller in the evenings for a 10-minute walk and talk before you launch into dinner. Relax together holding hands with no television on for 30 minutes after the baby goes to sleep. Fall asleep in each other's arms, even if you never quite summon the energy to make love. The point is to be sure you connect every day— physically, emotionally, and spiritually.

Initiatress of Love

Remember the focus of Tantric sex is not on climax—it's on the pleasure of the unfolding of life, moment by moment. So, too, with Tantric dating. There is no performing; there is no goal other than to enjoy each other, creating an ecstatic state of wooing and loving. Look upon this stage of your relationship as a new way of weaving yourselves together. You are new people—a mother and a father—so your intimacy has deepened, but at the same time you have become two different individuals. Let the changes you are both experiencing be invigorating.

The Sacred Bedchamber

Even if you can't always get out of the house, you can create a romantic sanctuary where you and your partner can have full intimate lives separate from your children. Let your bedroom be a retreat from the world. This means no television! Keep your bedroom clutter-free. Being surrounded by books, papers, bills, and folded laundry drains your love energy.

Indulge in luxurious sheets. For a change of pace, buy a new duvet cover or curtains. Buy beautiful pillows with beads and tassels, or whatever sparks your imagination. Surround your bed with candles on pedestals (be careful not to knock them over!).

Put a few drops of essential oil such as cedar, ylang ylang, or lavender in spray bottle, and spray your sheets. (Test a small, obscure area first to be sure it won't stain the fabric … or give anybody a rash!)

Also essential in the sacred bedchamber are sexual aids, such as lubricants and massage oil. And if you are concerned about not multiplying your family any more, certainly keep the birth control handy! As soon as your children are old enough to wander into your room on their own, you might also want to install a lock on your bedroom door. It can make you much more relaxed and able to enjoy yourself fully!

Create an altar to your sacred union in your room. This is a place where the two of you can come together and meditate. It can remind you of the aspects of your relationship that you treasure; it can signify your intention; and it can summon the energy you want to bring to your lovemaking session.

Items you might want to have on hand include:

♦ Photos of yourselves together that you like to look at.

♦ Found objects from your travels through life together—the shells from the beach you went to on your honeymoon, a strip of bark from the rain forest where you hiked together, tickets to a ballet you attended together.

♦ Items representing each chakra. Because each chakra is represented by a color, and color has powerful light energy, it could be stones of red, orange, yellow, green, light blue, indigo, and violet.

♦ Items representing the fire, earth, water, and air elements. Earth could be a stone, air could be a feather. Fire could be candles, while water could be a fountain.

♦ Statues or images of goddess you want to evoke—Venus of Willendorf, Kali, Shiva and Shakti, Isis, Aphrodite. Status or images of gods your partner wants to evoke—Shiva, Adonis, Osiris (with his golden phallus!).

♦ A lotus blossom.

♦ A wand.

Destination: The Love Shack

Mix up your private time together with time in your sacred bedchamber and time away at a romantic sanctuary. Get out of town. Get away! Though you may create a paradise in your bedchamber, it still may be too close to home. A change of scenery can free your spirits, and just loosen things up a bit. It can bring back that heady air element energy of romance. See Chapter 19 for more ideas that take you out of the bedroom for loving.

Sexy Mama: Your Changing Body

After childbirth, a woman's body changes. It's a pure and simple fact. Magazines and infotainment are chock-full of stories of celebrities who defy Mother Nature and snap their bodies back into sex goddess mode—a brief but necessary foray into mother mode, then right back to maiden.

Well, we're not quite sure how they do that, but we suspect a lot of very expensive makeup artists and personal trainers are involved. Women's bodies are meant to change as they go through the passages of life. Just because your body doesn't bounce back to the one you had before—at least not right away—doesn't mean you can't appreciate it for what it is now. Love your soft belly. Incorporate it into your lovemaking by letting your partner massage your tummy in clockwise spirals. Know that Buddhism encourages soft-belly thinking—a focus on compassion over self-armoring and conquering. So appreciate your new softness, and no doubt your partner will, too.

Learn the art of dressing naked. In the artwork of the original Kama Sutra and many other sacred texts on sexuality, the lovers are adorned with jewels. Find a special exotic necklace that you may wear only for lovemaking. Buy an ankle bracelet or toe rings. Get a tattoo. It's okay. You have a new body, so the rules have changed!

Painted toenails can also make you feel beautiful and exotic. The pedicure itself can feel luxurious, and the splash of color can enliven you. Next time you see a date night on the horizon for you and your partner, schedule a pedicure for the afternoon before.

Oracle Wisdom

Lakshmi, the Hindu consort to Vishnu the preserver, was born of the churning sea of milk, similarly to Venus. She emerged from the sea holding a lotus and proceeded to bestow blessings upon the universe. She dazzled all of the male deities, and they were in hot pursuit. She chose Vishnu. Together, they became the parents of Kama, the god of love. Worshippers who desire children often summon Lakshmi.

Revirginizing

You'll remember that Venus bathed in the foamy sea each time she shed a lover, emerging clean, pure, and radiant, like a virgin, ready to love again. This is likely what Venus was up to when Sandro Botticelli captured her in *The Birth of Venus*. After all, she is a full-grown woman, not a newborn. Symbols associated with Venus include golden apples, strawberries, dolphins, swans, herons, myrrh, roses, copper, gold coins, turquoise, emeralds, and seashells. Her color is green, the same as the heart chakra.

There can be something powerfully erotic about restoring the innocent mind. Of course, once you learn something, you can never unlearn it. But another way of looking at innocence is to see it as becoming open to any possibility, any discovery, as if experiencing life all over again for the very first time, as if you have no scars, no baggage, and no idea that anything can ever hurt you. You take chances because you don't know what can go wrong. Do you remember being that innocent?

Mirror the Venus revirginizing ritual with a long, luxurious bubble bath. Send your partner and the kids off to visit relatives for a weekend. Choose a Friday, because that is Venus' day. Here's how to do it:

1. Sometime in the week before the bath, spend some time looking at photos of yourself before you had children. This can be just delightful! You may realize you had a flat tummy all along, only you didn't know it then. Find some photos of yourself with your partner. Find some photos of yourself with your girl-friends. Dig up that senior prom photo.

2. Also that week, call up an old female friend from junior high, maybe one you went to slumber parties with. Recount some of your puberty misadventures, when you were first flirting with boys and wondering if they liked you. Reminisce about your first bra, the arrival of your first menstrual cycle. Giggle. (Remember how?)

3. Now you are ready. Fill up the tub with lots of bubbles. Don't hold back. You want to immerse yourself in mountains of white fluff, so use more than that "two capfuls" it says on the bottle. Remember, you rarely get to do this.

4. Add a few drops of essential oil. The combination of lavender, ylang ylang, and peppermint is a good one for revirginizing. Lavender helps you relax. It is very sensual and spiritual, earthy and high-minded. Ylang ylang activates the sexual chakra, and peppermint is rejuvenating. Or to mimic Lakshmi being born out of the churning sea of milk, add a cup of milk or cream to your bathwater. This will make your skin feel very soft.

5. Surround your bath with seashells.

6. Choose some soothing water-sounds music. Because Venus is associated with dolphins, you might try a tape of dolphin sounds, or you may want something more melodic and flowing.

7. Settle in with a glass of wine or a cup of spiced tea. (Spices such as cinnamon and ginger are associated with the sexual chakra.)

As you luxuriate in the bath, clear your mind. You may have a million-and-one things on your to-do list, but not now. Right now, your to-do list doesn't exist. Or it has one item on it: *you*. Let yourself sink into the water and luxuriate in your own being. Water can be very comforting. You are the nurturer for your whole family now. Let the bath nurture you, restoring you to innocence. Breathe.

Self-Pleasuring

After childbirth, one of the best ways to get your desire back is by engaging in a healthy dose of self-pleasuring. No, your doctor probably won't tell you this, which is why you are hearing it from us! You may find that your body has even more to offer to you in pleasure, or that things work for you that didn't work before. The best way to get to know the ins and outs of your "new" body is to discover it yourself with some gentle and self-loving hands-on research. Later, you can use this knowledge to enlighten your partner to your newly discovered erogenous zones.

Self-pleasuring may be more important than ever in closing the gap between the way you and your partner arouse your sexual energies separately. Men tend to be more genitally oriented, while women's arousal tends to originate from the heart chakra. After children, your heart chakra may be in high performance, and this gap may be even more pronounced. Self-pleasuring will get you back in practice for activating your arousal, bringing it quickly from your heart to your genitals.

When you self-pleasure, don't leave out the foreplay. After that long bubble bath, dry yourself with a big soft towel. Put on a silky robe or your favorite lingerie. Stand in front of a mirror and take it off again, sensuously unveiling your body. Dance. Caress your breasts; squeeze your nipples. Rub your body with oil. Stroke yourself all over. Let your hand slide down your belly. Scissor your fingers through your pubic hair. Let it tickle. Gently part your labia. Tease yourself. Lubricate your outer and inner labia, your clitoris, your perineum, the opening and inside of your yoni. Explore with different touches, strokes, and pressures. As you explore your clitoris, try different strokes, circular, brushing, pressure, as if you've never touched it before. Remember, today it is all new. Which part is the most sensitive? As you explore your yoni, experiment with fingers. If you are comfortable with it and if your doctor has already given the okay for sexual intercourse, you can also use sexual aids in the great tradition of Cleopatra or Isis—an artificial lingam such as a vibrator. (Don't do this if you are still healing from childbirth.)

As you hold yourself on the edge of orgasm, visualize drawing your sexual energy, your earth, and your fire, up through your Inner Goddess Channel. Try the Butterfly Pump we described in Chapter 15. As you feel your sexual energy expanding and rising up through your body, stroke your belly in slow circles. Continue self-pleasuring until you reach a near-peak. Stop pleasuring and breathe deeply, holding your pleasure energy, allowing it to fill your pelvis. Relax, exhale, and draw this energy up through your entire body, up through all your upper chakras. Direct energy up to the third-eye chakra by rolling your eyes upward or pressing your fingers on the center of your forehead as you continue to self-pleasure. Continue breathing. When your energy reaches your crown chakra (use your intuition, feel it), release, and let yourself reach the peak.

Initiatress of Love

To invoke the sexual mysteries of the Hindu goddess Kali, use sensual smells such as sandalwood, musk, patchouli, and camphor. She also likes garlands of red flowers, drumming, erotic dance, and wine. Kali can be summoned through spontaneous laughter, ballads, passionate love, and a "live life to the fullest" attitude.

All Kegels, All the Time

Now more than ever, it's vital to do those Kegel exercise (contracting and releasing the PC muscles we described in Chapter 15) to tone up your muscles again. During pregnancy, your muscles may have weakened due to the pressure of your baby's head on your cervix. During childbirth, you stretched a few things out. Remember, you can do these exercises anywhere, anytime.

Giving When You Are Depleted: Help Me, I'm Drowning!

"Weekend to myself? Ha!" you might be thinking. "Send the husband and kids to a relative? Ha!" Sure, time alone, dates with your husband, all of that may seem like a pipe dream, especially if you live away from family and don't have a network of support in place. Sometimes the demands of parenthood can be more than stressful, they can feel all-consuming. You may wonder sometimes how much you have to give. After children jump on you and grab you and ask for things all day, having your husband touch you may seem like the last thing on Earth you would want. You are nurturer all the time, and although you get hugs and cuddles from your little ones, the giving mostly flows from one source—you. That can get exhausting, depleting, sometimes even irritating. And sometimes it can be enough to make you break down and cry. (Yes, we know. Been there, done that.)

You may also feel so focused on your children that you lose sight of where you end and they begin. You may sometimes forget to notice how you feel. You may stay up late at night to pack the diaper bags and the lunches, then forget to pack one for yourself. Or you may bundle up little ones with hats and gloves and go out the door without a coat for yourself. And you may never even notice you're cold until you are already 10 miles down the road. Sometimes you may wonder where *you* went. You may carry around the feeling that you have lost something. And it may be you.

It can be a challenge to give to your partner when you have so little time to give to yourself. You may just want to collapse into bed every night as soon as the children are tucked in. It may seem like opposite-thinking, but the way back to giving to your partner is to give to yourself first.

Revitalizing with Yoga

No time for yourself? Well surely you have time for a little exercise. Even your doctor would agree! Yoga is one of the best exercises for new mothers because it is gentle on bodies that need to ease back into physical activity but grows in its challenges as you get back into shape. Plus, nearly every discipline of yoga can be revitalizing. Many women find they can't live without it once they begin to practice it.

Yoga has immense benefits for the body, mind, and spirit, bringing you back into balance and harmony. The Tree Pose, or vrikshasana, is a particularly centering pose that may help you replenish yourself. It is an excellent reminder of our connection to Earth, the creation and fertility goddesses. It reminds you that the mother goddess sustains and nourishes all living beings. This pose improves your posture and helps stabilize the pelvis, or sexual energy center. It elongates the spine, strengthens the legs and ankles, and increases the flexibility of the inner thigh muscles.

1. Stand with your eyes fixed on a focal point in front of you, bearing the weight of your body on your right foot. Tighten your thigh muscle.

2. Inhale and raise your left leg, placing the sole of your foot on the calf or inner thigh of the standing leg. You may want to hold your ankle with your left hand to keep it from slipping.

3. Stretch the groin of your bent leg by externally rotating the knee and upper thigh, aligning it with the hip. Breathe through it.

4. When balanced, raise your arms over your head, palms together. Hold for 8 to 10 breaths.

5. Return you raised leg to the floor and lower your arms.

6. Repeat on the other side.

Incorporate yoga into a lifestyle of healthy eating and regular exercise, and you are doing your part to replenish yourself. You are doing it for yourself, your partner, and your children. For more on yoga, check out *The Complete Idiot's Guide to Yoga*, *Third Edition*, by Joan Budilovsky and Eve Adamson (see Appendix B). You might also like *The Complete Idiot's Guide to Yoga with Kids*, which includes sections on yoga for infants, small children, preschoolers, and up, by Jodi Komitor, M.A., and Eve Adamson (Alpha Books, 2000).

Source of All: Womb Breathing

The secret Tantric technique of womb breathing is extremely vitalizing to mothers at any stage (and to women who aren't mothers, too). It can attract energy to you when you need replenishment. Womb breathing involves lying in a fetal position, taking only very shallow breaths into your abdomen. As you breathe, imagine taking in nourishment through your belly button. This draws sexual energy into your solar plexus.

Loss of Desire

What if it seems that no matter what you do, you cannot summon your desire? What if you have totally lost interest in sex? Remember, this is mostly hormonal and only temporary. If you are breast-feeding, that may help. Breast-feeding releases a hormone called oxytocin in the bloodstream that has amazing benefits. It's a love drug in and of itself. You can feel the rush of oxytocin as you begin to nurse, and it feels great. Oxytocin is the hormone that produces the "let-down" that occurs when breast-feeding, when the milk really flows. It produces such a sublime feeling of contentment that some women feel they don't really need sex.

Coupled with the nurturing overload we've already mentioned, many women feel they can only handle so many demands on their bodies. But eventually this subsides, and desire can return. Many women report when it's back, it's really back. Suddenly, they turn into vixens. Suddenly, they are wild with desire.

But again, if this isn't the case for you, you will want to look deeper. Look at it honestly: Many women who have lost interest in sex have lost interest in their husbands. At the root of this is respect. A woman who has lost respect for her husband cannot summon the desire she might once have had. Still other women find they need to examine events from childhood once they switch in the mother goddess role. If they hit a snag growing up, they are likely to experience a challenge when their children arrive at that same age.

Some couples find that children bring up feelings and attitudes they may not have known they had about mothers and sex goddesses—the so-called "madonna-whore" complex. Men who once burned with desire for their wives now see them as mothers and instinctively shrink away, because it's taboo to have sexual feelings for one's mother. Women may realize they, too, have a residue of this in their belief system. All of these issues can be examined in counseling with a licensed therapist. Don't be afraid to seek counseling if you are struggling with sexual or other relationship issues after childbirth. You won't be the first couple to seek such counseling, and you certainly won't be the last.

A Gallery of Role Models

As you move through this new segment of your journey, with its many challenges, don't forget the many other goddesses around you who have already traveled along the same road, or are doing so right now. By collecting goddesses around you as allies and role models, you can call forth the energy you need to remain yourself, nurture, your children, and infuse your sex life with renewed passion. It can all be better than ever! Look outside yourself for the answers. Your friends, your relatives, your teachers, celebrities who have had children and told their stories, and most of all your own mother are all fountains of goddess wisdom. And don't forget, of course, the many goddesses from the mythologies of cultures all over the world that have inspired and influenced goddesses all through the ages. We have mentioned many of them already in this book. Here's a partial recap for you to use as a road map:

- Venus, for bringing discovery and innocence back into passion.

- Venus of Willendorf, for appreciating the new voluptuous you.

- Gaia, for cultivating your earthiness, for finding your fecundity arousing.

- Kali, for channeling the deep intuitive wisdom that transforms, for fearlessness and passion, for embracing the changes of motherhood.

- Lakshmi, for invoking the earth goddess element (she was an earth goddess in early times), for bringing forth loyalty and friendship between you and your partner.

- Sarasvati, a patroness of the arts, for romance, for grace, for invoking the muse of creation, for bringing forth beauty and poetry. She is often depicted mounted on a peacock or seated on a swan.

- Pele, when you want some fiery passion. In Hawaii, people honor Pele by throwing hibiscus leis, sugarcane, or gin into her volcanic crater, Kilauea.

- Bast, the Egyptian goddess of pleasure, when you want to play wild cat or regal feline.

- Isis, the Egyptian patroness of loving wives and mothers, for restoration to your love.

- Hestia, Greek goddess of hearth and home, for honoring your devotion to family.

- Awitelin Tsita, for expanding your capacity for love and passion.

The Least You Need to Know

- Pregnancy and motherhood can deepen your intuitive sense, and you can channel that intuition into a transforming erotic charge.

- Your partner and you may lose sight of each other as parenthood crowds out your sex life. Seal the bond between you with techniques such as a heart chakra commitment, the loving circle, and Tantric dating.

- Recognize that your relationship is an ever-changing balance between romance, partnership, and friendship. All need to be nurtured to thrive.

- Honor your changing body through rituals such as the art of dressing naked and revirginizing. Rejuvenate yourself through yoga, exercise, and womb breathing. Remember to do your Kegels.

- When desire doesn't return after bearing children, look at the underlying reasons.

- Draw on a gallery of sex goddesses to guide you in your changing sexual energy.

Chapter **19**

On, and Off, the Pedestal

In This Chapter

- ◆ Alluring April and the festival of Veneralia
- ◆ The fun of flirting
- ◆ Take a (sex) vacation
- ◆ Coming out of the bedroom

It's kind of fun to stand up there, figuratively speaking, on the goddess pedestal, to indulge your goddess status. You feel and look mah-velous, dah-ling, and *everyone* knows it. It's amusing and empowering to know your sensuality affects so many people in so many different ways. Certainly your partner notices this goddess who is you. You awe and excite him; you are at the same time the stuff of his dreams and a significant part of his reality.

This pedestal is a metaphor for the way you, as a sex goddess, have become elevated above the mundane world as you come into your own, seeking passion, pleasure, and self-awareness. In a way, a pedestal puts you on display for others, which can be fun, empowering, and ego-stroking. But at times, you'll want to climb down from there, too. A sex goddess doesn't want to be on display *all* the time. A pedestal can even make you feel objecti-fied. There you are, up there, for the world to see and admire. "How does she do it all? So accomplished, so beautiful, so *sexy*."

A sex goddess knows that sometimes life is lovely on a pedestal, but only when it is easy to climb down. You don't want anyone to *put* you on a pedestal, or *keep* you on a pedestal. But if you can use this metaphorical pedestal for your own pleasure, go for it! When you are tired of being up there, being an icon, being that sex goddess everyone worships, climb on down and take some alone time or some partner time. You radiate womanness in all its layers and dimensions, whether on or off that pedestal. Your partner admires and honors you, and takes joy in knowing that you share your sexuality—and your pedestal—with him. (He can sit up there sometimes, too, can't he?)

When you look at your partner and smile with that certain look in your eye, and his eyes meet yours and your souls connect, pedestals dissolve into the bond between you. You're no longer out of reach, like an object of fine art; you are within reach, within touch. You are real.

Celebration of the Pedestal

Even if you aren't necessarily comfortable with the whole pedestal concept, we're going to talk a little bit about that pedestal, its tradition, and how you can learn to enjoy it and use it. Let's start with that goddess who particularly enjoyed life on a pedestal, that icon of love and beauty and pleasure: Venus.

Our modern month of April honors the Roman goddess of love and beauty Venus (Aphrodite in Greek mythology)—drawn from this goddess's Latin name Aprilis. And April First, our modern celebration of trickery and pranks, was no day for fools in ancient Rome. It was the Veneralia, an exuberant day of merriment and festivities for women to honor the aspect of the month's namesake known as Venus Verticordia— she who changes the hearts of men. The Veneralia was the one day every year when a woman could leave the demure and become the demonstrative. On this one day, it is the ordinary woman on display, with the goddess Venus supporting *her*.

Roman women started the day by bathing in the open and public men's baths. Wearing nothing but wreaths around their heads and the fragrance of incense upon their bodies, they immersed themselves in the warm water, offering prayers and praise to the lovely Venus Verticordia so the goddess would help them remain attractive and alluring to their husbands. In shedding their clothing, they symbolically cast off the constraints of everyday living and their outward presentation that conspired to squelch the fires of desire—doing laundry, scrubbing floors, raising children, planting the garden—showing themselves once again as sensual and beautiful. Bathing in the men's bath imbued the water with the women's essence—and literally, their fragrances—for the men to then soak up when they returned.

If the Roman women could "let it all out" once a year, we bet you can find ways to do the same! (Though we encourage you to indulge yourself far more often than yearly.) In the previous chapter, we suggested a Venus bathing ritual for new mothers to help reconnect them with fresh awareness to their "virgin" sexuality. Going public with your sensuality and your sexuality—whatever that means for you, and whatever your place on the arc of womanhood, from maiden to mother to wise women—restores and affirms this vibrant Venus sex goddess energy for you and for your partner. It helps you to embrace that pedestal for all it's worth.

Initiatress of Love

When April rolls around this year, forget the April Fool's jokes and instead turn your imagination to devising your own public celebrations (appropriate, of course) to honor Venus, the ancient sex goddess. You don't have to bathe in public as the Romans did, but you might consider sharing a sensuous private bath (fragranced with erotic oils such as sandalwood or ylang ylang) to remind your partner that you are, in all ways and all that you do, a sex goddess. Or lie skin-to-skin on a blanket in the spring sun (secluded from prying eyes, of course).

The View from the Diva Dais

Few would argue that legendary actress Sophia Loren is anything but a goddess among goddesses, a contemporary Helen of Troy. From her emergence as a curvaceous, sexy maiden, through the stunning decades as wife and mother, and now in her glory as a wise woman, Loren holds appeal for women and men across the spectrum of age. No question this woman lives her sensuality, in public and in private. And little wonder she captivated the heart of film director Carlo Ponti, who was so smitten by her charm and beauty that he was willing to engage the ire of even the pope.

As much as the marriage of Loren and Ponti seemed destined, it also appeared threatened by forces greater than the wrath of Hera. The Church determined that Ponti's Mexico divorce was not valid, annulled his marriage to Loren, and excommunicated him. The couple circumvented the situation by becoming French citizens and legally marrying in France. (Is it any coincidence that Ponti directed one of the world's most romantic dramas, *Dr. Zhivago*, during this time? We think not!) The result was a lifelong partnership and the couple's celebration in 2004 of their thirty-eighth anniversary (though 44 years together, if you count from their first, albeit annulled, wedding).

Aware of her beauty and its effects on others from the time of her adolescence (the teen beauty's teacher proposed marriage when Loren was 14), Loren has managed to keep balance and perspective throughout her life. "Being beautiful can never hurt, but you have to have more," she's quoted as saying on her official website (www.sophialoren.com). "You have to sparkle, you have to be fun, you have to make your brain work if you have one."

Balancing on the Pedestal

It isn't always easy for a woman to integrate her public image into her private life, though many women, both famous and ordinary, have tried to do so with varying degrees of success. Here are just a few examples from among the famous (and infamous):

♦ Jacqueline Bouvier Kennedy Onassis, the famed "Jackie O," was an icon of beauty, fashion, and grace whose difficult personal challenges—the loss of two infant children and two husbands—were painfully public.

♦ Princess Diana, whose life ended tragically early, found herself grappling every day to balance the storybook quality of her marriage to Charles, Prince of Wales, with the nitty-gritty of real life as a wife and mother in a difficult marriage—and often at odds with her mother-in-law, the queen. Diana shook up and transformed the conventions and traditions of the royal role.

♦ The Duchess of Windsor, a.k.a. Wallis Warfield Simpson, for whom the love of her life gave up the throne of England even though she was at the time married to someone else. He abdicated, she got a divorce, they married, and the royal family exiled them. The couple lived in quiet contentment until the duke's death 35 years after their marriage.

♦ Hillary Rodham Clinton has struggled to balance a very publicly difficult marriage, motherhood, and a high-powered career amidst both cheers and criticism.

How do you feel about these examples? Certainly this is a very short list from among the many, many public stories that could be included. Can you list more examples of women on public pedestals that you admire? What attributes do they display? To what extent can you identify with any or all these women? Do you think of them as epitomizing the modern sex goddess? Why or why not?

And of course, it's not only the famous who live outwardly sensual lives that are in synch with their internal sexuality. Can you think of some examples from among the ordinary … women like us? We bet you can list at least five women who stand out in your mind as personifying the sex goddess ideal in our contemporary times, women you know or see who live in the skin of their sensuality in ways that make it real and palpable to others around them.

Pygmalion's Pedestal: An Ancient Myth

The story of Pygmalion exemplifies the concept of the pedestal quite literally. In ancient Greece, there was a sculptor of unmatched talent, Pygmalion. Though Pygmalion had forsaken marriage (the mythology is unclear about the reasons but it seems he had an unpleasant experience as a young man that soured him on love), he carved a most exquisite woman from a block of ivory. So stunning was she, so perfect in every detail, that Pygmalion fell in love with her and named her Galatea.

Of course, even with a name the statue could not return his affections, and Pygmalion fell into a deep despair. He carved an elaborate pedestal upon which he placed his beloved creation. Every day when he left and when he returned, he kissed the statue on its pedestal.

On the festival of Veneralia, Pygmalion went to the temple of Venus to ask the goddess of love where he might find a maiden so fair. The goddess took pity on him and when the sculptor returned to his studio and kissed the statue, her lips softened and became warm. Astonished, he kissed an ivory arm. It, too, softened. Pygmalion kissed every inch of his statue, which came to life under the touch of his lips. Pygmalion took the hands of his creation to help her down from her pedestal, embraced her, and she became his wife.

Oracle Wisdom

You're like some marvelous, well, queen, I guess. You're so cool and fine and always so much your own. There's a kind of beautiful purity about you, Tracy, like, like a statue. … It's what everybody feels about you. It's what I first worshipped you for from afar.

I don't want to be worshipped. I want to be loved.

—John Howard as George Kittredge and Katharine Hepburn as Tracy Lord in *The Philadelphia Story* (1940)

Flirtatious Fun

It's not always easy to get back the thrill of first romance when you've spent the past *however* many years cleaning your husband's splatter stains off the rim of the toilet, washing his underwear, and trimming the little hairs in his ears. The mundane tasks of everyday life sometimes squelch the romantic right out of you, no matter how much you might prefer otherwise. Life can get pretty dull and routine when other forces take control of your life's direction.

But now that you've let your inner sex goddess out, the control is yours again! Remember the fun of flirting, of wondering whether he will kiss you or not? There are many ways the sex goddess in you can rekindle this excitement. Like Venus, you have the power to grant your deepest desires. All it takes is a little planning and imagination.

Pick Me Up

Early in her career, American actress Helen Hayes (1900–1993) sat alone and lonely at a party. A young playwright approached and handed her some salted peanuts. "I wish they were emeralds," he told her. What a wonderfully original pick-up line! Hayes thought so, too. "That was the end of my heart," Hayes is said to have recalled of her first meeting with Charles MacArthur. "I never got it back." The two wed in 1928. Legend has it that on their twenty-fifth anniversary, MacArthur handed his wife an emerald necklace and said, "I wish they were peanuts." Not a line that would have worked nearly as well 25 years earlier, we're willing to bet, but one that reflects a great sense of humor, not to mention memory, history, and undying love.

What were the first words your partner said to you when you met? What did you say in response? What would he be likely to say today, were he to meet you for the first time? What would you say to him? Can you match the originality of Charles MacArthur? Try picking up your partner like you've never met him before. You might have him sit at a table in a fine restaurant or alone at the bar of a glitzy hotel. Or reverse the roles and have him pick you up. Enjoy a glass of fine wine or a decadent dessert, and let him woo you like he did in the beginning (or if your "pick-up story" isn't so exciting, give him a chance to do an even better job!).

Delightful Dining

It's been said that food and sex are sensual pleasures that go together like, well, man and woman. A good meal can set the stage for good sex … and can *become* the stage with more on the menu than just food. Of course you can order foods reputed to be aphrodisiacs (see Chapter 9) and play with your food in suggestive ways.

When you want to let your fingers do the walking, sit adjacent to or beside each other so that lovin' feeling is within easy (and discreet) reach. Your actions may look as innocent (and sweetly romantic) as holding hands under the table—only you and your partner will know what's really going on down there.

Sitting across the table from each other? Shake off a shoe and try a little toe-tapping, letting your foot stroke and caress its way from your lover's foot to his … well, as far as your desire (and his clothing) allows. Whisper to him what you're wearing (or not wearing) underneath your dress and see how quickly his foot sidles up *your* leg.

Just remember, if these explorations culminate in ecstatic wriggles and moans, people will turn and stare and drop their eating utensils. This might be a good time to practice your eye-gaze breathing!

Initiatress of Love

Remember to keep a sense of humor in your amorous adventures. Sometimes there's nothing sexier than the ability to laugh at yourself. Sex, after all, should be fun. Relax and be willing to be a little silly now and again.

Tease Me, Tempt Me

Maybe you'd rather hint at pleasures to come instead of indulging on the spot. Maybe there's no tablecloth to shelter your wandering tootsies from the curious glances of other restaurant patrons. Maybe all you want to do is tease each other with the hints and previews of what may evolve when you return to the privacy of your boudoir.

Write naughty notes on napkins and pass them back and forth to each other. Use a fingertip dipped in ice water to draw suggestive images on the tabletop (they're easy to swipe away when the waiter comes to the table and will evaporate even if you forget about them). Whisper your desires in one another's ears when you get up to go to the bathroom or pick up a dropped napkin from the floor, or come up with any other contrived reason to be in close proximity (and maybe indulge a soft and teasing nibble on the earlobe while your lips are so temptingly close to this delightfully erogenous zone).

Knowing what potentially awaits when you finally get to somewhere private can be a most exciting and extended form of foreplay.

Anticipation … the Agony and the Ecstasy

Arousal and erotic play need not be merely foreplay. Turn them into the day's primary activities. You can be delicate and sensuous or outrageously tantalizing. Plan a day of erotic encounters just as you might plan any other kinds of activities for a day. Think about what you're comfortable doing, what settings you find romantic or erotic, and how you want the day to progress. Then just let things unfold.

> **Oracle Wisdom** _____
>
> Women! What can you say? Who made 'em? God must have been a … genius. The hair, they say the hair is everything, you know. Have you ever buried your nose in a mountain of curls, just wanted to go to sleep forever? Or lips, and when they touched yours were like that first swallow of wine after you just crossed the desert. Tits. Hoo-hah! Big ones, little ones, nipples staring right out at ya, like secret searchlights. Mmm. Legs. I don't care if they're Greek columns or secondhand Steinways. What's between 'em … passport to heaven. I need a drink.
>
> —Al Pacino as Colonel Frank Slade in *Scent of a Woman* (1992)

Public (In)Discretion

Not everyone appreciates public displays of affection. You might see a sunny summer day in the park as the ideal opportunity for a full-body embrace and tender kiss—which is sometimes all it takes for a passerby to call out, "Hey, get a room!" Even in these times when it seems that anything and everything goes, you need to be mindful of where you are and who might be watching when you snuggle up to your sweetie.

Discretion aside, what you can get away with baring and doing in public may be more a matter of edict than choice. From the time first woman Eve dusted herself off after her fall from grace to find a large leaf covering her yoni, decrees and conventions have defined what body parts can appear unclothed and in contact with someone else's body parts (and not always only in public, although it seems a bit foolish, not to mention intrusive, to monitor one's attire and actions behind closed doors—but we won't get into that discussion here!). Even in the early twentieth century laws in some parts of the United States forbade women from exposing even their arms and legs in public.

Though it does seem the pendulum of public acceptability is today on the far end of the scale from where it was a hundred years ago when the only skin a woman showed was above her neck, there is something to be said for leaving some visions to the imagination. Shroud your sex goddess in a little mystery, and you might be surprised at the outcome.

Private Indulgences in Public Places

Many people are intrigued with the thought of having sex in public places. Whether you'd actually do so or not, you may occasionally indulge the fantasy. And people have done the deed in every place imaginable, from secluded beaches to elevators in busy hotels to office buildings. (Think Samantha in *Sex and the City*.) For some people it's the thrill of possibly getting caught that's the big turn-on, and for other people it's simply the idea of bringing a little variety and creativity into their sex lives by choosing unusual locations.

As we said earlier, remain mindful of your surroundings and your potential audience. Stay appropriate. Jail jumpsuits are not especially sexy or attractive, even if you are the kind of sex goddess who can pull off bright orange.

When *No* Means Know

Being able to say "no" means you know your boundaries and your comfort zone. You know what you are eager to do, intrigued to try, and willing to consider. You also know what does not interest you, what you do not want to do, try, or consider. Everyone has such boundaries, and it's important for you to express yours, when need be, to your partner. Easier said than done, you say? You're right. This simple, two-letter word can be the hardest thing in the world to say to the love of your life (and sometimes even to yourself).

A friend told us, "A man I was dating once said to me, there is no graceful way to say 'no' to a man." Maybe so, but there's no grace in feeling forced to do what you don't want to do, either. Feeling forced to participate in anything that doesn't appeal to you is a sure-fire path to disaster, probably with the experience itself but certainly with its memory. The whole realm of "no" is a lot like a minefield where you never know whether your next step is the one that will set off an explosion. The best path is one of careful consideration.

So what do you do when your partner says, "Let's try ..." and your initial response sounds like you've got something caught in your throat? In a classic *Sex and the City* moment, Carrie grapples with her high-profile New York City politician boyfriend's request for a golden shower in the shower! (Yes, that means he wanted her to urinate on him.) Ultimately, after struggling with the idea and, of course, discussing it with Charlotte, Miranda, and Samantha (each with their *own* take on the situation), Carrie's answer is no.

If yours is a relationship or situation you want to continue to explore, first refrain from reacting reflexively with something like, "Are you nuts?!" when he asks you to say or do something a little bit outside your realm of experience or comfort. Take a moment to think through the words you want to use, and choose words that you can express in a soft and loving way. Often, your partner is putting himself out on the

Beyond Taboos

Even if yours is a long-term, committed relationship, it's important to know where your respective comfort levels are and to find a balance between them. If your partner wants you to do something that makes you uncomfortable, say "no." If your partner says "no" to your fantasies and desires, honor that. However, avoid becoming inflexible! Together, embrace small explorations that take you to new realms of intimate bliss.

proverbial limb to ask this of you and words that shut him down like a slap are sure to shake his confidence as well as jeopardize future sexual explorations.

If, like Marlon Brando in *Last Tango in Paris*, he asks you to "pass the butter," you want to be able to say "no" without destroying the moment. Be gentle in your response, and take enough time before responding so that you can offer an alternative that is more desirable to you yet accommodates in some way the intimacy your partner desires. Later, find an intimate but nonsexual moment to ask your partner, with the most loving kindness, what it is that he likes or needs from the experience he had asked for, so you can learn more about each other's desires. We all have fantasies and ideas that are appealing to our partners and others that are not. You want to keep your erotic encounters on a level you both can appreciate, handle, and enjoy.

This Vacation Is for Adults Only!

Whether you're fantasizing a romantic weekend tryst or an amorous month-long odyssey, escaping with your special someone can take you places you never dreamed you could go … in your imagination or in real life. One of a number of books that highlights vacation opportunities for loving couples is *Adults Only Travel: The Ultimate Guide to Romantic and Erotic Destinations, Second Edition,* by Louis James and David West (Diamond Publishing, 2003). This book tells you where the action is and how to get to it.

One If by Land, Two If by Sea

There's something alluring about the water, particularly water with waves. We can indulge a little water sex play in the ocean or a large lake without attracting attention, perhaps because it's a large enough body of water and it bobs us all around no matter what we're doing. Water, especially salt water, is quite buoyant. Moves you couldn't make on land become effortless in the water, adding to the adventures you can choreograph. Just remember to hold on to your swimwear lest it floats away during your moments of most heated passion. (That could make walking back up to the beach a little awkward.)

Another variation of sex and the sea is sex on a boat. Small boats, like sail boats or ski boats, rock on the waves in a rhythmic motion many people find arousing. Larger vessels, like cruise ships, experience the motion of the water less intensely.

Sex on the beach is enticing, too. With a towel or beach blanket between you and the sand, the sand feels warm and soft to lie on. Beaches are generally more exposed than the water, leaving you vulnerable to accidental discovery, so be aware of where you are and any local laws! And then there's the small detail of sand being in places it shouldn't be. But hey, you're on the beach. Hop in the water and rinse yourself off!

In many locations there are private beaches for those who want to enjoy the sand and surf in the buff. Most nudist beaches require membership as a means to help safeguard guests, though some (particularly in Europe) are open to the public. Just as there are tour guides to the best surfing beaches, there are guidebooks that describe the best nudist beaches. Check your local bookstore. (And remember that "nudist beach" doesn't mean "you can have sex in front of everybody beach." You still need to behave in front of people.)

> **Initiatress of Love**
>
> If you're of childbearing age and pregnancy is not in your plans, you'll want to make sure you have the contraception covered for your amorous adventures. Stash condoms in strategic places or carry some with you, or an extra diaphragm, in your purse, if these are your methods.

The Mile-High Club

Contemporary legend has it the first in-air copulatory connection between man and woman took place nearly a century ago, in 1916, pairing daredevil aviator Lawrence Sperry with an equally daring New York socialite who was taking flight lessons (and apparently more) from him. In those early days of aviation, it was a remarkable feat to fly a mile above the earth, though today's jets routinely cruise nearly seven miles into the atmosphere.

According to the story, Sperry's plane crashed in a boggy marsh from which duck hunters rescued him and his student—both naked. No official explanation was ever forthcoming. However, Sperry did invent the automatic pilot, derivations of which are in nearly all airplanes flown today, a few months before his erotic and fateful flight. Adventurous couples enamored of the idea of joining in passion high in the sky have reported indulging in similar feats (though not the crashing part) ever since.

Commercial airlines—and we—strongly discourage such amorous couplings on commercial flights, if for no other reason than the fact that they are now violations of U.S. law. Being arrested, even with a big smile on your face, is not exactly the way you want to end a passionate close encounter, not to mention a transcontinental flight. Instead, consider one of the many charter flights that will take you up for a romantic interlude.

Maybe you only want to sip champagne and hold hands as you drift through the clouds. Maybe you want to become one with each other as you cruise several miles above terra firma. Whatever your desire, be sure it's a permitted behavior for the flight. If you want to fly to new heights, literally, check out www.milehighclub.com for more information about charter flights that specifically accommodate aerial intercourse.

Beyond Taboos

In the years when air travel was coming of age, mile-high unions commonly took place in airplane lavatories (which clearly were larger than those on today's commercial aircraft) and other hideaway locations where passengers could duck and snuggle. The current climate, of course, precludes such rendezvous. Not only are lavatories smaller but passengers are no longer free to wander about the aircraft. You may need to be content with whispering subtleties to each other at 35,000 feet, with promises of follow-through at ground level. The anticipation carries its own sweet reward.

Home Is Where the Sex Goddess Lives

Vacations for passion are fun, though they eventually must come to an end. That doesn't mean your fun must end, too. When you're on vacation, you tend to be relaxed and carefree, traits that encourage the expression of sexuality in its many variations. There's no reason you can't take this aspect of your vacation home with you.

And who says sex has to stay in the bedroom? This is often the best option for privacy and to shape an environment that supports intimacy. But what better escape than an afternoon interlude of lovemaking in the living room? Or a before-breakfast quickie in the kitchen? As often as not, sex stays in the bedroom out of habit.

Consider planning a day of lovemaking that migrates from one room to another all through your home, like a banquet. You might start with a shower or bath together, enjoy an appetizer on the deck or in the yard (if you can be hidden from the view of neighbors and passersby), become the meal on the table. You'll never look at staying home for the day in the same way again!

It's *Your* Pedestal

As a sex goddess, you experience and enjoy the essence of your womanness, in many dimensions—through the physical sensations of your body, through your thoughts and emotions, through your spirituality. These are dimensions that will guide you to further discoveries and a sense of reverence and celebration about the sexual, sensual you. Within the boundaries of your comfort zone, explore and enjoy this essence that is you.

The Least You Need to Know

- As a sex goddess, you create your own pedestal for honoring and sharing your sexuality and sensuality.

- All women work and sometimes struggle to balance their public images and private lives, sometimes more successfully than others.

- Coming down from your pedestal (or inviting your partner up on to your pedestal) is to engage and evoke your sexuality in your everyday life.

- It's important to know your boundaries and limits in exploring the many dimensions of your sexuality and sex play, and to be able to say "no" with grace and loving kindness when your partner's desires look to carry you beyond your comfort zone.

- There's no rule that says you can only enjoy sex in your bedroom. You live in every room of your home; enjoy your sexuality in every room as well.

Chapter 20

A Touch of Sappho and Aphrodite

In This Chapter

◆ Focus on woman love

◆ The lesbian source

◆ Women first

◆ Spirit of the witch

◆ Special knowledge that women share

Sappho—you've probably heard of her. Her name has come to represent a certain kind of love. Sappho has been so influential in the course of our civilization that her name has even been made into an adjective. Sapphic love refers to the love between two women.

But what do you actually know about this woman? Who was Sappho really, and what is her importance? You probably know that Sappho is considered to be one of the great Greek poets. Although she gained fame through her work, much information about her life and most of her poems have been lost. You also may know that Sappho was born sometime between 630 and 612 B.C.E. She was born into an aristocratic family, married a wealthy merchant, and had one child, a daughter named Cleis. Sappho lived much of her life writing and studying the arts on Lesbos, an island in the Aegean Sea near the coast of Turkey.

Scholars are not in total agreement about how Sappho spent her time on the island. Many believe that she ran a school for young women or taught private poetry lessons. The poems, which were sung to the accompaniment of the lyre, may have been used in religious ceremonies as part of a women's mystery tradition that honored the goddesses. Sappho's own poems were unusual for the time because, instead of focusing on the gods and goddesses, she wrote about her own life and her personal feelings. Judging from Sappho's poems, or the fragments that remain, she had a tendency to fall in love with her female students. In her poems, she writes of love, yearning, and the beauty of women. She also addresses Aphrodite, the goddess of love, as a mentor and confidante. Sometimes she complains to the goddess. Other times she implores the goddess to help her secure the attention of the object of her affection.

After some time studying with Sappho, her young female students left the island to marry, and Sappho, who was considered the master of the genre, crafted each young woman's wedding song. Sappho's poetry was so well regarded that the island of Lesbos, which was considered a cultural center, minted coins bearing her image; the people of Syracuse, a city in Sicily where Sappho lived for a time, erected a statue in her honor; and the famed philosopher Plato referred to her as the tenth Muse. Over the period of more than 2,000 years since her death, Sappho has served as an inspiration for many poets, writers, women, lovers, and sex goddesses from all over the world. Today Sappho invites us to explore the sorority of the feminine and its place in the lives of modern-day sex goddesses like you.

In the Media

You can't seem to turn on the television these days without hearing about or seeing images of women's strong connection to other women. From Madonna's on-screen smooches with Britney Spears and Christina Aguilera to Jennifer Beals, Laurel Holloman, and Katherine Moennig starring in the new Showtime series *The L Word*, which focuses on the lives and loves of a group of sexy contemporary *lesbians* in Los Angeles, women are coming together on television, in movies, and in the news media like they never have before. And it's not just actresses that you see. With debate raging about same-sex marriage, real women are making the headlines, too.

Source of All

The word *lesbian,* which refers to a female person with homosexual tendencies, comes from the name of Sappho's home island Lesbos. Many women who primarily have sexual relations with other women call themselves lesbians, but not all do. Some women call themselves "gay," while others avoid that term because they feel it refers mostly to men. Some women identify themselves as "straight" (heterosexual) even though they sometimes have sexual relations with other women. The word *homosexual* is generally avoided because it sounds so clinical and old-fashioned.

In early 2004, thousands of same-sex couples flocked to municipal buildings all over the country to obtain marriage licenses. In San Francisco alone, more than 4,000 same-sex couples got married. Many of these couples stood in the rain for hours to obtain their licenses, and the images of this kind of devotion touched onlookers nationwide. Women like Del Martin and Phyllis Lyon, the first same-sex couple to obtain a marriage license and marry in the United States, have become icons and beacons of love. At the time of their marriage, Martin, 83, and Lyon, 79, had been together 51 years. (How many couples do you know who have stayed together that long?) Living and working together, Martin and Lyon have written numerous books and, in 1955, founded Daughters of Bilitis, the first national lesbian rights organization. The impact and the beauty of their love story have created a stir. Across the country, more and more people are starting to wonder why not allow same-sex couples the same legal recognition that male-female partnerships enjoy.

In many ways, fictional images of woman-to-woman love have proved more shocking and controversial than the real thing. Certainly Madonna was counting on the shock value of that kiss she planted on Britney Spears on national television! (Not to say we weren't intrigued …)

Of course, movies you may have seen, such as *The Hours* (2003), have portrayed the real tenderness and sexuality that can grow between women. In *The Hours*, which was based on the Michael Cunningham novel of the same name, Meryl Streep stars as book editor Clarissa Vaughn who lives with her longtime female partner, played by Allison Janney. In addition, 1950s housewife Laura Brown, played by the lovely Julianne Moore, shares an intense screen kiss with her best girlfriend, played by Toni Collette. Nicole Kidman, who won an Oscar that year for best actress for her portrayal of writer Virginia Woolf in *The Hours*, shares a kiss with the actress playing Woolf's sister, the artist Vanessa Bell; the kiss speaks volumes about a shared creative intimacy connecting two remarkable sisters. In real life, Woolf—like many famous female writers and artists—was also known for her affairs with women.

Beyond Taboos

If the idea of two women together makes you feel anxious, don't worry! Especially in the sexual arena, many people fear the unknown. We're sure that the more you learn about woman-to-woman love, the less fear you will feel. That doesn't mean you have to go out and kiss a girl! We only hope you will consider with respect those who choose to do so. Take it slowly if you need to, but we hope you will continue to read this chapter. Woman-to-woman love may not be for you, and that's okay. Nevertheless, as a sex goddess, you'll be able to appreciate how such relationships can be a source of joy, pleasure, and comfort for others.

Another movie you may want to check out is *Kissing Jessica Stein* (2002), an uplifting romantic comedy, co-written by co-stars Jennifer Westfeldt and Heather Juergensen. In the film, Jessica, a frustrated heterosexual copyeditor, answers a personal ad from a bisexual woman. Helen, Jessica's new date, is fairly relaxed, which is a good thing, because Jessica is anxious, in a funny Woody Allen–ish way. Despite their differences, the two young women fall sweetly in love. Another warm romantic comedy and coming-of-age story is *The Incredibly True Adventures of Two Girls in Love* (1995) directed by Maria Maggenti. Randy, a lesbian teenager is failing math and smoking too much grass. One day, her chic fellow student Evie drives up to the gas station where Randy works and changes her world forever.

Director Rose Troche's *Go Fish* (1994), a low-budget classic, stars the adorable Guinevere Turner and delivers a funny take on a young woman's attempts to find Ms. Right. In *Desert Hearts* (1985), directed by Donna Deitch, another warm, well-acted film that packs an emotional punch, opposites attract when the elegant Helen Shaver, playing a recently divorced college professor, arrives in 1959 Reno and meets the boyishly beautiful and sexy Patricia Charbonneau.

If you like your romance a little darker, you may like *The Hunger* (1983), a vampire film starring the agelessly elegant Catherine Deneuve. Perfectly cast as a vampiresse in search of a new mate, the sexy French actress seduces the gorgeous Susan Sarandon one silky, sunlit afternoon. *Bound* (1996), another skillfully crafted film that has attained cult status, features the squeaky-voiced Meg Tilly and the sultry Gina Gershon. Although violent at times, this film—part love story, part heist movie, and part gangster flick—is a delicious romp, and Tilly and Gershon are super sexy together. The beautifully filmed biopic *Frida* tells the story of Mexican artist Frida Kahlo who, though married for many years to the artist Diego Rivera, had many affairs with women and had a great aesthetic and sensual appreciation of the female form.

Even in the 1930s, Hollywood made use of the intrigue of lesbian love. A poster advertising Marlene Dietrich's film *Morocco* (1930) reads "Dietrich—the woman all women want to see." And in fact, Dietrich, who was rumored to have had many affairs with both men and women, appears in one scene dressed in a man's top hat and tails, then grabs a woman and kisses her on the lips. In *Queen Christina* (1933), Greta Garbo, another star thought to have had same-sex relationships, plays an androgynous role with lesbian overtones and another woman-to-woman on-screen kiss.

If you had been around before the birth of cinema in 1895, you would have found your images of women's love for women in paintings. *The Turkish Bath* (1862) by Jean-Auguste-Dominique Ingres (1780–1867), which hangs in the Louvre, captures the sensuality of a group of voluptuous bathing beauties (no waifs here!) who in turn have captured the imaginations of viewers for more than a century. So although you may see more images of lesbian sex goddesses and woman-to-woman love in recent times, such depictions certainly aren't new.

Initiatress of Love

In your journal, keep notes about what you find attractive about other women. Allow your observations to be wide-ranging, include the mental, emotional, and spiritual, as well as the physical. Feel free to note what you like about women you know and about those whom you don't know. You can even include celebrities. Which qualities and characteristics that you admire in others do you yourself possess? And which qualities would you like to cultivate in yourself?

Welcome to the Isle of Lesbos

As far as we can tell, ancient Greeks followed their hearts and did not worry about labeling their behavior or the gender of the individuals they loved. Many classics scholars believe that same-sex love was typical and accepted in the ancient world. On the island of Lesbos, Sappho's home, a phase of lesbianism seems to have been commonplace. Young women formed romantic bonds while they were students, and then left those relationships when they moved away from the island to get married. In Sappho's case, she seems to have continued to have same-sex affairs even while she was married. In addition to the young women, she may have been involved with a man named Phaon who worked as a ferryman.

What we admire about Sappho and her society is that they both cherished and educated women. On top of that, they recognized and celebrated the strong bonds of affection that can exist between women. Of course, ancient Greece is not the only culture to honor woman-to-woman relationships. As we noted in Chapter 6, ancient Chinese and Japanese cultures expected the principle wife in a household to sexually satisfy her husband's other wives and, in the Tantric tradition, sexual activity between two women is thought to strengthen a woman's yin essence and, thus, make her more attractive.

Unfortunately, during much of recent history in Western society, physical relationships between women, instead of being accepted, expected, and even celebrated, have been frowned upon or even persecuted. Many people today harbor so much *homophobia* that they could never consider admitting to any kind of sensual feeling for a member of their same gender. In fact, some people are so fraught with homophobia that they think no one should ever enjoy an intimate same-sex relationship. We think there is really nothing to be afraid of. We also think that, when it comes to intimate relations, everyone is different.

Source of All

Coined in the late 1960s by a psychologist, **homophobia** refers to the fear of homosexuality, fear of gay and lesbian people, or an aversion to the gay and lesbian lifestyle.

In the late 1940s and early 1950s, Dr. Alfred Kinsey, a sex researcher, developed a scale to measure the spectrum of sexual orientations. People, he discovered, are not just gay or straight, but are gay and straight to certain degrees. Kinsey found that each person can describe his or her sexuality by using his seven-point continuum, which ranges from exclusively heterosexual to exclusively homosexual. He also found that most people lie somewhere in between these two poles.

The Kinsey Scale

0 Exclusively heterosexual

1 Predominantly heterosexual, incidentally homosexual

2 Predominantly heterosexual, but more than incidentally homosexual

3 Equally heterosexual and homosexual

4 Predominantly homosexual, but more than incidentally heterosexual

5 Predominantly homosexual, incidentally heterosexual

6 Exclusively homosexual

When considering an individual's place on the scale, Kinsey took into account fantasies, dreams, thoughts, actual sexual activity, and emotions. He found that many people who live outwardly heterosexual lives actually lie somewhere between zero and three on the scale because sometimes they think, dream, or fantasize about sexual activities with members of their own gender or they occasionally act on these feelings of attraction.

The point of all of this is that many women have sexual fantasies about other women. And why not? As a sex goddess, you know that women are sexy! Having fantasies about women does not mean that you necessarily want to act on those fantasies. Maybe the woman in your head is the woman for you! But, perhaps, you do feel drawn to explore. Or perhaps you have explored Sapphic love in the past or are doing so in the present. Or maybe you just want to know more about the ancient woman-to-woman connection. Perhaps you just want to be able to answer that age-old question: What do two women do in bed?

The answer is: anything they want to! Some women who have sex with women enjoy receiving pleasure in the form of oral sex and some do not like this activity much. Some women who love other women sexually like to engage in *tribadism*. Some women who enjoy other women physically enjoy penetration and the feeling of having something—whether it be a finger, an object, or a whole hand—inside of them. And others do not take to this form of sexual expression. Some women like to perform oral sex, and some women do not. Some women derive pleasure from penetrating their partners, while others are left cold by the idea. Just like heterosexual women, some women who enjoy sex with women like everything, some women are satisfied by only a few types of sexual activity, and some prefer one method of loving over all others. Of course, ultimately the emotional bond between partners, whoever you are, is the *real* bond, not what you do in bed.

Oracle Wisdom

The sex act itself is neither male nor female: it is a human being reaching out for the ultimate in communication with another human being.

—Del Martin (1921–) and Phyllis Lyon (1924–), pioneers in the lesbian movement

Source of All

Tribadism, which comes from ancient Greek, refers to rubbing of the genitals. Two women can engage in tribadism together by adopting the "missionary position" and rubbing their yonis against each other. Alternatively, you can rub your yoni against your partner's thigh while stimulating her with your own thigh.

The Cult of Diana

Because she is an ancient Greek goddess we don't really know what Diana did in bed—but we can imagine! Known in the Greek tradition as Artemis, Diana, as you may remember, is the great huntress who gallops through the forest with quiver of arrows hanging from her shoulder. Surrounded by her nymphs, she avoids the company of men and pursues her own dreams and causes. She represents the hunt, wild places, women, and chastity. She is also associated with the moon.

You may know the story about Diana and Actaeon, son of King Cadmus of Thebes. Like Diana, Actaeon was considered to be an expert hunter. One day Diana and her nymphs were lounging in her favorite spot in the forest on the shores of a spring-fed pool. Actaeon, on an outing with his dogs and a party of his hunting buddies, stumbled upon them. Some say that he spied on them and saw Diana, stepping into the water, naked. Others say that he challenged her by claiming he was the better hunter. Still others think that he tried to assault her. With neither her arrows nor her javelin to defend herself, Diana splashed Actaeon with water. As soon as the drops hit him, he turned into a stag and bolted into the forest. His dogs and his friends, unaware that the beast they pursued was really Actaeon, gave chase and eventually killed him.

Of course, we're not suggesting that sex goddesses should turn people into animals or have them killed! What we do admire about Diana in this story is her ability to defend herself and her insistence on her right to have time to be alone with the girls.

Initiatress of Love

As you've probably guessed, *womyn* means "women." In the 1970s, when the term was coined, some womyn decided that they didn't like *woman* because that word comes from the Old English word *wifmann*, which means "wife of man." At the time, many women felt they had to totally separate themselves from men to find out who they were and what they wanted—personally, sexually, spiritually, and career-wise.

If you have ever attended an all-female high school or college, you know that there can be something really special and empowering about women-only spaces.

Or perhaps you have been to the Michigan Womyn's [*sic*] Music Festival, which has been held every year in August since the mid-1970s. For one week, women from all over the world gather in the Michigan countryside on a private plot of 650 acres to celebrate themselves, each other, and a woman-centered culture. In addition to music by popular performers (and sex goddesses!) such as Ani DiFranco, Ferron, Lucie Blue Tremblay, Toshi Reagon, Bernice Johnson Reagon, and Ubaka Hill, you might see performances by lesbian comedians such as Kate Clinton and Karen Williams. You also might take a workshop or two offered at the festival—yoga, women's sexuality, spiritu-ality, stilt walking, flirting, astrology, drumming, sacred singing, seduction, and div-ination are just some of the workshops offered. Most but not all the women who attend this annual event are lesbians. Many women feel a unique sense of freedom and empowerment, of being able to truly be themselves for the first time. Festival attendees also note an intense sense of connection to the enormous and powerful sis-terhood of women. As we're sure you see, this kind of empowerment, self-acceptance, and connection are all a part of the joy of being a sex goddess!

Margot Adler, a reporter and author of the influential *Drawing Down the Moon: Witches, Druids, Goddess Worshipers, and Other Pagans in America Today, Revised and Updated Edition* (Penguin/Arkana, 1997), has discussed her experiences of being a heterosexual woman at the Michigan festival. As such, she did feel part of a minority, but she also felt embraced, and as practitioner of a goddess-centered spirituality, she was both heartened and affirmed. If the Michigan festival had an official religion, it might just be goddess worship! Many women who attend the festival are in touch with their goddesses. And in fact, Diana is often central among them.

As you probably know, many pagan traditions including Wicca and other forms of witchcraft are major forms of goddess worship practiced in the United States today. Modern day witches hold themselves to a strict ethical code of conduct; avoid any-thing evil, including even the idea of Satan; and pay homage to the goddess. Because most witches see all goddesses as part of the great goddess, they can choose to focus on whichever goddess from whichever culture speaks to them personally.

In Dianic witchcraft, a tradition that was founded in the 1970s and derives its name from the goddess Diana, the goddess is honored in her three aspects—maiden, mother, and wise woman. Considered to be part of the feminist wave of witchcraft, many but not all practitioners of Dianic witchcraft meet in women-only covens. In the early days of Dianic witchcraft, most practitioners were lesbians. Today, that situa-tion has changed—some covens are all lesbian, some are mixed with members of all sexual orientations, and some are made up of heterosexual women. What all of these women have in common is their understanding of the sacred nature of women's bod-ies and a commitment to honoring women's experience—characteristics that you, as a budding sex goddess, will want to cultivate, nourish, and cherish.

> **Beyond Taboos** _____
>
> Some people have a hard time saying the words *lesbian, gay, bisexual,* or *homosexual* out loud. Do you feel embarrassed when you say these words? Do you feel awkward when you hear someone else say these words? Some people feel that the issues associated with these words should be kept private. Speaking these words in public can feel like breaking a taboo. Doing so may cause you to worry about what other people think of you. If you feel so inclined, practice saying these words out loud. The more you say them, the more easily and naturally they will roll off your tongue.

Girl Power, Goddess Style

One thing we can say about lesbian sex goddesses—from Sappho to some of the fictional characters we have mentioned to the real-life women in this chapter—they tend to be an empowered group, and you know that the old adage is true—knowledge is power. Woman-to-woman love has long been associated with a special knowledge. Just look at Anog Ite, the Dakota goddess, who was daughter of first Woman and first Man. This Native American deity taught a type of basket-weaving that was considered to conflict with a woman's traditional role. This special knowledge was said to lead women to lesbianism.

In feminist theology, Lilith, Adam's first wife in the Garden of Eden, was said to possess special, secret knowledge as well. In one version of her story, Lilith and Adam are created as equals. When Adam tried to control her, Lilith fled from the garden. This prompted God to create Eve. Adam told Eve stories about the evil Lilith and how she had to leave the paradise of the garden. One day, Eve, who was curious by nature, looked over the wall of the garden and came face to face with the woman she had been taught to fear. Eve was afraid of Lilith at first, but she also wanted to learn, so she stayed and listened to her. Lilith taught Eve what she knew, and the two became good friends. In one radical version of this story, Lilith even teaches Eve how to have an orgasm. Now that's some special and important knowledge!

But what is it that lesbians know? Women who are physically intimate with other women get a double dose of yoni power and greater reserves of yin essence. Female lovers, like many women who live together in close proximity, tend to get on the same schedule with regard to their menstrual cycles. Some people think that all this synchronized female energy increases a woman's receptivity to the womanly arts of intuition. We don't know if this is a scientific fact, but it feels like there could be something to this notion!

Perhaps lesbians hold the answer to that question of questions that Freud asked so long ago: "What do women want?" And perhaps the answer lies in the most obvious and personal of places. Maybe the special knowledge that lesbians hold is a true understanding and appreciation of the yoni, the source of all life, the doorway to the body and the spirit, and the center of goddesslike pleasure. Of course, as a sex goddess you know all of this, too!

Oracle Wisdom

Eleanor Roosevelt, first lady, writer, and campaigner for women's rights, had a close long-term relationship with journalist Lorena Hickok, who moved into the White House to be near her. In a letter from March 1933, Eleanor wrote to her good friend, "Hick darling … I want to put my arms around you, I ache to hold you close. Your ring is a great comfort, I look at it & think she does love me, or I wouldn't be wearing it!"

Ode to Aphrodite

Sappho's ode to Aphrodite is the only poem of hers that still exists today in its entirety. In the ancient world, choruses of young girls celebrated Aphrodite, as well as her sister goddesses Artemis and mother goddess Demeter, with poetry, song, and dancing. Aphrodite, of course, is the goddess of sexual love and beauty. In Sappho's ode, Sappho praises this sex goddess by remarking on her power and abilities to cause heartbreak. She also notes Aphrodite's "immortal smile" and asks for the goddess's help.

Praising another woman and cultivating an appreciation of other women in all their aspects is also learning to accept and appreciate yourself. We come in all colors, shapes, and sizes. We are old and young and somewhere in between. We are redheads and brunettes and blondes and some of us have mousy colored hair. Some of us have large, full breasts with soft pink nipples, while some have small compact ones with dark centers. Once you start looking, you will realize that every woman's breasts are as individual and beautiful as she is. Some of us have body and pubic hair that is dark; some of us have hardly any body hair at all. Your body, the amazing physical vehicle in which you have been placed to enjoy this earth and all of her gifts, is as unique and special and sexy as you are.

Oracle Wisdom

I will be quiet, be still, and know that it is God who put the love for women in my heart.
—Brigitte M. Roberts, U.S. writer

Are you ready for another sex goddess exercise? Well, we are! Why not write an ode to the sex goddess of your choice? If you're not much one for writing poetry, don't worry. We'll help you every step of the way!

First, to get in a poetic mood, you may want to read some of Sappho's work. Although much of Sappho's creative output has been lost, you can find what has remained into the present day in a number of good translations. Check out Mary Barnard's version, *Sappho: A New Translation* (University of California Press, 1986). Or if you want some great sensuous details about a real woman, look for Andrew Marvel's poem "To His Coy Mistress," which has been widely anthologized and included in many "great" poem collections. Let the words of these poets serve as a jumping-off point and an inspiration for what you appreciate about the female form and her spiritual essence.

If you haven't already, take a look at a few of the movies mentioned in this chapter. Make some notes about what you like and find attractive about the characters that you see. You also may want to visit the website of the Louvre Museum in Paris (or maybe take a field trip and bask in the presence of amazing artwork in the "flesh") and see Ingres's painting *The Turkish Bath*. Go to www.louvre.fr/louvrea.htm for the English language version of the site. Under "Collections," click "Selected works." Then click "Paintings," "Selected works," and "France: 19th century." You'll see a small image (which you can enlarge by clicking yet another link) of *The Turkish Bath* and those very voluptuous and sexy bathing beauties.

If there is a particular characteristic about yourself that you don't like, see if you can find that same "fault" in others and see how sexy it really is. We think it is interesting that lots of women who hate their own large hips can find Jennifer Lopez's full hips sexy. Spend some time appreciating Jennifer's amazing caboose. Or what about that little pillow of fat on your tummy? One of our friends hated hers until she realized that one of the really cute girls she kept seeing at the gym had one, and on her it looked inviting, sweet, and sexy.

Now gather your notes and your thoughts. Start by making a list of all the wonderful and sexy details that characterize the sex goddess in your mind. Remember to include sensuous details that make use of all five senses—sight, sounds, touch, taste, and scent. And include any details about the sixth sense—intuition—that feel important to you. Arrange the words from your list. Allow the sounds and the sense of the words to guide you, but don't worry about trying to rhyme. You may want to keep your poem in list form. (Many poets write list poems.) If you like, start your poem with these words:

"O great sex goddess, I praise your …"

Once you have written your poem and polished it to your satisfaction, get ready to celebrate your own inner sex goddess. You will need some quiet alone time with your sex goddess poem. (If writing a poem right now seems like it will just turn into one more task hanging on your to-do list, select a published poem that celebrates women.) You will also need:

- A few candles

- Soft background music

- A full-length mirror

Stand in front of the full-length mirror. If you feel comfortable, you may want to take off your clothes. If this feels like too much, don't worry and remain dressed. Spend a few moments looking at yourself with love and appreciation. Be sure you keep breathing while you do this so you can really take yourself in.

When you feel ready, read your poem of praise out loud to yourself. While you do this, look in the mirror and admire the glorious sex goddess that you are. Repeat the poem to yourself a few times. Allow the words to sink in. If there is a particular area of your body that bothers you, spend some extra time lavishing love and attention there.

When you feel that you are done, put your clothes back on and relax. Reflect on your experience. Spend a few minutes writing in your journal, if you feel so moved. Make note of which aspects of your song of praise were easy for you to accept and which felt more challenging or hard to believe.

Done regularly, this exercise will help you develop greater self-confidence, and self-confidence is a huge aphrodisiac. And, yes, the word *aphrodisiac* comes from the name of the great sex goddess Aphrodite.

The Least You Need to Know

- Women who love women have been a part of human culture throughout history.

- Many cultures celebrate love and sensuality between women.

- People are not just gay or straight, but are gay or straight to a certain degree. Most people fall somewhere along the continuum of sexual orientation.

- Attending a women-only event can be empowering, and your empowerment fuels your inner sex goddess.

- Sometimes it's easier to appreciate others than it is to appreciate ourselves. Allow your celebration of the beauty of women to include all women, especially you!

Chapter 21

A Sex Goddess Is a *Love* Goddess

In This Chapter

- ◆ Can a sex goddess change the world?
- ◆ The power of love to strengthen the family, community, and planet
- ◆ What the sex goddesses can teach you
- ◆ You the Creatrix
- ◆ Be a light unto yourself

In mythology, the sex goddess is a potent source of power. Her actions can change the seasons, shape the fate of the human race, manipulate the destinies of other gods and mortals, decide who lives and who dies, determine professions and marital status, fertility and success in childbirth. She governs birth and leads the soul into the underworld at the end of its time on Earth. She is the source of all.

But what about you? If you are a sex goddess, too, then how much power can you have over the world? Probably a whole lot more than you might think!

Sex Goddess Energy to Transform Reality

The regular practice of sacred sex and the confident immersion into the persona of sex goddess can do more than improve intimacy and strengthen your love relationships. It can also transform other aspects of your life, and the lives of others. Sex goddess "training" actually teaches you how to live a more vibrant and meaningful life, and when you live with more presence, energy, and radiating love, then everyone around you can't help but feel the effects.

Remember the classic Christmas movie, *It's a Wonderful Life?* Whether or not you've seen it so many times that you don't plan to ever see it again, this movie illustrates a little bit of what we mean when we say that your energy can transform reality. And we don't just mean that Jimmy Stewart's character, George Bailey, changed the world. What would George have been without Mary Bailey, Donna Reed's character? She transformed a restless young man who didn't know what he wanted into a partner and community pillar, a loving father and devoted husband.

Goodness and love have a ripple effect and when you practice them, they take on a life of their own, their energy spreading over others and changing their actions, which in turn influence the reactions of still more people. One act of love can have effects too numerous and far-reaching to calculate. Just imagine what a thousand acts of love could effect!

You can influence your impact on others purposefully and with true sex goddess panache if you engage the world with conscious attention and meaningful action. Consider how the lessons you learn from the practice of sacred sex can impact your family, friends, work relationships, and community. Think of the ways in which the love energy you and your partner generate can infuse both of you to act differently out in the world. Then, become a proactive love goddess, in the great tradition of other feminine creators, protectors, and avengers of evil. Just imagine if we all did it. Imagine how we might transform the world.

Oracle Wisdom

Shandian Pozi, the Chinese goddess of lightning, holds a mirror in each hand. She directs lightning, or her "golden snakes," to strike humans to reveal what is truly in their hearts, so the god of thunder can decide how they should be punished. No one can escape the revealing electrical jolt of Shandian Pozi! Like Shandian Pozi, you can also demand truth in your relationships. Use your intuition to determine truth, and don't settle for anything less! (But be prepared to hear it, too. If "you can't handle the truth," don't ask!)

Love Energy to Fortify Family and Friends

As you get in touch with your inner sex goddess and become more and more skilled at transforming sexual energy into spiritual energy, you get a few other skills that come along for the ride. Not the least of these skills is mindfulness, which can have a profound effect on your family life and on those others you hold dear.

Most of us have relationships of several types—with our children, parents, friends, partners, and co-workers. But because we know our families so well and because we have known them for so long, these relationships are more prone to patterns, assumptions, and automatic reactions. We get wrapped up in certain ideas about our families. We have profiles about each of our family members all written up in our heads, and they have profiles written up about us. When we talk to our families or get together with them, we all expect each other to behave according to our expected profiles, and to engage in the same patterns. In some ways this is comforting, especially when the profiles and patterns are favorable or make us feel safe. But if anyone should act out of character, it can cause resentment, anger, irritation, or frustration. When the profiles and patterns are less favorable, these same negative emotions can surface when our family members behave *exactly* in the way we expect.

Whether you like or dislike your family in general or have questionable relationships with some of them, try stepping back and seeing them more objectively. How would you see your sister if she wasn't your sister, but someone you just met? How would you relate to your parents if they were somebody else's parents? What about your children? How would you see them if they weren't yours? These topsy-turvy perspectives can give you new insight on these people you label "family."

Friends are often similar, so we tend to label them in certain ways—"the introspective one," "the partying one," "the responsible one," "the immature one."

But mindfulness cuts through all that. Mindfulness encourages you to abandon assumptions, patterns, and expectations, living only in the present moment. During lovemaking sessions, this helps you to tune in to every sensation, to more fully experience the building tension and thrills of sexual ecstasy. But in everyday relationships with family and friends, mindfulness helps you to banish what you think someone will do or say in favor of truly tuning in to what they are really doing or saying.

The mindful mother can look directly at her children and really listen to them when they talk to her, rather than distractedly nodding and muttering "uh-huh" while doing three other things at the same time. The mindful daughter can talk with her mother and hear her, not as a mother who is supposed to say certain things but as another human being interacting with someone she loves. The mindful friend pays attention to what is really going on with her friends, reading all the signs, not just listening: body language, facial expressions, calls for help, or requests to share joy. The mindful partner also knows how to really listen and be present with her beloved so they can exchange ideas, support each other, and move through life together in equal partnership.

> **Oracle Wisdom** _____
>
> Ariadne, one of the Greek goddesses of love, gave Theseus a ball of string to unravel while traveling through the maze to find and kill the monstrous Minotaur. Because of Ariadne's cleverness, Theseus was able to find his way out of the maze and, along the way, rescued seven boys and seven girls meant to be food for the Minotaur. Theseus and Ariadne fled together with their 14 adopted children away from Crete to safety. Thanks to Ariadne's innovative and creative mind, coupled with her love for Theseus, everyone survived.

The love that suffuses you when engaged in regular sacred sex can also have a profound effect on your family and friends. You will probably feel calmer, less stressed, and more loving toward the people in your family, and that will help everyone else to feel calmer, less stressed, and more loving, too. Rising above the mundane helps you to feel compassion and empathy for others, which will encourage you to act on behalf of the people you love, and even people you've never met.

The behavior of every human being influences others, a natural effect of living in social groups. When you radiate positive energy, everyone will benefit. So why not live in the light of your inner love right now, today, like a true sex goddess does? You can change the world as you change your heart.

Life Lessons from the Sex Goddesses

In the same way your family and friends benefit from the positive energy of the sex goddess, so does the community, and even the planet as a whole. When you re-orient your perspective toward life to fall in line with the perspective of a sex goddess filled with love and the desire to protect, your actions can have untold influence.

Consider the ways in which you might act like some of these goddesses to have a positive and loving influence on your community, the world community, and the planet. These are the life lessons of the sex goddesses, and life lessons you can practice and live by, too. Remember, everything you do influences others, either by direct impact, indirect impact, or example. Live, fully and compassionately, and others will learn to live better, too.

Now, as a sex goddess, please know and remember these lessons:

- **Have many personas.** Gentle and beautiful as Parvati, loyal marital equal to Shiva as Devi, courageous and invincible as Durga, and bone-crushing avenger as Kali, this goddess is just one of many who could manifest in different aspects. Each aspect is a different side of the same goddess. In one story, Parvati appeared to soothe the gods that demons, attempting to take over the immortal realm, were of no concern to them. Once they relaxed, the next moment, she transformed into Durga and marched into battle to confront the demons. Then, she transformed again into the terrifying Kali, conquering the demons single-handedly by tossing them about, crushing them with her jaws, and decapitating them with her swords. Afterward, she could return home to Shiva for an evening of sacred lovemaking!

> **Oracle Wisdom**
> I prefer you to make mistakes in kindness than work miracles in unkindness.
> —Mother Teresa, Yugoslavian missionary

- **Enjoy life with gusto!** The Greek goddess Adephagia is the goddess of hedonism. She is portrayed eating and drinking with great joy. Why should Bacchus have all the fun?

- **Love the earth as both your mother and your charge.** Many sex and love goddesses were also goddesses of the fertile earth, such as Kaya-no-hime-no-kami, the Japanese vegetation goddess, sometimes called the "Ruler of the Grassy Plains." This goddess of herbs, fields, and meadows transformed vegetation into food for nourishment and also encouraged the regeneration of life from the earth. Consider her when working in your garden.

- **Love children, even when they aren't yours.** Many goddesses make it their business to be protectors of children. The nymph Adamanthea protected Zeus as a baby. The Roman goddess Adeona guarded schoolchildren as they traveled to school and while they played. Acca Larentia, the Etruscan earth goddess and female wolf, nursed Romulus and Remus, the gods who founded Rome. Artemis, the virgin moon goddess and a warrior goddess of the Amazons, was protector of infants in childbirth and of the

> **Oracle Wisdom**
> This earth is my sister; I love her daily grace, her silent daring, and how loved I am, *how we admire this strength in each other, all that we have lost, all that we have suffered, all that we know: we are stunned by this beauty,* and I do not forget: what she is to me, what I am to her.
> —Susan Griffin, U.S. poet

young. Admete the untamable, a Greek goddess of earth and nature, was a nymph who helped young boys reach manhood. (We won't ask how.)

♦ **Be true to your goddess friends.** Have a friend in need? Invoke the energy of Chaska, the Incan dawn goddess who causes flowers to grow and protects young women.

♦ **Be beautiful, both inside and out.** If you know you are beautiful, and especially if that beauty radiates from deep within you, you will be beautiful, like Lakshmi, who rose from the churning primordial sea of milk and was immediately sought after by all the gods. Invoking her also brings prosperity.

♦ **Be comfortable with your body, including its functions.** Adamu, the Mesopotamian mother goddess, was called the Red One. She represented menstrual blood and the blood that comes from childbearing.

♦ **Play music.** Call on gLu-Ma Ghirdhima, the Tibetan goddess of music and song. This Buddhist goddess is red and plays a lyre while she dances.

♦ **At some point, leave your parents and become a grown-up, but still hang out with them sometimes.** Remember Persephone, who was taken to the underworld to be the queen, at Hades's side? Her mother missed her and the earth was cast into winter in her absence, but she grew to love her life as underworld queen with her husband, so she spent half the year with her mother and half the year with her husband.

♦ **Sometimes it can feel like the first time.** Even when it isn't. Imagine you are the Mayan moon goddess Ch'en, who according to myth was the first woman ever to have sex.

Initiatress of Love

Although the practice of sacred sex may make you feel transcendent and may help you reshape your priorities for a more compassionate life, sex goddesses also like to have fun. Let yourself enjoy life beyond the bedroom. Eat with joy, bathe with joy, have fun with your friends, and indulge in all the sensual pleasures. Aphrodite did it. Why not you?

♦ **Things aren't always as they seem.** Egle, the Lithuanian Queen of Serpents, was a beautiful maiden who went swimming with her sisters one day and when she returned to dress, found a serpent coiled in her clothes. He said he would move if she promised to marry him, so she did. After the wedding, the serpent took her to his undersea castle and turned into a handsome prince.

♦ **You have male energy, too.** Remember Ardhanari-Ishvara, the Hindu goddess/god "Who Is Both Male and Female"? Each of us has the potential to access both yin and yang, active and receptive, dark and light, sun and moon, male and female energy, when we need it.

◆ **Sometimes, you can be the rescuer.** Like Ishtar, a Mesopotamian goddess who traveled through the underworld and endured many trials to rescue and bring back her husband.

◆ **Don't be afraid to enjoy men.** Metsanneitsyt, the Finnish forest virgin goddess, loved men and often flirted with them until they would have sex with her. She was beautiful and well dressed from the front, but from the back, she appeared like a stump or a bundle of twigs, signifying her dual nature: sophisticated and natural.

◆ **Don't be afraid to get mussed up.** Be like "Comb Hair Upward Girl," a Hopi goddess who carried a brush and messed people's hair, and brought the winter wind to help with her hair mussing.

◆ **You are creativity itself.** Like Goose goddess, the Egyptian creator of life and "The Great Cackler," who laid the comic egg from which the world hatched, you can also create amazing things that can evolve to truly transcendent creations.

◆ **Hold sex sacred.** Astarte, the Assyrian goddess of sacred sexuality, was called the Queen of Heaven because sacred sex was of the utmost importance and a primal part of the feminine principle. As you learn more about sacred sex and work on practicing it, invoke Astarte and also your own spiritual side, even if you don't practice spirituality very much. When sex becomes spiritual, it is more potent and more powerful than ever before.

Hold sex sacred not only by incorporating spiritual awareness, but by putting your partner first in your life, ahead of your parents, friends, and even your children! Although you are still responsible for your other relationships, especially the care and nurturing of your children, all will benefit from seeing your closeness with your partner and basking in the glow of your contact. Besides, your children will learn important life lessons about how to love well and how to respect adults, including their desire for conversation. If your child has to wait *just a minute* before chattering on for 30 minutes about the plot of a movie, he will begin to learn self-discipline as well as consideration.

Unleashing Your Creativity

Creativity is one of the primary forces inherent in sex goddesses throughout world mythologies, and you can find it within yourself, too. What good does it do to be creative? Not only is creativity the very source of life, but it can enrich and improve your own life and the lives of others who are exposed to the effects of your creative fire.

Whether you write, paint, sculpt, draw, sing, play music, act, or think, adding creativity to your life will help you to grow, broaden your thinking, sharpen your skills, and add a new dimension to your existence. Sex is about creative energy, so when yours gets fired up, why not use it?

Even if you haven't engaged in any purposeful creative pursuit for years, you may find that the urge to do so comes out of the regular practice of sacred sex and the sex goddess lifestyle. We say, *brava!* The more you engage in creative pursuits, the more you generate and inspire your inner creativity. Being creative is a satisfying and fulfilling pursuit. Let your inner sex goddess seep into all the corners of your life and find your inner artist, too!

> **Initiatress of Love**
>
> Too shy to keep a sex journal? How about a drawing journal? Draw what you see, and let your feelings percolate down onto the paper. Keep a sketch diary and record things like the shape of your partner's naked body, the shadow the lamp casts across the ceiling, or the way the sun looks as it sets behind that grove of leafless trees. Draw whatever you feel compelled to draw, but don't worry about your technique. This is just for you and the creative force within you.

Look Within to Change the World

Finally, what you see within you will happen around you. On his deathbed, the Buddha (not a sex goddess, but nevertheless an enlightened human being) said to his disciples, "Be a light unto yourself." Enlightenment, understanding, the ultimate apprehension of truth, fulfillment, happiness, love—all these important things we seek in life are within us. All we have to do is pay attention, focus, and find them.

To be a sex goddess means to immerse ourselves in the sensual world, turn inward to see who we really are, turn outward to focus on our partners in total absorption, and *live*, every moment of every day, in awareness. Never spinning along on automatic pilot. Always alive, always awake, always feeling, whether pleasure or pain, titillation or boredom.

To act, to change things, to make things happen in the world will influence others. How we live can inspire those who admire and rely on us to live more actively and with more life and awareness. What better way to "win friends and influence people," and effect real change in the world than to live, really live, according to the natural laws: with attention, with compassion, and with feeling?

If nothing else, a sex goddess trains, learns, and never stops learning how to live with real feeling. So join us. It's a lovely ride, full of pleasure and emotion, love and passion, physical and spiritual ecstasy. It is the life of a sex goddess, and now you are one of us. Welcome to the club.

The Least You Need to Know

♦ Mindfulness and a radiating love for others can cause a ripple effect that can dramatically influence the world around you.

♦ The skills of a sex goddess are related to the skills of a loving parent, a caring child, and a valuable friend: paying attention, being present in the moment, and having the capacity for great compassion.

♦ Sex goddesses throughout history teach many lessons about life, from "Don't be afraid to cause a little trouble" to "You are creativity incarnate."

♦ Recognizing who you are and what you can do in this world and then going out and maximizing your potential as a goddess of love will help you to lead the most fulfilling life possible, and that is the best gift you can give to the world.

♦ You're in the sex goddess club now. We're glad you joined us!

Glossary

agni The Sanskrit word for the inner digestive fire behind the navel, which is thought to be responsible for heating the body, digesting food, and processing experience.

archetype A model or prototype for an ideal. Influential Swiss psychologist Carl Jung (1875–1965) takes this idea a step further, defining archetype as a symbolic image that exists in the collective unconscious of humans and represents something all people automatically understand.

astrology The study of the influence of heavenly bodies such as stars and planets on human behavior and personality.

ayurveda An ancient Indian science of life that encourages specific lifestyle and health practices according to an individual's dosha, or type. Therapies include individualized diet, massage, yoga, and hygiene practices to balance the body's energies and maintain or improve health and well-being on all levels.

bisexual A person who is sexually attracted to people of both genders.

Book of the Dead An ancient Egyptian book of spells, prayers, and hymns written about 300 B.C.E. and designed to secure safe passage for the dead from this world into the next.

cervix The necklike muscle at the back of the vagina that is the entrance to the uterus.

chakras   Spinning energy centers in the body. Each chakra is the source of certain specific energies. The seven primary chakras are located along the center of the body, from the base of the spine to the crown of the head.

clitoris   A highly sensitive organ at the top of the labia that can retract and is a source of orgasm for many women.

cunnilingus   Oral sex given to a woman, specifically having her yoni and clitoris kissed, sucked, and penetrated with her partner's tongue, sometimes but not necessarily to the point of orgasm.

ejaculation   A series of reflexive rhythmic muscular contractions that propel semen through the urethra, sometimes occurring with orgasm and possible in both men and women.

erogenous zones   Areas of the body that are particularly sensitive to erotic stimulation. The clitoris, the head of the lingam, the G-spot, and the nipples are obvious erogenous zones; your entire body can be an erogenous zone.

fellatio   Oral sex given to a man, specifically having his lingam sucked, sometimes but not necessarily to the point of orgasm.

foreplay   Mutual physical stimulation to arouse desire before sexual intercourse, including but not limited to touching, kissing, embracing, talking, and looking.

G-spot   The highly sensitive spongy area inside the front wall of the vagina that separates the urethra form the vaginal canal. It is a source of orgasms in many women.

genitalia   The external sex organs.

Kama Sutra   An ancient text from India passed down orally through generations and first organized and edited by Indian sage Vatsyayana in the fourth century B.C.E. Most known for its array of sexual positions, the Kama Sutra also provides guidelines for living, relationships, and morality, as well as techniques for wooing the right partner and for making sex emotionally, spiritually, and physically fulfilling.

kundalini yoga   A type of yoga that awakens and channels kundalini, an intense psycho-sexual energy that can travel through the center of the body to the crown of the head and can bring enlightenment.

labia   The liplike folds around the outer vagina.

lingam   The Sanskrit term for the penis, or a stylized representation of the penis.

Lotus Position   One of the most well-known yoga poses. Designed for stability during prolonged meditation, the pose imitates the shape and symmetry of the sacred lotus flower. To sit in this position, cross your legs and pull each foot, upturned, onto the opposite thigh.

mandala   A circular design meant to help the consciousness focus on a single point, represented by the center of the circular design.

mindfulness   A meditation technique for being completely tuned in and focused on what is happening in the present moment, rather than letting your mind dwell on the past or linger ahead in the future.

neti   An ancient technique for cleansing the sinuses that involves pouring salt water from a neti pot into one nostril and letting it run out of the other, then blowing the nose to clear it and drying the nasal passages by breathing through the nose. Many people still practice neti and believe it can reduce or eliminate colds, sinus infections, and nasal allergies.

orgasm   An intensely pleasurable physical sensation that can be focused in the genitals or in the entire body, accompanied by a series of rhythmic contractions leading to the release of sexual tension.

perineum   The sensitive smooth tissue between the vagina and anus in a woman or between the scrotum and anus in the man.

prana   The Sanskrit word for universal life-force energy that animates all physical matter and that moves in and out of the body with the breath.

pranayama   A traditional yogic system of breathing exercises designed to maximize prana in the body for ultimate physical, mental, and spiritual health and balance.

Shakti   The embodiment of feminine or yin energy. In Hindu mythology, Shakti is a creation goddess.

shavasana or Corpse Pose   A basic yoga pose meant to simulate the complete lack of tension in the body of a corpse, as well as the spiritual state of one freed from the physical bonds of the material world. The yogi lies on his or her back, legs slightly apart, feet relaxed so they fall to either side, arms relaxed with palms up, eyes closed. The pose is commonly practiced after a routine of vigorous yoga poses, or after each yoga pose.

Shiva   A supreme deity and the embodiment of masculine or yang energy in Hindu mythology.

Tantra   A Sanskrit word meaning "weave" that refers to an ancient Indian system of philosophy and psychology that considers the realm beyond oppositions in the universe, to encompass a reality that is ultimately unified rather than opposed. One method for comprehending this unification is through certain sexual practices.

TM or transcendental meditation   A meditation technique popularized by the Maharishi Mahesh Yogi (1957–1998) and practiced worldwide. It is a type of mantra meditation, in which a word or phrase is repeated as a point of focus.

vagina   The muscular channel between the cervix and the vulva.

vulva   The external part of the vagina.

yang   Masculine essence.

yin   Feminine essence.

yin/yang   A Taoist concept of balance in the universe. All things are associated with either yin—female, dark, moist, lunar energy—or yang—male, light, dry, sun energy. The yin/yang symbol represents the balance of these energies in the universe.

yoni   The Sanskrit term for the vagina.

zazen   Literally "sitting meditation," zazen is the primary type of meditation practiced in Zen Buddhism.

Appendix B

Resources

This book is just a beginning. Many other books, videos, and websites can teach you even more about sacred sexuality and the ways of the sex goddess. Here are some resources to get you started on your continuing study of ecstasy.

Books

Anand, Margot. *The Art of Sexual Ecstasy*. Jeremy P. Tarcher/Putnam, 1989.

Baring, Anne, and Jules Cashford. *The Myth of the Goddess: Evolution of an Image*. Penguin Books, 1991.

Budilovsky, Joan, and Eve Adamson. *The Complete Idiot's Guide to Meditation, Second Edition*. Alpha Books, 2002.

———. *The Complete Idiot's Guide to Yoga, Third Edition*. Alpha Books, 2003.

Corn, Laura. *The Great American Sex Diet*. William Morrow, 1991.

Deida, David. *Dear Lover: A Woman's Guide to Enjoying Love's Deepest Bliss*. Plexus, 2002.

———. *Finding God Through Sex*. Plexus, 2002.

Dodson, Betty. *Sex for One: The Joy of Self-Loving*. Three Rivers Press, re-issued 1992.

Douglas, Nik, and Penny Slinger. *Sexual Secrets: The Alchemy of Ecstasy, 20th Anniversary Edition*. Destiny Books, 2000.

Feldman, Gail Carr, and Eve Adamson. *Releasing the Mother Goddess*. Alpha Books, 2003.

Feldman, Gail Carr, and Katherine A. Gleason. *Releasing the Goddess Within*. Alpha Books, 2003.

Joannides, Paul. *The Guide to Getting It On!* Goofy Foot Press, 2003.

Keesling, Barbara. *Discover Your Sensual Potential*. HarperCollins, 1999.

———. *Sexual Healing*. Hunter House, 1990.

Muscio, Inga, and Betty Dodson. *Cunt: A Declaration of Independence, Second Edition*. Seal Press, 2002.

Odier, Daniel. *Tantric Quest: An Encounter with Absolute Love*. Inner Traditions, 1997.

Osho. *From Sex to Super Consciousness*. South Asia Books, 2003.

St. Claire, Olivia. *227 Ways to Unleash the Sex Goddess Within*. Harmony Books, 1996.

Sarita, Ma Ananda, and Swami Anand Geho. *Tantric Love*. Simon & Schuster, 2001.

Sonntag, Linda. *The Bedside Kama Sutra*. Fair Winds Press, 2001.

Stone, Merlin. *When God Was a Woman*. Harcourt Brace and Company, 1976.

Tognetti, Arlene, and Lisa Lenard. *The Intuitive Arts on Love*. Alpha Books, 2003.

Wikoff, Johanina, and Deborah S. Romaine. *The Complete Idiot's Guide to the Kama Sutra, Second Edition*. Alpha Books, 2004.

Williamson, Marianne. *Enchanted Love: The Mystical Power of Intimate Relationships*. Touchstone Books, 2001.

———. *A Return to Love*. HarperCollins, 1996.

Woods, Margo. *Masturbation, Tantra, and Self-Love*. Mho and Mho Works, 1981.

Videos

Ancient Secrets of Sexual Ecstacy for Modern Lovers. Several well-known sexual teachers, including Margot Anand, Nik Douglas and Penny Slinger, Robert Frey and

Lori Grace, and Charles and Caroline Muir, offer lots of good information and demonstrations of Tantric techniques.

Becoming Orgasmic: A Sexual and Personal Growth Program for Women ... and the Men Who Love Them (based on the book by the same name by Julia Heiman). Designed for the beginner, this video is a good starting point for women who want to know how to become orgasmic. It is also worthwhile for any woman because it covers many things that even orgasmic women may not have considered.

Celebrating Orgasm: Women's Private Self-Loving Sessions, Betty Dodson. Betty Dodson's self-pleasuring workshops are the benchmark. In this video, we see five individual coaching sessions where women, guided by Betty, learn about their own orgasmic potential.

Female Genital Massage by Joseph Kramer. Female version with Annie Sprinkle.

Multi-Orgasmic Response (MORE) for Women and Their Lovers. These are based on Margot Anand's book, *The Art of Sexual Magic*.

Self-Loving: Portrait of a Women's Sexuality Seminar, Betty Dodson. Betty's video is one of the very best for women. This one is in a seminar setting.

Websites

www.bettydodson.com, the informational website of Betty Dodson, the mother of masturbation seminars and books.

www.spiritualsexuality.com is the website for Ina Laughing Winds, the secondary teacher of the Chulaquai Quodoshka, student of Harley Swiftdeer Reagan.

www.templepriestess.com is Stacy Clark's site. This website introduces you to Stacy and her beliefs and practices, including information on how to reach her for sessions or lectures. Also includes great links to other sights about spiritual sexuality.

Breathwork

www.bobmandel.com

www.lovingrelationshipstraining.com

www.rebirthingonline.com/htms/rebirth2.html

www.vivation.com

Tantra/Kama Sutra

www.tantra.com

www.tantraattahoe.com/kama-sutra/kama-sutra-online.htm

www.tantraportal.com

Others

Margot Anand, Skydancing Tantra: www.margotanand.com

Chulaquai Quodoshka (American Indian): www.spiritualsexuality.com

David Deida: www.deida.com/default.html

Osho (formerly known as Bhagwan Shree Rajneesh): osho.com/homepage.htm

Upping Your Sex Goddess IQ

Maybe you've already read our book, or maybe you are just flipping through, trying to decide if this book is for you. Whether you want to ground your knowledge, give yourself a review session, or test the waters by dipping your toe into the warm, sensuous pool of sex-goddess-hood, here are some quick quizzes and thought-provoking questions for you to consider. Don't worry, these quizzes aren't graded and you can't possibly fail Sex Goddess 101. Consider this a study guide, a review session, or a tantalizing tease to what's inside this book. Ready to have some fun?

True or False

Fold a blank sheet of paper and cover the answer column at the left; don't peek! Enter true or false in the spaces provided, then check your answers.

F _____ All creation stories tell of a masculine creator.

F _____ Only famous women can be sex goddesses.

T _____ Sex can be a sacred spiritual act.

F _____ The Kama Sutra is an obscure book of sexual positions.

F _____ We focus only on our sense of touch in sex.

T _____ Laughing and playfulness can be part of sex.

T _____ Ceres, Juno, Pallas Athene, and Vesta are all names of goddesses as well as names for asteroids.

F _____ The Greek goddess Baubo was coy and demure in her speech.

T _____ There are goddesses of sex, love, passion, fertility, creation, destruction, motherhood, spousal fidelity, spousal infidelity, death, and resurrection in various cultures.

T _____ Crocodile Woman is a Sudanese birth goddess who took the form of a crocodile to protect infants.

T _____ Chi, a Nigerian earth goddess and creator of life, is an androgynous goddess can help us get in touch with both the male and female energies within each of us.

T _____ Cocamama is a Peruvian sex goddess with many lovers and also the mother of the coca plant, which brings health and happiness.

F _____ Kokopell' Mana was a Hopi goddess of sex and a fertility charm. She liked to challenge men to a duel with swords.

T _____ In Egypt, sex goddesses had great powers, often rivaling or exceeding the powers of the male gods.

T _____ Isis was originally worshipped on her own. Her husband, Osiris, was added into her myth later.

T _____ Ken, the Egyptian equivalent of the Roman Venus, is the goddess of love and sex, and is mentioned in Hebrew scripture.

F _____ The Japanese goddess Iku-tama-yori-bime tied a thread to her lover's clothes and followed the string the next day, discovering that he was a poor peasant.

F _____ Aphrodite was one of the chief 12 gods of Olympus.

T _____ Amrit, a Hindu goddess of immortality and sex, had a magic belly containing the water of everlasting life. Anyone who drank it would become immortal.

T _____ Kali, a Hindu goddess of life and death, was both a creator and a destroyer, devouring humans and protecting them, depending on the situation.

F _____ Anasuya, a Hindu goddess, was ravished by Shiva, Vishnu, and Brahma.

F _____ A woman can only be the age that she is, never older or younger.

T _____ The word *virgin* originally meant "a woman who belongs to no man."

F _____ To experience the mother stage of femininity, one must have a child.

T _____ The mother recognizes that the nurture of relationship is the pursuit of the self.

T _____ The wise woman stage is marked by the pursuit of relationship to the world as a whole, to universal understanding and a unity, not just with the other, but with the all.

F _____ A woman can only experience one aspect of the feminine trinity of maiden, mother and wise woman at a given time.

T _____ It is possible that many women are out of touch with their natural cycles due to a modern lack of connection to the outdoors.

T _____ Yin is the feminine essence, and yang is the masculine essence.

F _____ There are no androgynous gods or goddesses in any culture.

F _____ It is impossible for women to enjoy sex during their menstrual period.

F _____ PMS stands for pre-marital sex.

F _____ A woman's body has to be a perfect size 8 before she can enjoy sex.

T _____ Women who are considered "overweight" by current standards can enjoy full and rewarding sexual relationships.

F _____ There is such a thing as being "too sexy."

F _____ All female genitals look the same.

F _____ Masturbation is just for kids or for those in between lovers or for old people who end up alone.

F _____ Yoni is the male sex organ and lingam is the female sexual organs.

T _____ According to Tantric thought, female sexual bonding circulated yin essence between two women, making them softer, more compassionate, and even more feminine.

F _____ Women only respond to verbal or written erotica, not pictures or visual fantasies.

F _____ All women respond to the same kind of touch stimulation.

F _____ Women never ejaculate.

T _____ The more you practice self-pleasuring, the more you will learn what you like and how your body responds to self-touch.

F _____ How a woman feels about her breasts has nothing to do with how she feels about herself.

T _____ Looking into a mirror at our own bodies can help us accept our size and shape, which will enhance our experience of ourselves, our pleasure, and our partner.

T _____ Women should do monthly self-examinations of their breasts.

T _____ Regular yoga practice can help keep our bodies and minds fit and aware, which enhances sexual pleasure.

F _____ Women should not initiate sex because it threatens the male partner.

F _____ Physical fitness and sexual health are different and separate things.

T _____ Our breath is a vital part of full sexual and sensual expression.

F _____ Rituals always make sex a stale and repetitive experience.

T _____ According to feng shui, the ancient Chinese art of placement, arranging a bed against a wall symbolizes resistance to having a partner, because access to one side of the bed is blocked.

T _____ Much of the emotional and spiritual bonding of sexual union happens during foreplay.

T _____ The Throbbing Kiss is a lip touch with the lower lip moving during the return kiss—a slight but significant move that says "more?"

F _____ One should never talk during foreplay.

F _____ Sexual rituals should be followed exactly as given and never varied.

F _____ You shouldn't tell your partner how you like to be touched and pleasured. This is domineering and aggressive.

T _____ Fantasies are an excellent way to share with your lover what you like.

T _____ Many sexual poses in the Kama Sutra are designed to imitate the postures animals use during copulation.

T _____ Unlike some forms of yoga that dull the senses, Tantra teaches that supreme immersion in and ultimate sensitivity of sensual awareness leads to enlightenment.

T _____ Legend has it that Cleopatra, a sex goddess if ever there was one, kept a large assortment of sex toys, such as polished stone or polished wood phalluses.

F _____ None of the Kama Sutra's positions are suggested for strengthening particular parts of the body and increasing health.

T _____ Mary Magdalene was so called because Magdalene was her Priestess title.

F _____ Once we learn many different sexual positions, we should practice each one every time we make love.

T _____ A female orgasm is a series of involuntary muscle contractions in the yoni (vagina) accompanied by intense feelings of pleasure and ecstasy.

F _____ There is only one valid type of orgasm for women and one for men.

T _____ Full-body orgasm without ejaculation can be one of the most powerful experiences a human being can have.

T _____ Many women claim to have clitoral orgasms, G-spot orgasms, cervical orgasms, breast orgasms, mental orgasms, and/or full-body orgasms.

F _____ Only the sexual chakra is important to spiritual sexuality.

T _____ Synchronizing your breathing as you move toward orgasm with your partner is one of the most powerful sexual-spiritual connections you can experience.

F _____ The secret to attaining a blissful union is based in technique and position.

T _____ Channeling the energy of your sexual ecstasy rather than letting it dissipate is one of the central principles of Tantric sex.

T _____ During an orgasm, your brain waves change.

T _____ Tantra extends and elongates the present moment.

F _____ The G-spot is in the same place on all women.

T _____ Orgasmic energy can go way beyond the genitals.

T _____ After orgasm, men's bodies and women's bodies react differently.

T _____ Talking after sex is often easier, freer, and more intimate than talking at other times.

T _____ When a woman's sexual energy moves down through her chakras and a man's sexual energy moves up, they meet each other halfway—at the heart chakra in an explosion of unifying energy.

T _____ Amrita is one of the names given to female ejaculate. It means the "nectar of the goddess."

T _____ The goddess Persephone knew all about this dance of together-apart, together-apart. She was forced to spend six months each year away from her husband, Hades, king of the underworld.

T _____ Male sexual energy is easily ignited, but quickly extinguished. Female sexual energy comes to a slow boil, but it builds in waves.

F _____ A woman's sexual desire is always diminished after she becomes a mother.

T _____ Planning and creating a regular "date night" is one way to reclaim the passion and intimacy of your relationship after childbirth.

T _____ It is especially important to practice PC (or Kegel) exercises after childbirth.

F _____ A sex goddess never says "no" to sex or to any sexual act.

T _____ Sappho is considered to be one of the great Greek poets.

T _____ The word *lesbian*, which refers to a female person with homosexual tendencies, comes from the name of Sappho's home island Lesbos.

F _____ Heterosexual women should not find other women beautiful, sensual, or exciting.

T _____ Praising another woman and cultivating an appreciation of other women in all their aspects is also learning to accept and appreciate yourself.

T _____ You can influence your impact on others purposefully and with true sex goddess panache if you engage the world with conscious attention and meaningful action.

T _____ The love that suffuses you when engaged in regular sacred sex can also have a profound effect on your family and friends.

Multiple Choice

Once again, fold a sheet of paper and cover the answer column. Circle your choice and then check your answer.

D _____ A Sex goddess is:

    A. Slender

    B. Voluptuous

    C. Her ideal weight

    D. Any of the above

D _____ Sex goddesses:

    A. Aren't typically educated

    B. Are more intelligent than average

    C. Are less intelligent than average

    D. Any of the above

D _____ Sex goddesses are:

    A. Happy

    B. Angry

    C. "In the mood"

    D. Any of the above

D _____ Sex goddesses:

    A. Don't clean toilets

    B. Have housekeepers

    C. Do their own housework

    D. Any of the above

D _____ Sex is:

    A. Creative, fun, and sacred

    B. Boring, a chore

    C. Difficult

    D. Whatever I make it

C _____ Sex:

    A. Is only for intimate relationships with one person

    B. Is something we can share with more than one lover

    C. Is a matter of personal choice about when and with whom

    D. Should only be had within a marriage

B _____ Lilith was:

    A. A character in a book by Tom Robbins

    B. The biblical Adam's first wife

    C. A child of Zeus and Hera

    D. Not mentioned in this book

A _____ Medusa is the snake-haired Gorgon goddess of magic, sex, and ugliness. Her startling appearance didn't keep this powerful goddess from:

A. Sleeping with Poseidon

B. Finding a job

C. Being included in the council of the gods

D. Marrying

B _____ Venus, the Roman incarnation of Aphrodite, a powerful goddess of sensual love, was considered to be:

A. Frigid

B. The mother of the Roman people

C. Quiet and shy

D. Desperate to get married

A _____ Walden Wip, a German forest goddesses who performed magic and healing, enjoyed:

A. Seducing men

B. Making bread

C. Flying on a broomstick

D. Playing in the sea

B _____ A detailed astrological chart will tell you exactly how Ceres, Juno, Pallas Athene, and Vesta influence your:

A. Chances in the lottery

B. Personality

C. Sexual prowess

D. Attractiveness to men or women

C _____ The female trinity in Chapter 3 is:

A. Venus, Athena, and Demeter

B. You, me, and us

C. Maiden (virgin), mother, and wise woman (crone)

D. Sleeping Beauty, Cinderella, and Little Red Riding Hood

D _____ To experience and understand the maiden (or virgin) life stage of the sex goddess:

    A. One must never have had sex

    B. Requires living with your mother

    C. One must be under 29 years of age

    D. Is something we can do at any age

D _____ Women past their child-bearing years may experience:

    A. More wisdom and understanding

    B. A sense of depth and connection to all

    C. A new sexual freedom

    D. All of the above

B _____ "Tantra" is a Sanskrit word meaning:

    A. Sex

    B. Weave

    C. Join

    D. Goddess worship

D _____ Examples of feminine trinities include:

    A. Deanna Troi, Beverly Crusher, and Guinan

    B. Lakshmi, Sarasvati, and Devi

    C. Clotho, Lachesis, and Atropos

    D. All of the above

C _____ A woman's menstrual cycle relates to the cycles of:

    A. The seasons

    B. The sun

    C. The moon

    D. None of the above

B _____ The yin/yang symbol is:

  A. A symbol of weaving

  B. A Taoist symbol of masculine and feminine balance within the whole

  C. A picture of sexual organs

  D. A Western symbol of mother and father energies

D _____ How I feel about my body:

  A. Has nothing to do with how I experience sexual pleasure

  B. Is unchangeable

  C. Isn't important

  D. None of the above

B _____ The word *chakra* means:

  A. Life

  B. Wheel

  C. Seven

  D. Girl

D _____ Each chakra relates to:

  A. A part of the body

  B. An energy center

  C. A color

  D. All of the above

B _____ The Kama Sutra describes three types of yonis, or vaginas. They are:

  A. The circle, the triangle, and the square

  B. The deer, the mare, and the elephant

  C. Pink, red, and blue

  D. Small, medium, and large

B _____ Anahita is the Persian goddess of sacred sexuality who rules over water and fertility. Her name means:

    A. Young Girl

    B. Without Blemish or Immaculate One

    C. Still Waters Run Deep

    D. Moon Child

D _____ Women may respond to touch stimulation that is:

    A. Gentle and slow

    B. Rough and fast

    C. Deep

    D. All of the above—and more!

D _____ The size of a woman's breasts:

    A. Indicates her capacity for sexual pleasure

    B. Matters to all men

    C. Are an important part of tantra rituals

    D. None of the above

D _____ Sex can be enhanced through the use of:

    A. Sensual foods and drinks

    B. Sensual clothing and fabrics

    C. Sensual music and movement

    D. All of the above

A _____ In the term *PC muscle*, the PC stands for:

    A. Pubococcygeus

    B. Politically correct

    C. Prolific coming

    D. Perfect cunnilingus

C _____ Unresolved tensions:

    A. Have no effect on our sex lives

    B. Keep us from wanting sex at all

    C. Will affect how sexy we feel

    D. Should always be dissipated before sex

D _____ Meditation:

    A. Can help us become deeply in touch with ourselves

    B. Can calm us and help us focus

    C. Can bring insights

    D. All of the above

B _____ Affirmations:

    A. Must be complex and lengthy to be valuable

    B. Are a simple way to focus ourselves on positive thoughts

    C. Never work

    D. None of the above

D _____ The bedroom:

    A. Should be neat and free of distractions

    B. Should be a sacred haven of love

    C. Should never be used for an office or other function

    D. All of the above

D _____ The Kama Sutra describes several kinds of kisses. These include:

    A. The Clasping Kiss

    B. Wrestling Tongues

    C. The Bent Kiss and the Straight Kiss

    D. All of the above

C _____ One of the best ways for your partner to learn what you like is:

    A. Make your partner guess

    B. Pretend to like things you don't really enjoy

    C. Self-pleasure (masturbate) in front of your partner

    D. Only do things to please your partner, not yourself

B _____ Author and relationship expert David Deida says that a man needs a woman's _____, while a woman needs a man's _____.

    A. Vagina/penis

    B. Responsiveness/presence

    C. Touch/sweet talk

    D. Housekeeping/income

B _____ Body mapping is:

    A. Drawing maps on each others bodies with colored pens

    B. Showing your lover where you like to be touched both in general and with regard to what turns you on

    C. Learning the parts of the body and their scientific names

    D. Lying in the snow and making an imprint of your body

C _____ Who wrote, "What this world needs more of is loving: sweaty, friendly and unashamed"?

    A. J. K. Rowling

    B. Dan Brown

    C. Robert A. Heinlein

    D. Candace Pert

D _____ Betty Dodson wrote that "A good lover is a good _____ lover."

    A. Body

    B. Man

    C. Woman

    D. Self

C _____ The Yawning Union pose is:

   A. The best way to make love when you are tired

   B. A way to make love with your mouths open fully

   C. The woman's open thighs, which yawn to accept her lover

   D. A way to tell your lover you are too tired for sex tonight

D _____ Sacred sex involves a discipline in which sexually energy is purposefully channeled:

   A. To generate the most creative energy

   B. To best activate the chakras

   C. To obliterate and transcend the perception of opposites

   D. All of the above

D _____ The G-spot:

   A. Was named after a modern man, even though ancient cultures knew of it centuries ago

   B. Can experience pain when touched, at first

   C. Feels rippled or rougher in texture than the surrounding area

   D. All of the above

D _____ A full-body orgasm:

   A. Can open you to another dimension

   B. Is a fusion of sexual and spiritual energy

   C. Is an experience of clarity and expansion

   D. All of the above

D _____ Being silent after sex can:

   A. Help us feel rather than analyze our experience

   B. Help us sense the presence and touch of our partners

   C. Help extend the pleasure and intimacy

   D. All of the above

D _____ In Tantric and Taoist teachings, breast milk was cherished as one of three sexual secretions of a woman. It was called:

A. White Snow

B. Essence of Coral

C. Immortality Peach Juice

D. All of the above

D _____ A sex goddess:

A. Influences herself

B. May influence her partner with her positive energies

C. May influence the world in a positive way through her self-awareness

D. All of the above

Thought Questions

List 10 (or more) ways in which you feel you are a goddess. Include physical, mental, emotional, and spiritual aspects of yourself.

1. _____
2. _____
3. _____
4. _____
5. _____
6. _____
7. _____
8. _____
9. _____
10. _____

Make a list of the things partners and other people have complimented you for, things they liked about you that made you glow inside. Reading these lists can be encouraging when you are feeling a bit low about your goddess qualities.

1. _____
2. _____
3. _____
4. _____
5. _____
6. _____
7. _____
8. _____
9. _____
10. _____

Make a list of the ways you want to enhance your sense of yourself as a goddess. Refer to the book for ideas. What would you like to do, be, have?

Do	Be	Have
_____	_____	_____
_____	_____	_____
_____	_____	_____
_____	_____	_____
_____	_____	_____
_____	_____	_____
_____	_____	_____
_____	_____	_____
_____	_____	_____
_____	_____	_____
_____	_____	_____

Who are your role models for the kind of sex goddess you want to be? Choose from books, movies, television, mythology, religion—anywhere you can think of. Include some of the goddesses described in the book who appealed to you.

_____

_____

_____

_____

_____

_____

_____

_____

_____

_____

_____

_____

Index

A

acceptance
  agreements for sacred
    couples, 217
  public displays of affection,
    264
accessing your own goddess
  powers, 6-7
Adamu, 290
Adephagia, 289
Adjusting the System technique, 157
adolescents, breast appreciation, 80-81
African sex goddesses, 14
afterglow period, 221-232
  chakra balancing visualiza-
    tion, 224-226
  energy of the moment,
    226-228
  goddess empowerment,
    228-232
  yin and yang energy of
    orgasms, 222-224
aftermath. See post-sex rituals
aging breasts, 83-84
agni, 55
agreements for sacred couples
  accepting each other, 217
  being the best you can be,
    217-218
  daily physical contact, 218
  honesty, 216-217
  worshipping each other,
    216

Ahalya, 19
airplane sex, 267-268
Aisha Qandisha, 14
Akaru-hime, 16
Ala, 14
alternate nostril breathing,
  108
Amaterasu, 111
Amrit, 19
Ananga Ranga, 229
Anasuya, 19
Anatha Baetyl, 16
ancient masturbation tradi-
  tions, 66-68
Anog Ite, 15
aphrodisiac foods, 115-116
Aphrodite, 7, 18
  Ode to Aphrodite, 281-283
  symbols, 231
April (month), Veneralia
  celebrations, 258-259
archetypes, 7
Ardhanari-Ishvara, 126, 290
Arethusa, 225
Ariadne, 288
arousal, flirting techniques,
  263-264
Art of Sexual Ecstasy, The, 178
Artemis, 12
Arundhati, 19
assessing your man's attitudes,
  136-137
Astarte, 291
astrology
  asteroid representations,
    20-21

Athena, 21
  Ceres, 21
  Juno, 21
  Vesta, 21
  influences on sacred
    unions, 181-182
Athena, 12, 21
Atropos, 33
Autyeb, 16
Awitelin Tsita, 15, 238, 256
ayurveda, 104

B

Baba Yaga, 12
Bai Mundan, 17
Bak, Robert, 200
balance
  Balancing the Elements
    technique, 157
  pedestal concept, 260-261
Bast, 179, 256
Baubo, 12
beach sex, 267
Bear Maiden, 15
Beauvoir, Simone de, 186
bedrooms, creating a sacred
  bedchamber, 247-248
Benefits for the Internal
  Organs technique, 157
Bent Kisses, 119
bhramari (humming breath),
  107-108
Blow of the Boar penetration
  method, 166

Blow of the Bull penetration method, 166
body
    appreciating your sexiness, 58-59
    body mapping exercise, 137-140
    chakras, 53-58
    cleansing rituals, 104-106
    connection to moon cycles, 40-42
    developing a positive body image, 50-53
    erogenous zones, 127
    full-body orgasms, 167
    honoring your changing body following child-birth, 249-252
    rhythms of, 194-195
Book of the Dead, 44
Bound, 274
breasts
    adolescents, 80-81
    aging breasts, 83-84
    breastfeeding, 82-83
    explorations, 84, 86
    grown-up breasts, 81
    meanings, 74-77
    orgasms, 167
    pregnancy, 82
    self-exams, 84
    size concerns, 77-80
    universal nurturers, 86
breathing exercises
    Golden Breath meditation, 52-53
    pre-sex rituals, 106-108
    sacred breathing exercise, 179-180
    sacred chakra breathing exercise, 177-178
    womb breathing, 254
Buddha Dakini, 57

Butterfly Pose, 149-150
Butterfly Pump, 198-199

C

Ca-the-na, 15
Cavillaca, 15
Central America sex god-desses, 14-15
Ceres, 21
cervical orgasms, 167
Ch'en, 290
chakras, 53
    afterglow period, visualiza-tion exercise, 224-226
    channeling sexual energy, 175-178
    fifth chakra (communica-tion), 57
    first chakra (primal urges), 54-55
    fourth chakra (heart chakra), 56
    heart chakra ritual, 242-243
    kundalini energy, 151
    second chakra (inner fire), 55
    seventh chakra (universal unity), 58
    sixth chakra (intuition), 57
    third chakra (meeting the world), 56
channeling sexual energy
    chakra coordination exer-cise, 175-177
    Inner Goddess Channel, 178-179
    sacred breathing exercise, 179-180
    sacred chakra breathing exercise, 177-178
Chaska, 290

Chi, 14
children and motherhood
    affects of motherhood on sexual energy, 238-242
    honoring partners after having children, 242-244
    rekindling the flame with your partner, 244-245
        creating a sacred bed-chamber, 247-248
        romantic get-aways, 248-249
        Tantric dating, 245, 247
Chinen, Alan, 230
Chinese sex goddesses, 16-17
Churning penetration method, 165
circles, loving circle ritual, 243-244
Clasping Kisses, 119
Clasping Union position (Kama Sutra), 152
cleansing rituals, 104-106
climax, sacred unions, 185-186
Clinton, Hillary Rodham, 260
clitoral orgasms, 167
Clotho, 33
Cocamama, 15
colostrum, 82
communication
    assessing your man's attitudes, 136-137
    body mapping exercise, 137-140
    determining what pleas-ures you, 132-133
    fifth chakra, 57
    how to be treated like a sex goddess, 140-142
    pillow talk rituals, 211-212
    showing your partner what you like, 134-136

Concentration of Semen technique, 156
Consuming the Lingam Kiss, 121
couples
    agreements for sacred couples, 216-218
    importance of individuality, 218-219
creation, Phoenician creation myth, 107
creative energies
    affects of sex on, 8
    unleashing, 291-292
    vagina, 63-65
Crocodile Woman, 14
cunnilingus, 120
Cupid, 141

D

dating, Tantric dating, 245-247
deer yoni, 65
Deida, David, 183
Demeter, 203
depression, post-partum, 240
desire
    communicating your sexual desires, 132-142
    desire meter quiz, 92-96
    loss of sexual desire following motherhood, 254-255
Devi, 33
Diana, 32
Dianic witchcraft, 278-281
dining experiences, flirting techniques, 262-263
Dodson, Betty, 65
double shavasana pose, 209-210
Drinking from the Fountain of Life Kiss, 122

Duchess of Windsor, 260
Durga, 19

E

Egle, 290
Egyptian sex goddesses, 16
Eight Benefits of various sexual positions and techniques for health (Plain Girl), 156
    Adjusting the System, 157
    Balancing the Elements, 157
    Benefits for the Internal Organs, 157
    Concentration of Semen, 156
    Harmonization of Blood Circulation, 157
    Increasing the Blood, 157
    Resting the Spirit, 156
    Strengthening the Bones, 157
ejaculation
    female, 228-229
    withholding, 201-202
Ekineba, 14
elephant yoni, 65
Endymion, 18
energy
    chakras, 53-58
    creative energy
        affects of sex on, 8
        unleashing, 291-292
        vagina, 63-65
    kundalini energy, 151
    love energy. See love energy
    sexual energy
        affects of motherhood on, 238-242
        channeling, 175-180
    prolonging pleasures, 195-197

erogenous zones, 127
erotic play, 263-264
Erzulie, 14
European sex goddesses, 20
Eurydice, 18
exercises
    body mapping exercise, 137-140
    channeling sexual energy, 175-180
    Kegel exercise, 252
    love your breast exercise, 79-80
    self-pleasuring exercise, 69-70
expressing your sexuality
    mindfulness, 98-99
    tips for living a sensual life, 99-100
eyegaze breathing, 108

F

families, radiating love energy to others, 287-288
fantasies, self-pleasuring techniques, 68-69
Far East sex goddesses, 16-17
fellatio, 120
female ejaculation, 228-229
female trinity, 25-34
    ancient and contemporary representations, 32-33
    determining your stage in the cycle, 33-34
    maiden stage, 27-29
    mother stage, 29-30
    wise woman stage, 31-32
fifth chakra (communication), 57
first chakra (primal urges), 54-55
Five Essentials ritual, 161-162

flirting techniques, 261-264
    arousal and erotic play,
        263-264
    dining experiences,
        262-263
    picking up your partner,
        262
    teasing, 263
Flower and the Jewel ritual,
    173
Flutter of the Butterfly Kiss,
    122
foods (aphrodisiacs), 115-116
foreplay, 117-128
    kissing, 118-120
    oral sex, 120-122
    rituals, 123-126
    role of music, 122
    self-pleasuring, 122-123
    Shakti and Shiva union,
        128
    talking to your partner,
        121
    touching each other,
        126-128
fourth chakra (heart chakra),
    56
Frau Welt, 20
friends, radiating love energy
    to others, 287-288
Frigga, 20
Frithiof, 20
Full Pressed Union position
    (Kama Sutra), 152
full-body orgasms, 167,
    202-203

G

G-spot
    orgasms, 167
    prolonging orgasmic
        pleasure, 199-200

Gaea, 6
Gaia, 255
Ganesha (Indian elephant
    god), 150
Geion, 20
genital compatibility, 180
get-aways
    airplane sex, 267-268
    beach sex, 267
    vacation sex, 266
    water sex, 266-267
goddesses of sex
    accessing your own god-
        dess powers, 6-7
    Africa, 14
    building your personal sex
        goddess pantheon, 21-22
    Central and South
        America, 14-15
    Egyptian, 16
    embracing your inner sex
        goddess, 4-6
    European goddesses, 20
    Far East, 16-17
    female trinity, 25-34
    Greek goddesses, 17-18
    history, 6-7
    how to be treated like a sex
        goddess, 140-142
    Indian goddesses, 18-19
    invoking your goddess
        powers, 12-13
    life lessons from, 288-291
    North American, 15
    partnerships, 9-10
    pedestal concept, 257-261
    sexual secrets of, 146-158
Golden Breath meditation,
    52-53
gratitude ritual, 213
Great Cackler, The, 291
Greek goddesses, 17-18, 146
Grimhild, 20
grown-up breasts, 81

H

Harmonization of Blood
    Circulation technique, 157
Hathor, 12
Haumea, 12
heart chakra, 56
    afterglow period, visualiza-
        tion exercise, 224-226
    heart chakra ritual,
        242-243
heartlight meditation,
    110-111
Hecate, 32
Hestia, 256
Hiding in the Crevice sexual
    position, 165
history
    ancient masturbation
        traditions, 66-68
    sex goddesses, 6-7
Hnoss, 20
homosexuality
    Isle of Lesbos, 275-277
    Kinsey Scale of sexual
        orientations, 276-277
    lesbian relationships
        Dianic witchcraft,
            278-280
        media portrayal,
            272-275
        Ode to Aphrodite,
            281-283
        special sharing of
            knowledge, 280-281
        tribadism, 277
honoring
    menstrual cycle, 47
    partners after having
        children, 242-244
    relationships, 214-219
Hours, The, 273
humming breath exercise,
    107-108

Hunger, The, 274
hydrotherapy ritual, 211
hygiene rituals, 104-106

I

Ichpuchtli, 14
Iku-tama-yori-bime, 17
Inari, 17
Increasing the Blood technique, 157
Incredibly True Adventures of Two Girls in Love, The, 274
Indian elephant god (Ganesha), 150
Indian sex goddesses, 18-19
individuality, importance of, 218-219
Ingeborg, 20
initiating sex, 96-98
Inkosazana (Princess of Heaven), 14
inner fire (second chakra), 55
Inner Flute, 178
Inner Goddess Channel, 178-179
Inner Yoni Tongue Strokes Kiss, 122
Inside Pressing Lingam Kiss, 121
intercourse. *See* sexual intercourse
intuition, sixth chakra, 57
intuitive wisdom-energy (motherhood), 240-242
invoking your goddess powers, 12-13
Ishtar, 6, 291
Isis, 16, 256
Isle of Lesbos, 275-277
Ix Chel, 14
Izushi-otome-no-kami, 17

J-K

Japanese sex goddeses, 16-17
Jiutinan Xuannu, 17
Jung, Carl G., 183
Juno, 21
Juno Coelestis, 14

Kali, 6, 19, 195, 255
Kama Sutra, 8
    sexual secrets of goddesses, 151-154
    Work of the Man penetration methods, 165-166
    yoni types, 65
karma, 186-187
Kaya-no-hime-no-kami, 289
Kegel exercises, 252
Ken, 16
Khir Bhawani, 82
Khotun, 7
Kinsey Scale of sexual orientations, 276-277
kissing
    foreplay, 118-120
    Kiss of the Penetrating Tongue, 122
    Kiss of the Upper Lip, 119
    Kissing the Lingam Kiss, 121
    Kissing the Yoni Blossom Kiss, 122
    Nine Kisses ritual, 210
    oral sex
        lingam kisses, 120-121
        yoni kisses, 120-122
    types of kisses, 118-119
Kissing Jessica Stein, 274
Kokopell' Mana, 15
Korawini?i, 16
Kuan Yin, 6
kundalini energy, 151

L

Lachesis, 33
Lakshmi, 33, 249, 255, 290
lesbian relationships
    Dianic witchcraft, 278-280
    Isle of Lesbos, 275-277
    Kinsey Scale of sexual orientations, 276-277
    media portrayal, 272-275
    Ode to Aphrodite, 281-283
    special sharing of knowledge, 280-281
    tribadism, 277
life cycle (female trinity), 25-34
    ancient and contemporary representations, 32-33
    determining your stage in the cycle, 33-34
    maiden stage, 27-29
    mother stage, 29-30
    wise woman stage, 31-32
life lessons from sex goddesses, 288-291
Lilith, 12
lingam (penis)
    alternative names for, 171
    Flower and the Jewel ritual, 173
    Lingam Tongue Strokes Kiss, 121
    oral sex, 173-175, 120-121
    penetration methods, 165-166
    sacred unions, 171-172
Lotus-Like Union position (Kama Sutra), 153
love energy
    looking within to change the world, 292-293
    radiating to others, 286-291
    unleashing your creativity, 291-292

love your breast exercise,
79-80
loving circle ritual, 243-244
Lucina, 32
Lu-Ma Ghirdhima, 290
lunar cycles, connection to
menstrual cycles, 40-42

M

Maia, 18
maiden stage (female trinity),
27-29
Man-on-Top position, 180
mandala, 109
mantra meditation, 109
mare yoni, 65
Mariana, 15
masturbation. *See also* self
pleasuring
techniques, 66-70
views of Betty Dodson, 65
Maya, 185
media portrayal of lesbian
relationships, 272-275
meditation techniques
Golden Breath meditation,
52-53
heartlight meditation,
110-111
mantra meditation, 109
mindfulness, 98-99
relation meditation,
109-110
sensuality meditation,
111-113
transcendental meditation,
109
zazen meditation, 109
Medusa, 18
men
assessing your man's attitudes, 136-137

meaning of breasts, 76-77
penis (lingam)
alternative names for,
171
Flower and the Jewel
ritual, 173
Lingam Tongue Strokes
Kiss, 121
oral sex, 173-175,
120-121
penetration methods,
165-166
sacred unions, 171-172
Work of the Man penetra-
tion methods, 165-166
menstrual cycle
connection to moon cycles,
40-42
having sex during, 45
honoring, 47
pre-menstrual syndrome,
46
recognizing how your
cycle affects your body,
44, 46-47
mental orgasms, 167
Metsanneitsyt, 291
Mile-High Club, 267-268
Milk Lake Mother (Khotun),
75
mindfulness, 98-99
moon, connection to men-
strual cycle, 40-42
moon goddesses
representations, 42
yin-yang connection, 42,
44
Morocco, 275
mother goddesses
affects of motherhood on
sexual energy, 238-242
honoring your changing
body following child-
birth, 249-252

honoring your partner-
ships, 242-244
loss of desire, 254-255
rekindling the flame with
your partner, 244-249
revitalizing techniques,
252-254
role models, 255-256
mother stage (female trinity),
29-30
Mother Water, 82
Moving Forward penetration
method, 165
Music, role in foreplay, 122
Mystic Mother, 82
Mythology, goddesses of sex,
13-20

N

Natarajanasana (Shiva Pose),
148-149
Native American sex god-
desses, 15
Nayikas, The, 19
Nine Kisses ritual, 210
Nominal Kisses, 118
North American sex god-
desses, 15

O

O-ichi-hime, 17
Ode to Aphrodite, 281-283
Olokum, 15
Onassis, Jacqueline Bouvier
Kennedy, 260
oral sex
cunnilingus, 120
fellatio, 120
lingam kisses, 120-121
sacred unions, 173-175
yoni kisses, 120-122

orgasms, 168
   afterglow period, 221-232
   breast orgasms, 167
   cervical orgasms, 167
   characteristics of female
      orgasms, 192
   clitoral orgasms, 167
   full-body orgasms, 167
   G-spot orgasms, 167
   mental orgasms, 167
   post-sex rituals, 207-214
   prolonging pleasure,
      191-204
   self-pleasuring, 166
   simultaneous climax,
      185-186
Orpheus, 18
Outer Yoni Tongue Strokes
   Kiss, 121
Outside Pressing Lingam
   Kiss, 121

P

Packed Union position
   (Kama Sutra), 152
partnerships, 9-10
   agreements for sacred
      couples, 216-218
   honoring partners after
      having children, 242-244
   importance of individual-
      ity, 218-219
   rekindling the flame with
      your partner following
      motherhood, 244-249
   saying "no" to your part-
      ner, 265-266
Parvati, 289
pedestal concept, 257-261
   balance, 260-261
   Pygmalion's pedestal, 261
   Veneralia celebrations,
      258-259
   views from divas, 259-261

Pele, 224, 255
penetration methods, 165-166
penis (lingam)
   alternative names for, 171
   Flower and the Jewel
      ritual, 173
   Lingam Tongue Strokes
      Kiss, 121
   oral sex, 173-175, 120-121
   penetration methods,
      165-166
   sacred unions, 171-172
Persephone, 12, 203, 232, 290
Phoenician creation myth,
   107
Pierce penetration method,
   165
pillow talk rituals, 211-212
Plain Girl, sexual secrets of,
   155-158
   Eight Benefits of various
      sexual positions and
      techniques for health,
      156-158
   Ten Stages of Loving,
      155-156
pleasures
   prolonging, 191-204
   self-pleasuring
      after childbirth,
         251-252
      foreplay, 122-123
      orgasms, 166
      showing your partner
         what you like, 134-136
      techniques, 65-70
poses (yoga)
   Butterfly Pose, 149-150
   double shavasana pose,
      209-210
   reclining spinal twist, 196
   Shiva Pose
      (Natarajanasana),
      148-149
   Spider Pose, 196

tree pose, 147
vajrasana pose, 70, 72
positions (sexual positions)
   Butterfly Pump, 198-199
   Eight Benefits of various
      sexual positions and tech-
      niques for health (Plain
      Girl), 156-158
   Kama Sutra, 151-154
   Man-on-Top position, 180
   Pressing Position, 197
   sacred sex, 162-165
   Side-by-Side position, 180
   Splitting Position, 180
   Woman-on-Top position,
      180
post-partum period
   affects on sexual energy,
      239-240
   depression, 240
post-sex rituals, 207-214
   double shavasana pose,
      209-210
   gratitude ritual, 213
   hydrotherapy ritual, 211
   Nine Kisses ritual, 210
   pillow talk, 211-212
   returning to the real
      world, 214
   rite of refueling, 211
   silence ritual, 212-213
pranayama breathing exer-
   cises, 106-108
   bhramari (humming
      breath), 107-108
   eyegaze breathing, 108
pre-menstrual syndrome, 46
pre-sex rituals
   affirmations, 113-114
   aphrodisiac foods, 115-116
   breathing exercises,
      106-108
   cleansing rituals, 104-106
   heartlight meditation,
      110-111

preparation of lovemaking spaces, 114

relation meditation, 109-110

sensuality meditation, 111-113

pregnancy

affects on sexual energy, 238-239

breasts, 82

preparations. *See* pre-sex rituals

Press penetration method, 165

Pressed Kisses, 119

Pressing Position, 197

Pressing Yoni Kiss, 121

primal urges (first chakra), 54-55

Princess Diana, 260

Princess of Heaven (Inkosazana), 14

private indulgences in public places, 264-265

prolonging pleasures, 191-204

body's rhythms, 194-195

energy of orgasms, 195-197

focusing on own sexual needs, 203-204

full-body orgasm, 202-203

heightening sensation, 193-194

orgasms, 197-200

screwing, 197

withholding ejaculation, 201-202

public displays of affection

private indulgences in public places, 264-265

public acceptability, 264

saying "no", 265-266

Pygmalion's pedestal, 261

Q-R

Quadriviae, 33

Queen Christina (itis), 275

Rajneesh, Bhagwan Shree, 177

reclining spinal twist, 196

refueling ritual, 211

regular sex versus sacred sex, 159-160

relation meditation, 109-110

relationships

agreements for sacred couples, 216-218

importance of individuality, 218-219

keeping your relationship sacred, 214-215

lesbians, 272-283

radiating love energy to others, 286-293

representations

asteroids, 20-21

female trinities, 32-33

moon goddesses, 42

Resting the Spirit technique, 156

revirginizing ritual, 249, 251

revitalizing techniques (mother goddeses), 252-254

womb breathing, 254

yoga, 253-254

rite of refueling, 211

rituals

Five Essentials ritual (sacred sex), 161-162

Flower and the Jewel ritual, 173

foreplay, 123, 125-126

heart chakra ritual, 242-243

loving circle ritual, 243-244

post-sex rituals, 207-214

pre-sex rituals, 104-116

revirginizing ritual, 249, 251

role models, 255-256

romantic get-aways, 248-249

Rub penetration method, 165

Rumi, 197

S

sacred breathing exercise, 179-180

sacred chakra breathing exercise, 177-178

sacred sex

agreements for sacred couples, 216-218

Five Essentials ritual, 161-162

importance of individuality, 218-219

keeping your relationship sacred, 214-215

orgasms, 166-168

penetration methods, 165-166

post-sex rituals, 207-214

sexual positions, 162-165

versus regular sex, 159-160

sacred unions

astrological influences, 182

channeling sexual energy, 175-180

Flower and the Jewel ritual, 173

genital compatibility, 180

lingam, 171-172

oral sex, 173-175

simultaneous climax, 185

yoni, 170-171

same-sex relationships. *See* lesbian relationships

Sappho
  Isle of Lesbos, 275-277
  Ode to Aphrodite, 281-283
Sarasvati, 33, 229, 255
Sarton, May, 6
saying "no" to your partner, 265
screwing, 197
second chakra (inner fire), 55
secrets
  sacred unions, 184-185
  sex goddesses, 146-158
Selene, 18
self breast exams, 84
self-pleasuring. *See also* masturbation
  after childbirth, 251-252
  foreplay, 122-123
  orgasms, 166
  showing your partner what you like, 134-136
  techniques, 66-70
  views of Betty Dodson, 65
senses
  prolonging pleasures, 193-194
  stimulating, 193
sensuality
  appreciating your sexiness, 58-59
  sensuality meditation, 111-113
  tips for living a sensual life, 99-100
seventh chakra (universal unity), 58
sexual intercourse
  afterglow period, 221-232
  as a source of creative energy, 8
  foreplay, 117-128
  influences of the four asteroids on, 20-21
  loss of desire following motherhood, 254-255

menstruation and, 45
positions
  Butterfly Pump, 198-199
  Eight Benefits of various sexual positions and techniques for health (Plain Girl), 156-158
  Kama Sutra, 151-154
  Man-on-Top position, 180
  Pressing Position, 197
  sacred sex, 162-165
  Side-by-Side position, 180
  Splitting Position, 180
  Woman-on-Top position, 180
post-sex rituals, 207-214
pre-sex rituals, 104-116
prolonging pleasures, 191-204
sacred sex, 159-168
sacred unions, 170-187
saying "no" to your partner, 265-266
vacation sex, 266-268
sex drive fitness, 100, 102
sex goddesses. *See* goddesses of sex
sexiness, appreciation of, 58-59
sexual energy
  affects of motherhood on, 238-242
  channeling, 175-180
  prolonging pleasures, 195-197
sexual secrets of Taoist, 155
Sexual Secrets: The Alchemy of Ecstasy, 77
sexuality
  communicating your sexual desires, 132-142

desire meter quiz, 92-96
  expressing yourself, 98-100
  initiating sex, 96-98
  sex drive fitness, 100-102
Shakti and Shiva union, 128
Shandian Pozi, 286
Shiva and Shakti union, 128
Shiva Pose (Natarajanasana), 148-149
Siddhi, 150
Side Nibbling Lingam Kiss, 120
Side-by-Side position, 180
silence ritual, 212-213
Simic, Charles, 187
Simpson, Wallis Warfield, 260
simultaneous climax, 185-186
sitting meditation, 109
sixth chakra (intuition), 57
Sky Mother, 76
Soatsaki, 16
South America sex goddesses, 14-15
Spider Pose, 196
Splitting Position, 180
Splitting the Bamboo sexual position, 163
Sporting of the Sparrow penetration method, 166
Straight Kisses, 118
Strengthening the Bones technique, 157
Strike penetration method, 165
Sucking a Mango Kiss, 121
Sucking the Yoni Blossom Kiss, 122
Supported Union position (Kama Sutra), 154
Supta Padangusthasana (reclining spinal twist), 196
Supta Padangusthasana (Spider Pose), 196
Suseri-bime-no-mikoto, 17

Suspended Union position (Kama Sutra), 154
Swooping Shakti sexual position, 163-164

T

talking during foreplay, 121
Tantric traditions
  dating, 245-247
  defining characteristics, 32
  self-pleasuring exercises, 69-70
  sexual secrets of goddesses, 150-151
Taoist concepts
  ejaculation schedules, 201
  sexual secrets of goddesses, 154-158
  yin-yang connection, 42, 44
teasing your partner, 263
Ten Stages of Loving, 155-156
third chakra (meeting the world), 56
Throbbing Kisses, 118
Tiger's Tread sexual position, 163
tongue, Wrestling Tongues Kiss, 119
touch
  foreplay
    self-pleasuring, 122-123
    touching each other, 126-128
  self-pleasuring techniques, 68-69
Touching Kisses, 118
transcendental meditation, 109
transforming reality with love energy, 286-293

fortifying family and friends, 287-288
life lessons from sex goddesses, 288-291
looking within to change the world, 292-293
unleashing your creativity, 291-292
tree pose (yoga pose), 147
tribadism, 277
trinity (female trinity), 25-34
  ancient and contemporary representations, 32-33
  determining your stage in the cycle, 33-34
  maiden stage, 27-29
  mother stage, 29-30
  wise woman stage, 31-32
Turned Kisses, 119

U

Union Like a Pair of Tongs position (Kama Sutra), 153
unions
  Kama Sutra positions, 151-154
    Clasping Union, 152
    Full Pressed Union, 152
    Lotus-Like Union, 153
    Packed Union, 152
    Supported Union, 154
    Suspended Union, 154
    Union Like a Pair of Tongs, 153
    Yawning Union position, 152
  sacred unions
    astrological influences, 181-182
    channeling sexual energy, 175-180
    Flower and the Jewel ritual, 173

genital compatibility, 180
  karma, 186-187
  oral sex, 173-175
  secrets to blissful unions, 184-185
  simultaneous climax, 185-186
  yin/yang flow, 182-184
  yoni, 170-172
  Taoist unions, 154-155
universal nurturers (breasts), 86
universal unity (seventh chakra), 58

V

vacation sex, 266-269
  airplane sex, 267-268
  beach sex, 267
  water sex, 266-267
vagina (yoni), 47
  alternative name for, 170
  as a source of creative energy, 63-65
  exploring, 62-63
  Flower and the Jewel ritual, 173
  oral sex, 121-122, 173-175
  protecting, 63
  sacred unions, 170-171
  self-pleasuring techniques, 66-70
  types, 65
  yoni-waves, 229
  yoni yoga, 70-72
vajrasana pose (yoni yoga), 70, 72
Veneralia celebrations, 258-259
Venus, 6, 18, 255
Venus of Willendorf, 74, 204, 255